How Brands Grow
Part 2
Revised edition

This book is dedicated to Gerald Goodhardt, developer of the Dirichlet model and the duplication of viewing law—Gerald, you have taught us so much: your wisdom and wit have been much appreciated.

how brands grow

Part 2

including emerging markets, services, durables, B2B and luxury brands

Jenni Romaniuk
Byron Sharp

Revised edition

OXFORD
UNIVERSITY PRESS
AUSTRALIA & NEW ZEALAND

OXFORD
UNIVERSITY PRESS

Oxford University Press is a department of the University of Oxford.
It furthers the University's objective of excellence in research,
scholarship, and education by publishing worldwide. Oxford is a registered
trademark of Oxford University Press in the UK and in certain other
countries.

Published in Australia by
Oxford University Press
Level 8, 737 Bourke Street, Docklands, Victoria 3008, Australia.

© Jenni Romaniuk and Byron Sharp 2022

The moral rights of the authors have been asserted

First published 2016
Revised edition published 2022

A catalogue record for this
book is available from the
National Library of Australia

ISBN 9780190330026

Reproduction and communication for educational purposes

The Australian *Copyright Act 1968* (the Act) allows educational institutions
that are covered by remuneration arrangements with Copyright Agency
to reproduce and communicate certain material for educational purposes.
For more information, see copyright.com.au.

Edited by Jennifer Butler
Typeset by Newgen KnowledgeWorks Pty Ltd
Proofread by Peter Cruttenden
Printed in China by Leo Paper Products Ltd

Disclaimer
Indigenous Australians and Torres Strait Islanders are advised that this publication may include
images or names of people now deceased.

Links to third party websites are provided by Oxford in good faith and for information only.
Oxford disclaims any responsibility for the materials contained in any third party website
referenced in this work.

Contents

Introduction

'My market is different.' It's a common refrain, and not untrue—every market has its peculiarities that have to be experienced and learnt on the job. This said, there are fundamental similarities about the way brands compete and buyers buy, and hence how marketing works.

This edition of *How Brands Grow Part 2* is about how the fundamentals of buying behaviour and brand performance apply to a wide range of conditions, such as services, durables, luxury and business-to-business (B2B) categories; countries such as China, India, Russia, South Africa and Indonesia; and circumstances such as launching a new brand. These fundamentals provide a consistent roadmap for brand growth and improved marketing productivity.

The major changes from the first edition include substantially revised content on physical availability (Chapters 8 and 9) that captures key advances in knowledge since the publication of the first edition, and a new chapter (Chapter 11) specifically on B2B marketing to test and apply laws of growth to this context. In addition we expand on category entry points and their role in building mental availability, and broaden the scope of our investigation into whether brands' or buyers' luxury categories behave differently from other categories.

Readers of the first *How Brands Grow* can learn more about key concepts and their application. These concepts include:

- the three pillars of physical availability
- how to build and measure mental availability

- what to do when launching a new brand
- metrics to assess the strength of your distinctive brand assets.

How Brands Grow Part 2 is also for marketers operating in emerging markets, services, B2B, durables and luxury brands. We show how the laws of growth apply in these categories and can be used to grow brands more efficiently and effectively.

We hope you enjoy this updated edition of *How Brands Grow Part 2*.

Jenni and Byron

Acknowledgments

We would like to thank the following people who reviewed early manuscripts pointing out errors and confusing writing: Dr Zac Anesbury, Dr Abou Bakar, Vivien Chanana, Professor Francesca Dall'Olmo Riley, Dr Margaret Faulkner, Associate Professor Kesten Green, Dr Nicole Hartnett, Associate Professor Richard Lee, Professor Larry Lockshin, Dr Cathy Nguyen, Sarah Patrick, Associate Professor Anne Sharp, Dr Lucy Simmonds, Dr Arry Tanusondjaja, Quin Tran, Dr Kelly Vaughan and Dr Amy Wilson. We would also like to thank Sarah Patrick and Emily Primavera, whose research assistance helped bring the data to the page. Thank you also to our colleagues at the Ehrenberg–Bass Institute for their general support and encouragement throughout the process of putting *How Brands Grow Part 2* together. Thank you as well to the Institute's corporate sponsors who provide feedback and data and constantly ask the difficult questions—in particular the members of our advisory boards in Europe, the USA and Australasia.

About the Authors

Jenni Romaniuk

Dr Jenni Romaniuk is Research Professor and Associate Director (International) of the Ehrenberg–Bass Institute at the University of South Australia. Jenni's research covers brand equity, mental availability, brand health metrics, advertising effectiveness, distinctive assets, word of mouth and the role of loyalty in growth. She is the developer of the Distinctive Asset Grid, which is used by companies around the world to assess the strength and strategic potential of their brand's distinctive assets. Her book on this topic, *Building Distinctive Brand Assets*, is also published by Oxford University Press. She is also a pioneer in mental availability measurement and metrics, as well as the identification and use of category entry points.

Jenni is a past executive editor of the *Journal of Advertising Research*, and now sits on the Journal's Senior Advisory Board. She was awarded the University of South Australia Business School's Distinguished Researcher in 2020.

<www.JenniRomaniuk.com>

Byron Sharp

Dr Byron Sharp is Professor of Marketing Science and the Director of the Ehrenberg–Bass Institute at the University of South Australia.

Byron's book *How Brands Grow* was voted marketing book of the year by AdAge readers in 2013 and has sold over 100,000 copies. He has published over 100 academic papers and is on the editorial board of five journals. With Professor Jerry Wind, he hosted two conferences at

the Wharton Business School on the laws of advertising, and co-edited the 2009 and 2013 special issues of the *Journal of Advertising Research* on scientific laws of advertising.

His university textbook *Marketing: Theory, Evidence, Practice* (Oxford University Press) was released in 2013 and the second edition was released in 2017.

<www.ByronSharp.com>

Magda Nenycz-Thiel

Professor Magda Nenycz-Thiel leads the Industry Growth Initiative at the Ehrenberg–Bass Institute at the University of South Australia. Magda's main research areas are category growth and physical availability management and metrics. She has published in international journals such as *Marketing Letters*, *Psychology & Marketing*, the *Journal of Business Research* and the *Journal of Advertising Research*. She is a past associate editor of the *Journal of Consumer Behaviour*.

Robert East

Robert East is Emeritus Professor of Consumer Behaviour at Kingston Business School, London, and Adjunct Professor at Ehrenberg–Bass Institute at the University of South Australia. He trained as a social psychologist and is a postgraduate of London Business School. Now retired, Robert's past research focused on store use, consumer loyalty and brand switching and word-of-mouth patterns. Robert is the founding author of an evidence-based textbook, *Consumer Behaviour: Applications in Marketing* (2013), published by Sage.

About the Ehrenberg–Bass Institute

The Ehrenberg–Bass Institute at the University of South Australia Business School is a university-based R&D think tank devoted to advancing marketing science. Its research is used and financially supported by many of the world's leading corporations, including Mars Incorporated, LinkedIn, Suntory Beverage & Food, Red Bull, Lindt & Sprüngli, Colgate Palmolive, Unilever and HSBC.

For more on the Institute, go to www.marketingscience.info.

1

How Brands Grow

Byron Sharp and Jenni Romaniuk

This chapter addresses the debate about whether more sales growth comes from *penetration* (getting more customers) or *loyalty* (getting customers to buy more). It documents the law of double jeopardy across a diverse range of areas:

- emerging markets
- services
- durables
- local and global brands
- a wide range of loyalty metrics.

We explain *why* double jeopardy occurs, and describe the conditions under which brands do, and do not, conform to the double jeopardy law.

How to grow

Marketing is about providing for customers; so, the pursuit of growth, to address the needs of more customers, is noble. In a competitive market where rivals seek to serve your customers, it is also a necessity. Indeed, 'grow to survive' is a marketing mantra. Even in high-growth markets, growing market share is necessary to gain scale, to gain the resources to match the marketing budgets of rivals, and to have a positive momentum story to explain to intermediaries why they should supply your brand.

It's easy for managers of small brands to waste time on inconsequential efforts or even damage the brand through unnecessary change. Likewise, it is easy for managers of large brands to be lulled into complacency by consistently high metrics and allow a more nimble competitor to erode their share. Throughout *How Brands Grow Part 2*, we highlight the important strategies marketers can use, but also the pitfalls that marketers can face.

In this chapter we'll provide evidence to highlight how much striving to increase penetration matters for growth, and how loyalty metrics can normally be predicted from a brand's penetration. We'll also show this evidence is apparent for brands in emerging markets, services and durable categories, just as it is for packaged goods categories in developed markets.

Can you engineer your brand loyalty?

A fundamental question of marketing strategy is how much to focus on improving the loyalty of existing customers or to try to win new customers. Logic says that both are ways to grow but logic alone can't tell us if both are equally attractive or viable options for growth.

The loyalty path delivers extra sales revenue through existing customers buying more (and therefore less of competitors' brands). Such a strategy might focus on improving the attractiveness of the brand to current customers: for example, through better service, loyalty rewards such as incentives or points, or providing existing customers additional opportunities to buy via related products or services (cross-selling). For example, in personal insurance, cross-selling home insurance products to car insurance customers (and vice versa) is common.

Loyalty strategies are thought to lower marketing costs through having a much narrower advertising target, as existing customers are just a fraction of the market. Further, it is thought that, given these customers already buy the brand, they need less encouragement or inducement to buy something else—or buy the same product or service again—compared to non-buyers buying the brand for the first time. If these buyers are cheaper to reach and cheaper to convert, these additional sales are cheaper to acquire.

A similar strategy, popular in services categories, is to focus on customer retention. This strategy offers the promise to increase the size of the customer base through a reduction in customer defections. While not focusing on acquisition might sound like an odd way to grow a customer base, it is often claimed that an effective retention strategy will create brand advocates who generate positive word of mouth that attracts new customers. Coupled with greater retention, then, this strategy should grow the customer base.

It turns out that all this speculation is for naught. *How Brands Grow* (2010) presented decades of evidence that renders the question 'Can you engineer brand loyalty?' largely moot: brands grow by improvements to both penetration and loyalty, though typically far more sales growth comes from gains in penetration than improved loyalty. The question of whether strategy should therefore aim for loyalty or penetration has a very clear answer. Brands can enjoy higher loyalty, *but only if they very substantially improve their penetration.* A loyalty-first approach is simply not a growth strategy. Given the overwhelming evidence, it is surprising that many marketing consultants and academics still propose the sort of logic (and hopes) presented in the previous paragraphs, and unfortunate that marketers believe them.

The use of laws to build wondrous things is normal and need not stifle creativity. Engineers build aeroplanes in different ways, but all aeroplane designers must work within the laws of motion and gravity. Similarly, marketing choices—about what media to advertise in, who to target, the price points covered by the brand's portfolio, the distribution channels to sell in—need to work within the law-like patterns of competitive markets. Different marketers can make different choices, but all of these choices, if successful, will result in the same underlying pattern of growth. As a brand grows, it gains a predictable amount of penetration and loyalty for its market share. This real-world pattern is known as *the law of double jeopardy.*

The law of double jeopardy

Double jeopardy was discovered at the NBC television network and later named by a sociologist, William McPhee (McPhee, 1963). His book *Formal Theories of Mass Behaviour* documented this phenomenon in attitudinal data: for example, less well-known radio announcers (the first jeopardy) are also less liked by those who know them (the second jeopardy). A decade later Andrew Ehrenberg (1972) and Claude Martin (1973) independently documented this same pattern in brand choice: smaller share brands have fewer sales because they have many fewer customers (the first jeopardy) who are slightly less loyal (the second jeopardy).

Since then the law of double jeopardy has been observed for industrial brands, services, stores, store chains, comic strips, newspapers, radio stations, television networks, television programs and politicians. More recently, researchers have documented double jeopardy in fruit and vegetable buying, political polls and Twitter (Graham et al., 2017; Kooyman & Wright, 2017; Rogers et al., 2017). Table 1.1 contains examples from three service categories, in three different countries, with three different loyalty measures.

Table 1.1: Double jeopardy in service categories

	China personal banking		USA music streaming		Hotels (multi-country)	
	Penetration (%)	Average number of products	Penetration (%)	Average listening frequency	Penetration (%)	Solely loyal (%)
A	64	2.3	57	6.2	20	18
B	62	2.2	48	6.6	16	14
C	52	2.3	28	5.2	15	8
D	43	1.9	23	6.4	15	5
E	41	2.3	22	5.9	15	5
F	38	2.1	22	4.8	12	4
G	23	2.0	15	5.6	11	4
H	17	1.9	16	5.4	11	3
I	17	2.0	14	5.0	9	2
J	13	2.1	12	5.1	9	4

When brands are ranked by market share we can easily see that both penetration and loyalty metrics decline in line with lower market share. This holds for local and global brands: see Table 1.2, where Colgate in China has about double the market share of LSL (a local brand). It also has double the penetration (46% versus 23%). However, loyalty differences are much smaller, with Colgate having a purchase frequency of 2.5 compared with 2.2 for LSL and share of category buying of 26% compared with 23% for LSL.

Table 1.2: Illustration of the double jeopardy law—toothpaste in China (annual figures for 2011)

Brands	Market share (%)	Household penetration (%)	Average purchase frequency (number of times purchased)	Average share of category purchases (%)
Crest	19	57	2.8	29
Colgate	14	46	2.5	26
Zhonghua	12	43	2.4	25
Darlie	11	35	2.7	26
LSL	6	23	2.2	23
Hei mei	3	14	1.9	18
YNBY	3	14	2.2	20
Bamboo	2	9	2.0	19
LMZ	2	9	1.7	17
Sensodyne	0.3	2	1.5	13
Average	**7**	**25**	**2.2**	**22**

Source: Kantar Worldpanel China

A brand could, theoretically, enjoy similar sales to a rival brand but have a much smaller but more loyal customer base—the classic niche brand—*but this hardly ever happens*. Small market-share brands practically always have the penetration and the loyalty metrics expected of small brands. Even the few small brands that are slightly niche rarely have the loyalty levels of larger brands in the category.

However, what we see, time and time again, is that two brands with similar market share will typically have:

• very similar penetration levels—that is, the number of people who buy them, at least once, during the time period of interest

- highly similar levels of loyalty—that is, the people who buy them will, on average, buy them at similar rates or hold a similar number of products, or devote similar proportions of their repertoire, repeat-buy at the same rate, and so on. Loyalty metrics change with category types, but the double jeopardy pattern holds irrespective of the loyalty metric chosen.

Table 1.2 also counters the myth that Chinese consumers aren't loyal to brands and generally shop on price (for example, Lavin 2018). One of the pioneers in buyer behaviour research in China, Professor Mark Uncles, set up a panel of buyers in China over a decade ago to observe their retail and brand buying behaviour. His team was amongst the very first to report double jeopardy in China, with smaller retailers and brands having systematically lower penetration and loyalty than larger share brands (Uncles, 2010; Uncles & Kwok, 2008). Over ten years ago, Bennett (2008) reported double jeopardy in the durable sector; namely, for buying televisions in China, and these patterns continue in electronics today. In Table 1.3 we show double jeopardy for mobile phone handsets in China across two 'loyalty' metrics—repeat buying and attitude to the brand. Knowing the double jeopardy pattern will allow you to see the deviations easily (for example, 70% of Nokia customers say the brand is their favourite, which is much higher than for Lenovo, which has a similar penetration). But don't let the deviations distract you. Most brands, for most loyalty metrics, follow a normal double jeopardy pattern.

Table 1.3: Double jeopardy for mobile phone handsets in China (2014)

	% current ownership	% repeat-buy	% say it is their favourite
Apple iPhone	35	64	81
Samsung	31	57	58
Huawei	8	57	38
HTC	7	41	39
Nokia	5	52	70
Lenovo	5	37	30
Motorola	3	47	27
Average	**13**	**51**	**49**

Chinese customers are loyal to brands, just not 100% loyal (few people are). Armed with the knowledge of double jeopardy, you can see the brand loyalty patterns for Chinese consumers for what they are—largely normal, with occasional typical exceptions.

Double jeopardy occurs for packaged goods, services, durables—a wide range of categories and in every country where it has been examined. This is why the pattern is a scientific law. In Figure 1.1, we show examples from Nigeria and Kenya in soft drinks and, in Table 1.4, we see the double jeopardy pattern in Indonesian banking—across different loyalty metrics such as number of products bought, attitudes and defection rates (with the pattern in reverse, where big brands have smaller defection rates).

Figure 1.1: Double jeopardy chart for soft drinks in (a) Nigeria and (b) Kenya (2014)

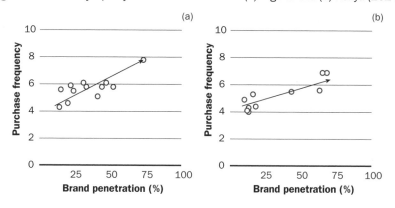

We see double jeopardy in every category we explore, such as banking, insurance, retailers, social media sites, mobile phones, and in every country from China to Russia, from Nigeria to South Africa, from Turkey to Indonesia. Indeed, tests have only been limited by data access. But don't just take our word for it: look in your own data—all you need to do is organise the brands by market share and have a loyalty metric that is generated from the customer base for each brand.

Table 1.4: Double jeopardy across metrics for personal banking in Indonesia (2014)

Brands	Penetration (%)	Average number of products per customer	Customers who say brand is their favourite (%)	Potential defection p.a. (%)
Bank Central Asia	64	1.8	57	13
Bank Mandiri	63	1.9	48	17
Bank Rakyat Indonesia	50	1.6	41	17
Bank Negara Indonesia	49	1.7	43	17
Bank Tabungan Negara	20	1.5	19	36
Average	**49**	**1.7**	**42**	**20**

How brands change in penetration and loyalty over time

When brands grow or decline, their movements do not depart from the double jeopardy pattern. Gains (or losses) in market share conform to double jeopardy—so as brands gain (or lose) penetration their loyalty metrics also simultaneously adjust. This means a single annual or quarterly snapshot of brand performance metrics won't reveal which brand is growing or declining. Researchers have looked at deviations from double jeopardy to see if this might foretell a brand's movement and have found that it doesn't (Kearns, Millar & Lewis, 2000). Brands do not, as commonly asserted, kick off growth with high loyalty for their current size. Nor do we see brands develop low loyalty (for their penetration) before they decline. Another marketing myth dies. Instead, Barker (2021) finds that small brands have a greater propensity to grow when they move from deficit loyalty to expected ('normal') loyalty for their size; and a greater propensity to decline when moving from normal to deficit loyalty. That is, penetration drives most change in share.

This is another nail in the coffin for loyalty-focused growth strategies. If they did work, we would surely by now have substantial evidence of small brands who achieved excess loyalty before parlaying that deviation into market-share growth.

What we have is clear evidence that the growth and decline in the size of a brand's customer base (penetration) is due largely to unusual acquisition levels. Both brands that grow and decline lose customers in line with expected defection rates (as dictated by their respective market shares). It's the level of acquisition that largely determines a brand's trajectory. If acquisition is higher than expected, the brand will grow; if it is lower than expected, the brand will decline (Riebe et al., 2014). Detroit's loss of US market share to Japanese and then Korean brands was not due to a collapse retention rates, but rather because US car brands failed to win their usual share of customer acquisition (Sharp, 2009). It's as if you can only control one lever to grow penetration, and that is your acquisition rate.

Penetration rules!

Most changes in market share will show up as larger movements in penetration and smaller increases in loyalty metrics. Studies of typical smaller but celebrated market-share changes (such as 0.3 or 0.5 percentage points from one year to the next) that have shown growth and decline reveal changes much more in penetration than brand loyalty (Anschuetz, 2002; Baldinger, Blair & Echambadi, 2002; McDonald & Ehrenberg, 2003; Nenycz-Thiel, Dawes & Romaniuk, 2018; Romaniuk, Dawes & Nenycz-Thiel, 2014; Sylvester, McQueen & Moore, 1994).

Table 1.5 shows a brand that doubled its share in Brazil over a four-year period. Penetration almost doubled (82%), which explains most of the increase in sales, while changes in loyalty metrics over this period were less dramatic (around 35%). The brand had many more customers buy it somewhat more often.

Table 1.5: An example of a growing brand over time—toothpaste in Brazil (2006–09)

Year	Market share (%)	Household penetration (%)	Average purchase frequency	Average share of category requirements
2006	6.3	22	2.3	16
2007	10.1	31	2.8	19
2008	11.7	35	2.9	20
2009	14.1	40	3.1	22
% change 2006–09	124	82	35	38

Source: Nielsen Household Panel Brazil

This is the way double jeopardy says it has to be, because most brands are a long way from owning most of the market (that is, more than 70% market share) and so have modest levels of penetration even if the metric is calculated for a whole year.[1] The exceptions to double jeopardy can occur when brands have extremely high penetration, or are genuinely trapped in a niche, with a very high penetration of a very limited market (for example, brands that have only been able to secure regional distribution). In these circumstances, brands will see their growth (or decline) reflected mostly in loyalty metrics simply because of the ceiling on penetration.

A niche brand simply has restricted growth potential. This makes large marketing investments unwise unless these limitations can be dealt with (such as securing more distribution). Niche brands should be pitied for their lack of potential, rather than celebrated. Small brands are in a better position than niche brands—they *can* become big.

However, most brands sit on the low to middle part of the double jeopardy line (Allsopp, Sharp & Dawes, 2004; Ehrenberg, Goodhardt & Barwise, 1990; Uncles et al., 1994). A move from one position to another on the double jeopardy line then typically means larger changes in penetration accompanied by smaller changes in loyalty.

---

1   We now generally advise brand managers not to use annual penetration, but rather use quarterly (three-monthly) brand metrics. This gives a more realistic picture and fits with the frequency of new marketing interventions.

Why does double jeopardy occur?

In competitive choice situations, where buyers have a range of not-too-dissimilar options to buy, brands still have large differences:

- *mental availability*—the propensity for the brand to be thought of in buying situations; and
- *physical availability*—how easy the brand is to buy and find.

Large popular brands have excellent mental and physical availability amongst the buying population. This means more people will buy them (higher penetration). Small brands will have far less mental and physical availability. Indeed some people don't even know these brands exist, and many potential buyers seldom, if ever, notice them. Therefore fewer people buy them (lower penetration) in any time period.

But why do brands also vary in their loyalty scores, and vary systematically in line with their size? Again, the answer lies in mental and physical availability and the fact that these combine to be the dominant driver of a brand's market share. It means that very popular brands are thought of by more people across more category-buying occasions and are available to buy in some places where they are the sole brand (or one of very few). Similarly, many light or infrequent buyers of the category don't know of many brands, and the few brands these buyers do know are much more likely to be the more popular brands.

Small brands unenviably find themselves in the opposite position. Fewer people know them and fewer know them well, while the people who do know them tend to be heavier category buyers—and these people also buy many other brands, including the big brands. Small brands are available in fewer outlets and these tend to be common locations where they are displayed alongside many other (larger) competitors.

The higher competition faced by small brands is illustrated in Figure 1.2 for fast food brands in Russia and South Korea. In both cases, a small brand's customers *buy many more other brands* than the customers of big brands do. For example, in Russia, customers of the biggest brand, McDonald's, also buy from 2.6 other quick-service food brands; while in the same time period, customers of the much smaller Sbarro's buy from more than twice as many brands (5.6). This law-like pattern is known as the *natural monopoly law*, a title that refers to the fact that larger share brands have a greater proportion of their customer base made up of light category buyers, and therefore monopolise the light category buyers (also see Dawes 2020).

Figure 1.2: Smaller share brands attract heavy category buyers for fast food in (a) Russia and (b) South Korea (2014)

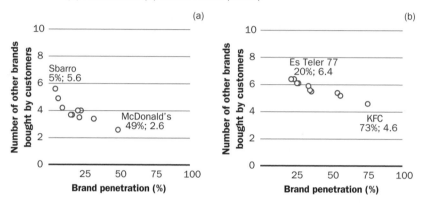

These differences mean that the customers of smaller brands know about and buy many more options. Even if you try a small brand for the first time and really like it, its competitive conditions make it a bit harder to remember that brand (mental availability) and, even if you do, a bit harder to find it (physical availability). Likewise, if you sit in McDonald's and decide that you really didn't like the burger you ate, the odds are you'll still probably eat there again one day because it's just so easy—McDonald's is in your head, and it is widely physically available.

If the big difference (in terms of what drives choice) between the brands is their availability (mental and physical) then we have to have double jeopardy, where high penetration brands also enjoy slightly higher loyalty metrics.

If we refer back to our Indonesian banking example in Table 1.4, we can see that Bank Tabungan Negara (BTN) has a defection rate much higher than the other Indonesian banks listed. This is not because BTN's customers are particularly unhappy or its service is bad—but simply a function of two factors:

- a limited product range focused on loans for subsidised housing, rather than the more traditional product mix aiming towards transaction account customers, which constrains mental availability; and
- fewer branches (only 100 branches), compared to Bank Mandiri (around 2000 branches) and Bank Rakyat Indonesia (around 4000 branches), which constrains physical availability.

Much of the defection in financial services is driven by customers changing their circumstances—they move, get married, have children—and smaller brands with fewer locations, fewer branches and less well-known product ranges are particularly vulnerable to these changes, so they get more defection (lower loyalty).

A brand's loyalty level relates to its penetration level; both are underpinned by mental and physical availability. This double jeopardy pattern wouldn't occur if brands were really differentiated from others, such that they appealed to or 'locked in' a specific type of customer.

Truong (2014) documented double jeopardy deviations across six emerging markets (Brazil, China, India, Indonesia, Malaysia and the Philippines). Across more than 450 brands in twenty repeat purchase categories, only 10% of brands deviated substantially from their expected loyalty level. *No systematic exceptions* existed in any of these brand types:

- local brands
- global brands
- higher priced brands
- discount brands
- country of origin.

Half of the exceptions were dominant market leaders with a little 'excess loyalty', similar to that sometimes observed in developed markets (Fader & Schmittlein, 1993; Pare & Dawes, 2011). The remaining exceptions were split, with some having higher and others lower than expected loyalty, with no clear patterns or explanation.

Deviations from double jeopardy are therefore relatively unusual and, when they are present, they are not usually terribly dramatic or insightful. For example, the geography of many emerging markets means that local brands are often regionally based, and lack full distribution across the country; this restricts their total market penetration, so their loyalty level can look high for this (low) penetration, similar to store brands only distributed in a single retail chain. This is often mistaken for strong loyalty.

On rare occasions brands have low loyalty for their level of penetration; this tends to be because they are bought for a particular occasion, need, or time of year. This often reveals an issue with category definition. For example, premium whisky brands (which are typically purchased for special occasions such as fiftieth birthdays or given as gifts), when analysed alongside standard whisky brands, look different. But, when only analysed alongside other premium whisky brands, these brands look normal.

Interestingly, the conditions that would make a category depart from double jeopardy—highly differentiated brands each with appeal to particular segments—are widely assumed by marketing theorists to be normal or commonplace. If this really were the case, we would not have a double jeopardy law—but we do. In the real world, double jeopardy is everywhere. Differentiation turns out to be slight, and of far less consequence than thought (for further evidence, see *How Brands Grow*). In line with this, substantive deviations from double jeopardy are uncommon and tend to be easily explained.

Double jeopardy is clearly evident in most markets, for most brands. This is not a pattern exclusive to the stable, mature markets that dominate the developed world. It is also evident in dynamic emerging markets, services, durables and even when markets suffer from disruption, such as transport or accommodation. Even in categories with obvious functional differences between brands, we tend to see surprisingly small exceptions to the law of double jeopardy.

For example, 1st for Women insurance in South Africa claims to design insurance products especially for women, and indeed 90% of its customer base is female (compared to an average of around 50% for other brands). This is pretty atypical, yet its loyalty, expressed as the number of products held, is 1.9, only a little higher than expected given its low penetration (see Table 1.6). Its loyalty is a little higher because it really is a larger brand in a smaller market.

Table 1.6: Double jeopardy in insurance in South Africa (2012)

Brands	Penetration (%)	Insurance products held with company
Outsurance	27	2.3
Mutual & Federal	13	2.3
Santam	12	2.5
ABSA idirect	11	2.1
Auto & General	10	2.0
Budget	7	1.9
AA	7	1.3
Dial Direct	6	1.9
St Bank/Stanbic	5	2.0
Miway	4	1.8
1st for Women	3	1.9
Average	**10**	**2.0**

Source: National Advertising Bureau Roots Survey, 2012

(Back to) How to grow

Double jeopardy provides a clear strategy lesson. It is not possible to grow market share without expanding your customer base, which means reaching out to category buyers who never or very seldom buy your brand. A focus on your current consumers, particularly your heavier consumers, sounds efficient. It's human nature to prefer to talk to those who already know and like us. This idea is even more popular in services where companies have customer details on databases making communication with 'friends' easier. However, this strategy won't deliver much in the way of sales growth, and could indeed set you back as you lose the customers you neglect, and fail to acquire new ones. We talk more about this in Chapter 2.

In emerging markets, a focus on current customers misses a great opportunity to capitalise on category expansion and attract these new category buyers to your brand. Winning a share of these new buyers is essential in order to enjoy the category growth. If a 10% share brand wants to stay a 10% share brand it must continuously win 10% of the new buyers entering the category.

The good news is that if you recruit them, *and* you have a product that is good enough to do the job it was bought to do, *and* you keep up mental and physical availability, then you will get repeat purchases. Loyalty will be a natural consequence of effective marketing that builds the customer base and grows penetration. The more effective your marketing is at building the customer base, the more loyalty you will receive.

Dismantling barriers to market-share growth

The first step towards an evidence-based growth strategy is to remove any self-inflicted barriers. A growth-oriented strategy has to be a market penetration-oriented strategy. And tactics to reach out to new customers can't help to also reach existing customers, who have a heightened tendency to notice the brand's marketing activities (Harrison, 2013; Vaughan, Beal & Romaniuk, 2016). Reaching out to non-customers and light customers does not neglect your current customer base, but strategies only aimed at your brand's existing customer base can easily exclude non-buyers.

Beware of consultants selling you loyalty initiatives that promise to deliver growth by targeting your existing customers, or worse, your heaviest existing customers. One fad that was popular in developed economies was to sell loyalty programs and customer relationship management (CRM) software and staff training on the basis that it would stem defection and result in existing customers buying many more services. But both before and after this all started, cross-selling metrics obeyed the double jeopardy law.

For example, in spite of all their efforts, banks vary only a little in terms of how many products their customers have with them—and this in line with their size, whether or not they have adopted a particular CRM system or whatever their customer satisfaction scores were. The bigger banks with much higher penetration have slightly higher cross-product loyalty, as double jeopardy says should be the case (see Figure 1.3, which shows metrics for banks in India).

Figure 1.3: Double jeopardy in banks in India (2014)

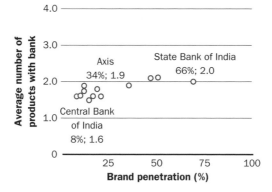

The conclusion is clear. The first place to look for growth barriers is your own marketing strategy—it may be holding you back. Another place to look for penetration barriers are impediments to purchase. Is anything making it difficult to buy or use your brand? Do you have varieties to suit most buyers? Are you too expensive for the mainstream customer?

In the USA people live in houses and drive cars that are very large by emerging market standards. This allows them to buy large packages and in quantities that are impractical in other countries (where in the house could they be stored?)—these are barriers to penetration in some countries. In Thailand, a great market for haircare products, premium Western brands are desirable, but large bottles were beyond the weekly budget of many households. Companies like L'Oréal, Unilever and Procter & Gamble found success in offering much smaller packages of their brands. This might seem slightly counter-intuitive from a developed market perspective, as smaller packages mean that the product is more expensive per gram. Why would you market a more expensive product to people who weren't wealthy? But the smaller product lowers the overall price of purchase, the *entry cost*, which was a key barrier to penetration. Now millions could buy it as an occasional treat, and it could be bought more regularly by hair-conscious teenagers, who were never going to save up for a large, pricey bottle.

Meaningful loyalty metrics

Knowing about double jeopardy has the added practical value of giving loyalty metrics context and meaning. It provides the foresight to be able to predict how penetration and loyalty will change if the brand grows. It can also help identify and troubleshoot problem brands. For example, it reveals if you have a niche or change-of-pace brand: both are deviations you may need to try to fix. If these deviations can't be fixed, then investment can be structured to reflect the brand's limited potential for growth.

Conclusion

The law of double jeopardy holds in emerging and developed markets, for services and products, for consumables and durables. It has held for decades and continues to do so even as the markets globalise, and digital and mobile offerings change how we engage with and buy brands. Even in categories such as financial services, with state ownership of banks and much regulation, we see double jeopardy.

Consequently, for a brand to grow it needs to grow its market penetration, through broadening mental and physical availability. Focusing too much on loyalty, either by trying to build it or imagining it doesn't exist and thinking that you therefore need to 'buy' customers every time with price promotions or loyalty incentives, are costly distractions that brands can ill afford.

Don't assume that any special characteristics about a brand will confer on it a loyalty advantage. If the brand does deviate from double jeopardy, search for impediments to penetration (such as lack of distribution in key regions or channels) as these may be what makes the loyalty metrics look high. And these impediments will limit growth potential.

The double jeopardy law tells us that brand growth depends on reaching non-customers and light customers. In Chapter 2, we'll look at these buyers. We'll discuss their strategic importance and the marketing challenges of reaching and refreshing the mental structures of many low-value customers.

FURTHER READING ON THE DOUBLE JEOPARDY LAW

Important claims require serious evidence, hence the many data sets in this chapter. Those interested in delving deeper or simply seeing the wide range of conditions under which the double jeopardy law has been documented (for example, attitudes, behaviour, industrial, services, durables, retail stores, voting, media) may wish to read the following peer-reviewed sources.

Bennett, D & Graham, C 2010, 'Is loyalty driving growth for the brand in front? A two-purchase analysis of car category dynamics in Thailand', *Journal of Strategic Marketing*, vol. 18, no. 7, pp. 573–85.

Bhat, S & Fox, R 1996, 'An investigation of jeopardy effects in store choice', *Journal of Retailing and Consumer Services*, vol 3, no. 3, pp. 129–33.

Donthu, N 1994, 'Double jeopardy in television program choice', *Journal of the Academy of Marketing Science*, vol. 22, no. 2, pp. 180–5.

Ehrenberg, A 1972, *Repeat Buying: Theory and Applications*, American Elsevier, New York.

Ehrenberg, A 1991, 'Politicians' double jeopardy: a pattern and exceptions', *Journal of the Market Research Society*, vol. 33, no. 1, pp. 347–53.

Ehrenberg, A & Goodhardt, G 2002, 'Double jeopardy revisited, again', Marketing Insights, *Marketing Research*, Spring, pp. 40–2.

Ehrenberg, A, Goodhardt, G & Barwise, P 1990, 'Double jeopardy revisited', *Journal of Marketing*, vol. 54 (July), pp. 82–91.

Jürkenbeck, K, Anesbury, Z, Bogomolova, T & Bogomolova, S 2019. 'Analyzing double jeopardy pattern among fresh fruits and vegetables', European

Marketing Academy Conference (EMAC), 28 May, University of Hamburg, Hamburg, Germany.

Kooyman, C & Wright, M 2017, 'Double jeopardy benchmarks for political polls', *Australasian Marketing Journal*, vol. 25, no. 3, pp. 180–4.

McDowell, W & Dick, S 2005, 'Revealing a double jeopardy effect in radio station audience behavior', *Journal of Media Economics*, vol. 18, no. 4, pp. 271–84.

Martin, C, Jr 1973, 'The theory of double jeopardy', *Journal of the Academy of Marketing Science*, vol. 1, no. 2, pp. 148–56.

Michael, J & Smith, P 1999, 'The theory of double jeopardy: an example from a forest products industry', *Forest Products Journal*, vol. 49, no. 3, pp. 21–6.

Riebe, E, Wright, M, Stern, P & Sharp, B 2014, 'How to grow a brand: retain or acquire customers?', *Journal of Business Research*, vol. 67, no. 5, pp. 990–7.

Rogers, A, Daunt, K, Morgan, P & Beynon, M 2017, 'Examining the existence of double jeopardy and negative double jeopardy within Twitter', *European Journal of Marketing*, vol. 51, no. 7/8, pp. 1–35.

Solgaard, H, Smith, D & Schmidt, M 1998, 'Double jeopardy patterns for political parties', *International Journal of Public Opinion Research*, vol. 10, no. 2, pp. 109–20.

Uncles, M & Lee, D 2006, 'Brand purchasing by older consumers: an investigation using the Juster scale and the Dirichlet model', *Marketing Letters*, vol. 17, no. 1, pp. 17–29.

Wright, M, Sharp, A & Sharp, B 1998, 'Are Australasian brands different?', *Journal of Brand and Product Management*, vol. 7, no. 6, pp. 465–80.
(A full reference list is at the end of this book.)

2

Target the (Whole) Market

Byron Sharp and Jenni Romaniuk

In Chapter 1, we talked about the double jeopardy law, which says that for a brand to grow, it needs to increase its penetration: that is, to win more customers in each time period. In this chapter we explore the nature of brand customer bases in more detail. We show why reaching non-buyers of the brand (in the time period), and infrequent buyers of the category, are essential for growth. Along the way we further expose the heavy-buyer fallacy.

The scientific laws revealed in this chapter have major implications for brand strategy—from brand equity to media planning, to what to put in advertising. These laws explain why successful marketers are sophisticated mass marketers who have a deep and evolving understanding of *both* the commonalities *and* differences in their buyers, and use this understanding to appeal to a wide range of category buyers.

All that glitters …

When the market is large, and full of unknowns, it is tempting to retreat from battling the whole market and focus on protecting what you have: your current customers, and particularly the ones who buy the brand often. Similarly, return on investment (ROI)–driven thinking encourages a focus on heavy or current customers. In this chapter we provide evidence to help prevent falling for loyalty myths.

We'll start by explaining why heavy customers are a poor source of *growth*.

The heavy-buyer fallacy

Heavy buyers look attractive from a marketing perspective, particularly in repeat-purchase markets. They buy more and therefore are worth more, much more, than the typical buyer of the brand. But, and this is very important, this isn't what matters from a growth perspective. What matters for growth is how much more they can be encouraged to buy from you. The answer turns out to be not much.

The first, and rather obvious reason, is that these people are few. A typical packaged goods brand might have an average purchase frequency of only three times annually, and the top 20% might buy it at a rate of around five or six times annually. If all these heavy buyers made one more purchase in a year, which is a lot for that group (an increase of around 20%), this will actually deliver only a few per cent of sales growth because they are few in number. Simple maths.

If we look at buying of durables, a survey of 1205 adults in the UK conducted in 2019 found that of those who had bought at least one washing machine in the past five years, 85% had bought just one, 10% had bought two washing machines and the remaining 5% bought three or more times (five people had bought five or more washing machines, so at least one a year!). In the more exciting category of televisions, 67% had bought just one television in five years, 23% had bought two, and only 10% had bought three or more televisions in the last 5 years. Heavy buyers are few, and them buying one more durable will not contribute much to the bottom line.

Which brings us to the second, less obvious, reason why you won't be able to encourage your heavy buyers to buy much more from you. Contrary to popular belief, it isn't easy to boost the purchasing of these buyers. A brand's heaviest customers are already highly likely to be heavy buyers of the category, so it is unlikely that they will increase their category buying rate and buy even more, and you can't steal from competitors as they are already very loyal to the brand (Sharp, Trinh & Dawes, 2014). How do you make someone who takes three international holidays a year take another international holiday? Where would the extra sales come from?

A brand's existing favouritism with heavy buyers puts a ceiling on how many more sales you can ever hope to gain from them. Heavy buyers aren't new to the category; this isn't something they are getting into; they are mature buyers of the category (think of them like a mature, saturated sub-market); and they already favour your brand. If a brand grows, we find surprisingly little of this is due to a brand's heaviest buyers.

Of course we want to retain these people as buyers of our brand. We want to reach them with our marketing efforts—and we almost always do. These buyers are vastly more likely to notice any marketing we do: they see our discounts; they notice our service improvements. Their brains are also far more attuned to noticing and recognising our brand, and its advertising. We hardly have to worry about giving these people extra attention: we are already in their sight line.

It would be nice to think that by focusing on these heavier buyers we could somehow reduce their defection risk but, in the original *How Brands Grow*, we saw that most customer defection is for reasons completely outside our control—for reasons such as customers moving house, getting married or dying. For example, in an Ehrenberg–Bass Institute study of business clients who had defected from their financial services provider, about 60% of defection occurred for reasons completely beyond the influence of marketers (Bogomolova & Romaniuk, 2009). For the remaining 40%, the key reasons were getting a cheaper offer from a competitor or joining some corporate buying group to gain cheaper services. Only 4% of business owners changed financial service provider because of a service issue—not exactly an incentive to introduce costly service improvement initiatives!

It would be nice to think that we could cross-sell other services to our customers to grow, but again the empirical evidence suggests this is very difficult as service brands vary little in the number of products their customers hold (Mundt, Dawes & Sharp, 2006). Besides, these people are a small part of your customer base, and a tiny part of your total potential market.

These strategies directed at heavy buyers are hit and miss at best and, even if you hit, the rewards are small.

Finally, it would be nice to think our heavy buyers become advocates and help us grow by recommending the brand—but the reality is that most word of mouth comes from lighter buyers, because these people are many. For example, we surveyed customers of Matahari, a popular department store chain in Indonesia, and found that the 11% of its heavier shoppers, who visit it three or more times a month, accounted for only 15% of the word of mouth given about the retailer. Less frequent shoppers were responsible for five times more word of mouth, because many of them exist. This pattern is typical: other retailers such as upmarket SOGO and online retailer Lazada have similar results. Any small segment equals a small effect on word-of-mouth levels, and heavy buyers are a small segment of any brand's buyer base.

An analogy would be if we thought that people with red hair give ten times more negative word of mouth because of their volatile temper. This might justify efforts to target redheads and given them extra special service to avoid their bad temper! But, as only 1–2% of the global population have red hair, the volume of negative word of mouth from this segment will be small, even at ten times more likely—hardly worth rolling out the red carpet for them! The incidence of people with red hair, and their contribution to the total volume of negative word of mouth, are both needed to work out if this segment is worth special attention. It's the same with heavy buyers: even if their propensity to buy and to give word of mouth is substantially higher, this rarely generates enough volume to compensate for their small segment size.

Any customer can give word of mouth, but for this to happen it requires the right circumstances, such as talking to someone who asks for advice. Heavy buyers are few, which lessens the likelihood that any one of them will be in an appropriate situation to give word of mouth. Light and medium buyers are many, so it is more likely one of them will be in a situation with the opportunity to give positive word of mouth. Cultivating relationships with heavy buyers in the hope they will generate large, sustained, volumes of word of mouth is a costly distraction from the path to growth. (In Chapter 7 we talk more about word of mouth.)

Why light/infrequent buyers really matter

Our heaviest, most loyal buyers aren't a great source of growth because they are unlikely to buy much more and their low numbers don't make a major difference to the bottom line. In the case of light buyers, yes, it's the opposite, but the story is more interesting than that. Let's start with how many light buyers a brand normally has.

We (repeatedly) find that brands in categories bought often enough to generate data across multiple brand purchase opportunities follow the same reverse-J shaped distribution of how many people buy once, twice, three times and so on. This means many infrequent buyers and a long tail of a few (very) frequent buyers. Andrew Ehrenberg first identified this in 1959, and today we see this reverse-J-shape for brands from all corners of the earth, including emerging markets. We see this distribution across countries, categories and over time. When designing a marketing strategy, this distribution is one of the most important pieces of information that any brand manager can arm themselves with.

Figure 2.1 illustrates the shape for different countries (Brazil, Philippines and Turkey), categories (toothpaste, beer and soft drinks) and functional qualities such as local or global brands (compare Cola-Turka with Coca-Cola Light).

Larger share brands have more people buying them, and at a slightly more frequent rate (the law of double jeopardy). This law is because of this negative binomial distribution. The big potential shift in the frequency for all brands is the proportion of buyers in the zero columns, which (inversely) records each brand's penetration (see Figure 2.2). When a brand grows, the main change will usually be the zero buyer column shrinking; if the brand declines, the main change will be the zero column growing—that is, penetration will change.

Figure 2.1: Buying frequency distributions for a range of categories, countries and brands

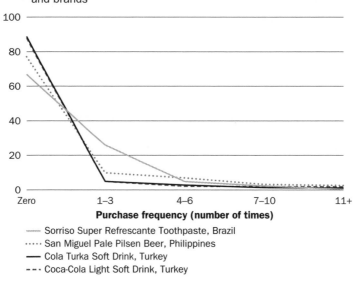

Purchase frequency (number of times)

— Sorriso Super Refrescante Toothpaste, Brazil
····· San Miguel Pale Pilsen Beer, Philippines
— Cola Turka Soft Drink, Turkey
- - · Coca-Cola Light Soft Drink, Turkey

Figure 2.2: Buying frequency distributions for fuel brands in the UK (2012)

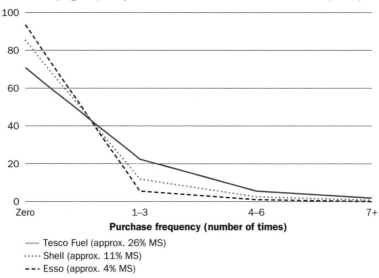

Purchase frequency (number of times)

— Tesco Fuel (approx. 26% MS)
····· Shell (approx. 11% MS)
- - · Esso (approx. 4% MS)

When brands grow, more light brand buyers are gained than heavy ones (see Table 2.1) and when brands decline, more light brand buyers are lost than heavy ones. In terms of influencing people, successful marketing activities therefore create more light buyers than heavy buyers. That is, we need *many* people to buy the brand once, and a *few of these* to also buy the brand again and again in the time period. By only focusing on the heavier buyers, we miss that we also need to influence the behaviour of many lighter/non-buyers.

Table 2.1: Chinese toothpaste brand that increased by 1.5 percentage points in market share

Brand buying frequency	Year 1 (%)	Year 2 (%)	Change (Y2 – Y1)
Zero	91.7	89.8	– 1.9
Once	5.0	6.3	1.3
Twice	1.6	2.0	0.4
Three times	0.7	0.8	0.2
Four times	0.6	0.5	– 0.1
Five or more times	0.5	0.5	0

A brand that moves from one market share to another also moves from one negative binomial distribution to another: its new frequency chart looks rather similar to its old one. It will still have mostly light customers, a few heavy buyers, and most customers will be lighter than average. The greater a brand's penetration—that is, the more buyers it has—the more heavy buyers it has.

To illustrate this, if Brand A and Brand B have the same market share, they will usually have same amount of heavy brand buyers. But if Brand B is a smaller brand than Brand A, it will have fewer heavy buyers. This can be mistakenly interpreted to mean that Brand B is small because it lacks the heavy buyers of Brand A. Actually, Brand B is smaller because it lacks the number of customers that Brand A has in all buying weights—light, medium and heavy. Compare Tesco and Esso in Figure 2.2—Tesco has more of all types of buyers than Esso except, of course, non-buyers.

The ubiquity of this pattern means an absence of evidence that brands have succeeded by attracting or holding on to a disproportionate amount of heavy brand buyers.[1]

---

1   This highlights the importance of correct metrics. We unfortunately see cases where consultants misinterpret metrics by only focusing on one small part of the picture.

The negative binomial distribution also gives you a crystal ball. It means you can predict your brand's (potential) future. That is, you can predict the future frequency distribution of your brand, should it grow in market share. If the brand's current share is 1.5% and your objective is to become a 3% share brand, you can predict how many light, medium and heavy buyers the brand will have if it reaches 3%.

Pareto says you can't ignore lighter buyers

The Pareto law is usually stated as 'the top 20% of a brand's customers generate 80% of its sales'. This extreme magnitude is used to justify investments in targeting existing customers, and ignoring, or even 'firing' light buyers. But the Pareto law is not 80:20. Sharp and Romaniuk (2007) comprehensively documented the Pareto law as closer to a 50:20 pattern: that is, the top 20% of a brand's customers (the Pareto share) account for 40–60% of sales. In Table 2.2 we document additional results from a range of emerging markets to show further evidence from different countries and categories.

This law has profound strategic implications for resource allocation, just not in the way it is typically used—which is to justify concentrating resources in the very valuable customers. If 80% of a brand's customer base generated only 20% of its sales we would not be writing a chapter now on the importance of light customers. This 80% could perhaps even be largely ignored. But who wants to walk away from almost half their sales?

Looking over time reveals more to this story. The Pareto share is the proportion of *this year's sales* that come from the heaviest 20% of all the people who *bought the brand this year*. And this Pareto share is usually close to as much as 60% (Sharp, Romaniuk & Graham, 2019). But, if we track these same 'top 20' buyers next year, they will always be worth less. Some have changed their preferences, or left the country, or even died. A

Table 2.2: Examples of average annual brand Pareto shares across a variety of categories and countries

Country	Category	Brand's Pareto share (average)
India	Biscuits	64
Malaysia	Soft drinks	64
Philippines	Alcoholic beverages	60
Malaysia	Instant noodles	57
Malaysia	Biscuits	55
Malaysia	Detergent	55
Malaysia	Bar soap	53
Malaysia	Toothpaste	51
Kenya	Soft drinks	50
Nigeria	Soft drinks	50
Indonesia	Fashion retail	49
Malaysia	Shampoo	49
Turkey	Soft drinks	49
Brazil	Toothpaste	47
China	Toothpaste	45
Mexico	Soft drinks	45
Average		**53**

big driver of this is what statisticians call *regression to the mean*: over time, extremes in any cohort, such as heavy buyers, move closer to the average. In this case we can explain it very easily.

Some (but not all) of these heavy buyers really are different from most other people at least in terms of buying this brand and this category. Say the category is shampoo: perhaps they have oily hair (and need to shampoo a lot) or perhaps their hair is their crowning glory, and either of these reasons means they buy the category a great deal. Coupled with this, for whatever personal reason, one brand has dominant mental and physical availability for them (perhaps it was the one their mother used?). This makes them one of the brand's very heavy users.

But other people just happened *that year* to buy the brand enough to qualify as 'heavy' (compared to other buyers). They don't usually, but this particular year they did. Many reasons are possible for this, such as an extended stay by a house guest or a fitness fad, but serendipity is a reasonable explanation. Somehow (largely unpredictable) factors came together that year that meant they bought (a bit) more than they usually do.

Yes, much 'heavy buying' is due to happenstance. Remember, it often doesn't require a huge jump in purchasing to move from being an average buyer to a heavy buyer. In many cases, even just one single additional brand purchase will do it. For example, look at Table 2.3: to move into the top 50% (the heavy half) of buyers requires only buying four times; for 16% of buyers that's just one more purchase. To move into the top 20% requires only a few more. Of course, this happens all the time. One year a buyer might buy Fanta twice, another year only once, another year four times—they are hardly likely to even notice these changes (remember four times a year is only once every three months). The buyer's ongoing propensity is to buy Fanta about twice a year, with a bit of wobble: some years more (our friends' kids come to stay), some less (our kids go away to visit relatives). What this means is that some of the people whom we thought were committed heavy buyers (because they bought us a lot in the time period we were looking at) aren't really; they just looked heavy this year, and next year it is very likely that they will buy closer to their normal rates. This will drive much of the regression to the mean.

Movement in the opposite direction is also apparent, when some of our heavier buyers will next year just happen to have a lighter than average (for them) year. Serendipity strikes again! Put this all together and we actually see that around half of the people we class as our heaviest buyers based on a particular period of buying do not meet this criteria in the next period—and they are (perfectly) replaced by 'light buyers' who next period happen to buy at a heavy rate.[2]

---

[2] The fact that they are perfectly replaced—that is, the number of people who drop out of the heavy buyer group is exactly matched by the number elevated into the group—seems almost magical, but of course it has to be for any brand that is stable in sales amongst these buyers. This 'magic' is because the effect is entirely statistical, due to random chance. It's the same sort of magic that allows us to make astonishingly accurate predictions about how much money casinos will take and how much they will pay out. It's the same sort of magic that allows us to predict the distribution of heights, weights and student grades from simply knowing the average.

Table 2.3: Purchase frequency distribution for Fanta in Mexico (2014)

Frequency of purchase	Buyers (%)	Cumulative (%)	Weight
10+ times	13	13	
9 times	1	14	Top 20%
8 times	3	17	
7 times	3	20	
6 times	7	26	
5 times	9	35	Top 50%
4 times	10	45	
3 times	16	61	
Twice	21	82	
Once	18	100	

A relative consistency of 50% stability across brands and categories is apparent in Table 2.4, which shows the results across brands in two different categories in Malaysia.[3] About half the people who were classified as heavy buyers in one period also qualified as heavy in the subsequent period—meaning about half *weren't*.

Table 2.4: Stability of heavy buyers in Malaysia (2011–12)

Soap	Top 20% stability	Noodles	Top 20% stability
Dettol Regular	47	Maggi	59
Lux	42	Cintan	49
May	29	Mamee	42
Orchid Fruitale	46	Mie Sedaap	59
Lifebuoy	30	Vits	38
Protex	37	Private Label	53
Antabax	48	Eka	42
Palmolive Naturals	34	Jasmine	42
Average	**39**		**48**

Source: Kantar WorldPanel Malaysia

---

3   Our testing included Top 10% and classifying people by buying weight as per Romaniuk and Wight (2014). The results were consistent across heavy buyer classification approaches.

We find this level of stability applies to Western brands introduced to the country (such as Pantene, Colgate or Coca-Cola) and specialist, strongly positioned brands such as Safi, 'specifically designed to meet the need of the modern Muslim women and men' (Safi, 2015), which has around 40% heavy-buyer stability in shampoo and 50% heavy-buyer stability in toothpaste.

This makes it hard to correctly classify heavy buyers using any snapshot of buying data, even a snapshot that covers a whole year. This rampant misclassification creates problems for any database-driven targeting of heavy customers. We risk interpreting this misclassification as indicators of success or failure of our marketing activities.

Of course we can more generally profile our customers, and it doesn't take sophisticated market research to realise that the heavy buyers of luxury European clothing brands are going to be people with a certain amount of discretionary income and an interest in fashion. But, we have to accept the following points:

- many of the people who fit this profile won't be heavy buyers of our brand (though they obviously have potential)
- quite a lot of our heavy customers at least in a particular time period won't fit this profile
- much of our sales won't come from heavy buyers, anyway.

What about heavy category buyers?

In the quest for marketing efficiency the often-cited next question is: surely our best targets for acquisition are the heaviest buyers of the category? It's true that if these people have the highest potential they *could* buy you more often. From an efficiency or ROI perspective it probably makes sense to reach out to these customers.

In India, when Inorbit Mall opened its first Bangalore mall, no one was surprised they choose the exclusive suburb of Whitefield even if it is quite removed from the centre of the city. Inorbit Mall of course needed to be close to wealthier shoppers—people who spend more on expensive clothes and restaurants. But there were other considerations: Whitefield also has good transport infrastructure and can be reached by road, bus and rail, which is important for shoppers to shop there, and for the delivery of goods and supplies (the Container Corporation of India has a large inland container depot just off Whitefield Road).

'Fish where the fish are' can be a sound maxim. You might as well *start* where many fish are pooling together—particularly when the ocean is huge. But to grow you need to reach all sorts of category buyers—light as well as heavy. Given that a large proportion of category buyers are infrequent, even in a frequently bought category (see Figure 2.3) then they are going to be your main type of customer.[4]

When a brand is small, more of its customer base is made up of heavy category buyers. Partly this is because heavy category buyers have bigger repertoires—they buy lots of brands including small ones.

Figure 2.3: Category purchase frequency for biscuits in India (2011)

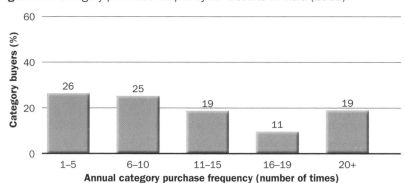

If a brand is fortunate enough to grow, then its customer base will change—a greater portion of its customers will be lighter category buyers, and a smaller portion will be heavy category buyers.

The natural monopoly law

This advantage of big brands is known as the *natural monopoly law* (Ehrenberg, 2000; Dawes, 2020). Bigger brands have a greater monopoly over the light category buyers. Think of it this way—low-rating television

---

4   It is important to avoid confusing the frequency distribution with the number of purchases or time frame or both. Over a longer time frame, everyone will buy the category more. Over a shorter time frame, everyone will buy the category less. The absolute numbers for what classifies someone as a light buyer may change, but the distribution doesn't.

programs are, by definition, watched by very few people. When we look at many of these programs it is rather obvious why few people would waste time watching them. More of a mystery is why anyone would, yet they do attract viewers. Who are these people watching these low-rating shows?

Well, the viewers of low-rating programs tend to be people who watch an awful lot of television. But, like all categories, the heavy television viewers are in the minority. So for a program to gain high ratings it must reach well beyond the group of heavy television viewers and attract light television viewers. This is why top-rating shows are valuable to advertisers: they attract people who hardly ever watch television. This story, the natural monopoly law, is the same for brands and retailers.

To be a big brand you *must* reach out and attract many light category buyers. It's not that some big brands monopolise light category buyers and some don't—*all* attract light category buyers. If you want to be a big brand, you therefore need to attract light category buyers as well. If you want to *remain* a big brand, you need to extend your marketing activity to reach these customers, otherwise they could slip away.

This is one reason that an ROI focus can keep a brand from growing: it distracts brand managers from the main game. It seems counter-intuitive to reach out to people who don't buy the category much, and so would appear to deliver lower ROI. Ironically, focusing on ROI can prevent a brand from benefiting from scale and earning larger, more secure, profits.

Resist the seduction of sole loyalty

The chase for loyalty quickly turns into a chase for the unicorns of target marketing: the heavy category buyer who buys only your brand. While buyers can be heavy category buyers who are solely loyal to one brand, these buyers are so few that they may as well be mythical.

We illustrate this with examples from soft drinks in Turkey and Mexico (see Table 2.5), where fewer than 1% of the heaviest category buyers (buying once a day or more often) are solely loyal. Sole loyalty is highest amongst those buying once a month or less frequently; however, unfortunately fewer than 5% of category buyers buy at this rate.

Table 2.5: The relationship between category purchase frequency and sole loyalty for soft drinks in Turkey and Mexico (2014)

Purchase frequency	Turkey % solely loyal	Mexico % solely loyal
Once a day or more often	0.5	0.3
Every 2 or 3 days	0.7	0.5
Once a week	7	6
2 or 3 times a month	14	20
Once per month	29	31
Less than once a month	40	33

This might not come as a surprise for soft drink buyers—after all, it is a low-value category, prone to impulse-buying and variety-seeking by consumers. What about a completely different category, such as financial services? We find the more financial services products someone holds, the less likely they are to be solely loyal. Figure 2.4 shows how, for banks in South Africa, buyer movement from one to two products quickly halves the number of 100% loyals.

Figure 2.4: The relationship between number of products purchased and sole loyalty for financial services in South Africa (2012)

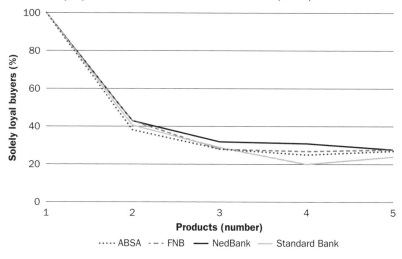

Source: National Advertising Bureau Roots Survey, 2012

To class sole-brand buying as the outcome of some deep customer intent or desire is questionable; 100% loyals are usually low-value customers who don't often buy the category. Much of what we observe as sole loyalty is happenstance, or because someone only bought the category once (and so by definition is 100% loyal to whichever brand they bought). If you extend the time frame, you see the proportion of solely loyals decline because with more opportunities to buy the category, people buy from more brands (as shown in Table 2.5).

Share loyalty (of which sole loyalty is the extreme) becomes more important for growth where it is impossible to expand the customer base. This is not a strategy to seek out but one to adapt to if the typical penetration-led path to growth is closed to the brand. The extreme idea that you should try to build a 100% loyal customer base is likely to lead to costly failure, even in subscription markets such as banking and insurance.

Sophisticated mass marketing

Marketing textbooks caricature mass marketing as offering a single marketing mix. This is nonsense. It's so silly that it's hard to think of a single real-world example. Even the Coca-Cola Company has hundreds of brands, distributed in different ways, in different places, with different advertising (in numerous languages), different prices even in the same store (cold cans are priced higher) and so on.

There is a difference between a product-range strategy and a segmentation strategy. Any successful marketer develops a product range to take into account the heterogeneity amongst category buyers. It's essential to do this if you want to reach all people in all buying situations (that is, target the market). But this does not require targeting specific buyers with each offer, as advocated by a segmentation strategy. Instead, a better option is for an 'anyone, anytime' sales approach. The aim is to reach everyone with a relevant, attractive offer in as many buying situations as possible, without generating over-the-top complexity and destroying scale advantages. The secret to doing this is to look for commonalities, and mass ways of reaching customers both physically and mentally.

Customers do vary a great deal in their lifestyles, interests, wealth, age and so on. It is easy to get distracted by these differences and to make things more complicated than they need be. The customer differences that matter, that are of any practical value, should be very obvious (for example, geographic differences); if they are not, they are unlikely to matter.

Sophisticated mass marketers can offer a great deal of customisation without having to identify and target different buyers. For example, a great deal of customisation occurs at the point of sale, where buyers choose between options for a number of different characteristics:

- payment
- delivery
- packaging
- volume of the order
- insurance, and so on.

This sort of customisation is offered to all customers and is not based on identifying particular types of people and targeting them. Customers are allowed individual expression, and vote with their wallet.

Don't shoot yourself in the foot with target marketing

Contrary to popular belief, target marketing is not clever. Nor is it customer-centric. Like salt in cooking, a little bit of targeting makes sense but tighter targeting than targeting category buyers is a recipe for negative growth.

The desire to target just a fraction of the market is often based on the idea that the brand is highly differentiated and so must appeal to some and not others—or that it must be made to (because Kotler or Aaker told me so). Data on real-world buying just does not support this view (see *How Brands Grow*, Chapter 5, and award-winning research such as Kennedy & Ehrenberg, 2001; Kennedy, Ehrenberg & Long, 2000; Uncles et al., 2012). Rival brands sell to highly similar customer bases, each made up of a very similar mixture of heterogeneous buyers. The stark difference is that some brands have bigger customer bases than others.

A really dangerous practice in modern marketing is to describe a market as a single person: for example, 'our target consumer is Nicole, she's 28 years old, is passionate about the environment and sustainability, shops at Whole Foods market, likes new experiences, reads classic literature but also watches *Keeping up with the Kardashians* as a guilty pleasure'. This is the height of inane target marketing: to treat all those very different customers as if they are clones of Nicole. In their defence, some will say this caricature is just to 'bring the customer alive', to 'help thinking', but it is lazy, dangerous thinking that often finds its way into advertising and media plans, and the brand ends up talking only to a tiny fraction of its potential market. Many new brands have failed to generate enough sales to justify their existence, not because they were bad products but because this sort of targeting guaranteed that they would undershoot their sales targets. A large share of a tiny (Nicole) market still equals very low sales.

America's biggest Hispanic-owned food company, Goya Foods, began in 1936 as a specialty distributor of basic products, such as beans, to Hispanic immigrants. Today it is one of the USA's fastest-growing food companies, introducing all sorts of Americans to a (wide) range of Hispanic-inspired food items. 'We like to say we don't market to Latinos, we market as Latinos', says CEO Bob Unanue (Wentz, 2013). In the UK, the brand Quorn offers a wide range of meat-free protein dishes. They could have targeted vegetarians, as these are the people for whom the brand had the most obvious appeal. Instead, as they explain, 'We started to transform the brand's positioning from a vegetarian substitute (relevant to around 7% of UK households) to a broader healthy eating brand (relevant to around 70% of UK households), thus opening up a significantly larger penetration-led growth opportunity' (Wragg & Regan, 2012, p. 33). By the end of 2011 Quorn were responsible for delivering 62% of category growth with sales up £6.8 million (Wragg & Regan, 2012). In 2020 Quorn's marketing director reported that the majority of Quorn consumers are meat eaters.

Goya Foods and Quorn are examples of marketers thinking about the category needs their brands could satisfy, and worrying less about who within the category is going to buy their brand. This thinking widened their potential markets and created sales opportunities that would have been missed if they had stuck to their 'target' markets.

Conclusion

This chapter explained why light buyers matter most, and the importance of sophisticated mass marketing to build a large brand. Most growth will come from light and non-buyers of the brand, simply because of how many of them there are, and the room they have to increase their purchasing. The natural monopoly law also highlights the importance of designing marketing strategies that reach out to light category buyers.

We also exposed many of the loyalty and targeting fallacies that are peddled to marketers. Next we look at what other brands your customers buy, and what can be learnt from this.

3

Where New Customers Come From

Byron Sharp and Jenni Romaniuk

We've seen that, to grow, a brand needs to recruit new buyers and encourage very light buyers to favour the brand a little more. This means winning buyers from other brands, which raises the question of which other brands' customers we should target. We now showcase an empirical law that makes managing a brand a little less complicated.

Insightfully examining differences between brands' customer bases leads to the realisation that your brand potentially competes with every other brand in the category for the same customers. We show how to use this knowledge to your advantage.

Then we turn to what can be learnt by monitoring the competitors' brands bought by your consumers. We show how to systematically analyse the competitive structure of the market from different viewpoints (for example, brand, product type, price point or region). Today's markets can have all sorts of variation, which needs to be understood in order to manage a portfolio of brands. The key to getting a handle on this complexity is to first understand the pattern of brand switching or sharing to expect. The *duplication of purchase law* provides this baseline.

Competitive brands have similar customer bases

If positioning-based targeting actually worked, we would see rival brands each selling to different types of customers. But this rarely turns out to be the case. When we compare the customer profiles of competing brands, they look strikingly similar (Hammond, Ehrenberg & Goodhardt, 1996; Kennedy & Ehrenberg, 2001; Kennedy, Ehrenberg & Long, 2000; Uncles et al., 2012; Truong, Faulkner & Mueller Loose, 2012; Anesbury, Winchester & Kennedy, 2017; Patrick et al., 2018). This is evident in a wide variety of categories, countries and over time as well (Anesbury, Winchester & Kennedy, 2017).

For example, if we look at the South Korean fast food market (Table 3.1) and compare brand-user profiles for ten of the top brands, we see that the average brand's customer base is about half male (48%); about a sixth of customers (15%) are aged 18–24 years; about a third of buyers (34%) are lower income and so on. Also immediately apparent, when you look at the data in this way, is how similar this story is for every brand. Lotteria, a large local chain selling burgers, has 47% male customers, similar to McDonald's (52% male) and so on—all very close to half. The variance, quantified in the mean absolute deviation, is between 1 and 3 percentage points. We also see very little difference in the user profiles of local and global brands: competing brands sell to similar customers.

South Korea's results are not unusual. We see this pattern play out in fast food across the world, as illustrated by Table 3.2, which shows the mean absolute deviations for key demographic variables across eleven emerging markets, ranging from China to Mexico to Nigeria.

Table 3.1: Fast food in South Korea eaten in the last six months—sample of demographic profiles

Brands (in penetration order)	Male (%)	18–24 years (%)	25–34 years (%)	Lower income (%)	Higher income (%)	Have children aged under 5 (%)	One person in household (%)	Work full-time (%)
*Lotteria	47	16	25	37	16	13	8	62
McDonald's	52	16	28	35	17	13	8	67
KFC	51	13	29	35	18	10	9	68
Pizza Hut	48	14	22	31	20	12	6	69
*Paris Baguette	46	15	24	36	14	11	9	63
Dunkin' Donuts	46	15	27	33	20	14	6	66
Domino's pizza	44	13	29	33	20	16	7	72
*Tour Les Jour	42	18	25	35	15	15	7	63
Burger King	53	16	29	31	21	11	6	66
*Kyochon	50	16	18	31	19	14	7	70
Average	48	15	26	34	18	13	7	67
Mean absolute deviation	**3**	**1**	**3**	**2**	**2**	**2**	**1**	**3**
Average (local brands only)	**46**	**16**	**23**	**35**	**16**	**13**	**8**	**64**

*Local brand

Fast food brands largely compete for the same type of customers. Over more than 3000 cross-tabulations involving more than 100 brands, only 2.5% of brands deviated more than 10 percentage points from the average brand on that characteristic, even though the brands sell very different types of food (including local cuisine, chicken, hamburgers, pizza and doughnuts).

Table 3.2: Mean absolute deviations (in percentage points) in fast food brand-user profiles across eleven countries

Country	Gender	Age	Household size (number of people)	Children at home	Work status	Income
Brazil	3*	3	2	3	5	3
China	5	3	2	3	1	4
India	2	3	2	3	2	2
Indonesia	4	2	2	2	2	2
Kenya	3	4	2	3	3	3
Mexico	3	3	2	2	3	2
Nigeria	4	3	2	2	2	2
Russia	6	3	2	2	3	3
South Africa	3	2	3	2	3	4
South Korea	5	4	2	2	3	2
Turkey	2	3	2	3	2	3
Category average	**4**	**3**	**2**	**3**	**3**	**3**

*Interpreted as, for example, fast food brands in Brazil varied in the percentage of males from the average brand by 3 percentage points—so if the average brand had 50% in its customer base, brands are between 47% and 53%.

What about service categories in emerging markets?

Similarity in customer profiles extends to categories such as financial services, telecommunications and insurance. Table 3.3 shows the results for personal banking in seven emerging markets. While we see larger variation between providers than we saw for fast food, particularly for income and work status variables, much of this variation is easily explainable.

Table 3.3: Mean absolute deviation variation (in percentage points) in banks'
customer profiles (2014)

Country	Gender	Age	Household size (number of people)	Work status	Income
Brazil	3	4	3	6	4
China	4	3	2	2	3
India	3	3	3	3	3
Indonesia	3	4	2	3	7
Russia	5	3	4	4	3
South Africa	3	2	2	4	6
South Korea	4	3	2	3	3
Category average	**4**	**3**	**3**	**4**	**4**

Let's dive a little deeper into the two countries with larger differences in the income levels of their banking customers: Indonesia and South Africa.

For Indonesia, the deviations were evident in foreign banks that had disproportionately more customers with monthly incomes over 7 million rupiah (Citibank, +17 percentage points; HSBC, +20 percentage points; Standard Chartered, +22 percentage points; ANZ, +14 percentage points) and several local banks having fewer higher-income customers (for example: BRI, −18 percentage points; BNI, −12 percentage points; BTN, −12 percentage points).

In South Africa, specific brands drive the variation. Postbank, which is a bank operated out of the South African Post Office, has more low-income customers (+29 percentage points), while Investec, an international specialist investment bank and asset manager, is a mirror image with more higher-income customers (+36 percentage points). The sources of the differences are thus unsurprising and based on the functional differences between the brands: in this case, the range of services they provide, their fees and where they have branches.

Before we wrap up discussion of this law-like pattern regarding the similarity of the customer profiles of competing brands, let's look at one more category: telecommunications. Growth in mobile phone usage means that telecommunications is becoming an increasingly important category in emerging markets. In some countries this category is just emerging from government regulation and opening up to foreign companies.

With many countries having only a few very large providers, the scene might be set for more specific targeting of customers as these competitors slice up the market. But, as Table 3.4 shows, we find across eight countries that, again, the user profiles of competitive brands differ very little, with mean average deviations of around 3 percentage points. In only 4% of cases did brands differ by more than 10 percentage points from the category average.

Table 3.4: Mean average deviation variations (in percentage points) in telecommunication services' customer profiles (2014)

Country	Gender	Age	Household size (number of people)	Age of children	Income
Brazil	2	4	2	5	3
India	4	3	1	3	2
Indonesia	2	5	4	3	3
Mexico	5	4	3	5	4
Nigeria	6	4	3	5	4
Russia	4	2	3	3	3
South Africa	2	1	1	2	2
Turkey	1	2	1	2	2
Category average	**3**	**3**	**2**	**3**	**3**

Loyal switchers

Your customers are much the same as other brands' customers. One reason for this similarity is that your customers also buy other brands. The customers who return to your store or repeat-buy your brand also buy your competitors' brands. This is a fundamental fact of competitive markets.

It is not uncommon for a brand manager to look at their Kantar or Nielsen report and, when they see that their customers only devote, say, a third of all their annual purchasing to their brand, exclaim with dismay 'my customers buy other brands most of the time'. They might then try to craft strategies to build up share loyalty. But such customer behaviour is normal. In the famous words of Andrew Ehrenberg, 'your customers are really other people's customers who occasionally buy you'.

In subscription markets, buyers allocate a large portion of their category buying to one brand: for example, we usually only have only one hairdresser and only one dentist (Sharp, Wright & Goodhardt, 2002). But, over time and purchase occasions, people have repertoires. Service firms offer many different products and services, but their customers seldom buy all of these from the same provider. Consequently, even a bank or an insurance provider may typically find that only around half of its customers consider that bank their main institution: so, the other half of their customers are largely another bank's customer (see Figure 3.1 for examples from Indonesia and South Korea). This is especially the case for smaller banks shown in Figure 3.1, such as Permata, the tenth-biggest bank in Indonesia, which is the main financial institution for only 15% of its customers, or Hana Bank in South Korea, which has only 26% of its customers say it is their main institution.

Nowadays, particularly in emerging markets, it is not unusual to have multiple phone handsets as well as SIM cards from multiple providers to take advantage of the different offers from telecommunications providers. Some people, when they hear this, throw their arms in the air and say, 'there is no loyalty any more'. This is very wrong, on two counts. Firstly, nothing has changed; this is how your grandparents, and their grandparents, bought brands. No past golden age of loyalty existed where people each bought only one brand religiously (except perhaps as a fairytale written in marketing textbooks). Secondly, while people buy from a repertoire, they are also very loyal: brands are not bought randomly. Loyalty appears to be a natural human behaviour (see Livaditis, Sharp & Sharp, 2012; and our university textbook: Sharp, 2017, pp. 40–4).

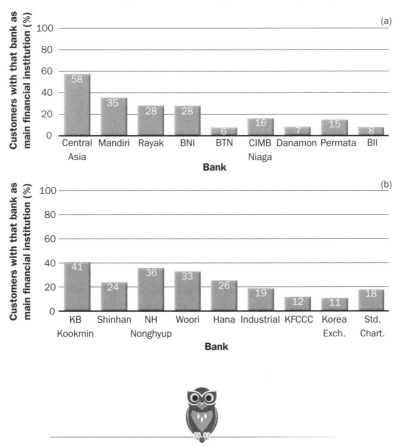

Figure 3.1: Percentage of bank customers with that bank as their main financial institution in (a) Indonesia and (b) South Korea (2014)

While people are not 100% loyal, this does not mean we need to jump to the opposite extreme and disclaim any loyalty. We see that not everyone who bought a category twice will have bought two brands—in fact, a good proportion will have bought the same brand twice. The pattern continues: people who bought three times bought fewer than three brands; people who bought four times bought fewer than four brands and so on.

If you look at the heaviest buyers, over a long time period, or at a category where people buy very frequently, like noodles, then some buyers have bought the category a great deal but their repertoire size, or the number of brands they actually bought, will be remarkably small. People keep returning to the same brands.

In Figure 3.2, we see two clear patterns from a South Korean alcoholic beverage category with more than 50 brands. The first is that as category purchase frequency increases, so does the number of brands bought (repertoire size). The second is that as category purchase frequency increases, the repertoire size as a percentage of category purchase frequency declines—signalling that the more people purchase a category, the more they tend to go back to the same brands to fulfil these additional purchases.

Figure 3.2: The relationship between (a) category purchase frequency and (b) repertoire size for alcoholic spirits in South Korea (2012)

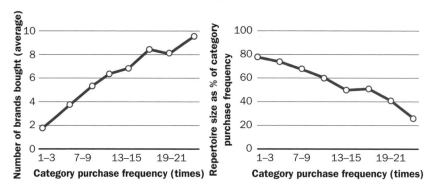

People are naturally loyal, yet it isn't normal for them to behave in either of these ways:

- buy only one brand over many purchase occasions; or
- buy a different brand for every purchase occasion.

Reality lies, somewhat unglamorously, somewhere in the middle of these two extremes.

Using predictable customer overlap

Your customers (and potential customers) buy other brands; indeed, they may mostly buy other brands. The *duplication of purchase* law predicts how many of your customers will buy each other competitive brand within any time period. Stated simply, the duplication of purchase law says that brands will share their customers in line with the other brands' penetration:

- A brand bought by most people in the market will also be bought by most of your customers.
- A brand that is bought by very few people in the market will be bought by few of your customers.

Put like this the duplication of purchase law sounds rather intuitive,[1] but what's surprising is its precision. It predicts that each brand will have a consistent level of customer overlap with all other competitive brands. The level of this overlap will also be correlated with the brand's share. A larger brand will have a higher overlap with all other brands than a smaller brand. This means that *if,* in a particular time period, 20% of all the people who bought fuel at Shell in the UK also bought from BP, *then* 20% of customers from other fuel retailers will also have bought from BP.

The duplication of purchase law says that competitive overlap, or the degree of competitive clout that a brand has over another, depends primarily on the brand's size. This also suggests that competition is largely about mental and physical availability, and not brand positioning, history, quality and so on.

Knowing that this pattern is the norm allows us to spot exceptions (referred to as *partitions*) that can provide additional insights and opportunities. But before we do that, we will show how to reveal the predictable patterns of customer overlap in a simple table.

A duplication of purchase table shows the degree to which brands within a category share their buyers with each of the other brands in the category (that is, what proportion of their customers also bought another

---

1   It has been referred to as 'fair share' and other terms, but this is often meant as a possible outcome rather than an empirical law.

particular brand during the period). Table 3.5 is a duplication of purchase table with no data.

Table 3.5: Duplication of purchase (no data)

Brand	% buying	Buyers who also bought other brands (%)			
		A	B	C	D
A	Highest	100%			
B	...		100%		
C	...			100%	
D	Lowest				100%

The 100% cells are a brand's level of customer overlap with itself, which logically must be 100%. In terms of the presentation of the data, it is good practice to blank out these cells, because they will distract from the key patterns, as well as distort the column averages.

In repertoire markets, the duplication of purchase tables refer to a particular time period: for example, the people during the year who bought brand A and who also bought brand B. Note that a buyer of brand A needs to only make one purchase of brand B to be counted. Consequently, duplication analyses that apply to very long periods can be misleading, because every brand may show very high levels of sharing with every other brand. This obscures who competes more or less closely. At the other end of the time spectrum, little duplication occurs in very short time periods, because most customers only bought the category once. This is also misleading. The analyst should choose a period long enough to capture a degree of repeated purchase: that is, a period long enough to allow most people to have revealed their repertoire of multiple brands. Fortunately, this is usually easy—the analyses aren't overly sensitive to the time period outside the two extremes mentioned. However, readers of duplication tables in repertoire markets need to note that they refer to a particular period, rather than an absolute metric; one can't simply say, '20% of Shell shoppers also buy fuel at BP'; it's 20% *in a month* or *in a year*.

In subscription markets, there needs to be capacity for multiple purchases. This can be through a broad definition of the category, such as any personal insurance (which covers home, car and even health insurance) instead of a single category such as home contents insurance. Or the category can be examined over time, which allows for multiple purchases across brands due to switching behaviour.[2]

A duplication of purchase table from annual purchases in the haircare category in China (Table 3.6) shows customer overlap in this time period varies from about two-thirds of every brand sharing customers with Pantene, down to less than a fifth sharing with Clear, the smallest brand in the table.

With the brands ordered by declining penetration, the duplication of purchase law becomes easy to see. Every brand shares more of its customers with larger competitors, and less with smaller competitors. It is also apparent just how accurate the duplication of purchase law is in this market; the brand scores running down the columns are very close to one another (and to the average) in spite of all the things going on in the market in that year (promotions, new SKU launches, natural disasters, marketing mistakes)—and, of course, sampling error on any market research sample.

Now that we can see the duplication of purchase law so clearly, we can also spot a few partitions. These would be difficult without arranging the data like this, or knowing about the duplication of purchase law. Four figures are emphasised, to make them easy to see. L'Oréal Paris and Lancôme share customers with each other more than expected, as do Avène and Clarins. L'Oréal Paris and Lancôme are marketed by the same company, a common reason for higher-than-expected customer overlap (cannibalisation).

---

2   As a technical note, because switching levels are typically low (under 10%) this approach requires large sample sizes to get enough multi-brand buying to see the patterns.

Table 3.6: Duplication of purchase table for skin care in China (2017)

Buyers of	Buyers who also bought (%)											
	Estée Lauder	L'Oréal Paris	Lancôme	Olay	Shiseido	SKII	Clinique	Kiehl's	Avène	La Mer	Laneige	Clarins
Estée Lauder		27	21	20	15	17	7	6	4	8	4	6
L'Oréal Paris	28		**31**	22	9	8	3	5	5	5	3	3
Lancôme	24	**34**		20	15	11	5	2	5	3	6	7
Olay	25	16	21		15	12	6	5	6	5	4	5
Shiseido	26	17	23	22		8	9	6	11	8	5	10
SKII	38	14	22	21	10		7	13	7	7	5	5
Clinique	32	21	18	23	23	14		16	14	5	9	9
Kiehl's	26	21	9	19	14	26	16		9	7	7	5
Avène	20	23	23	25	30	15	15	10		5	3	**15**
La Mer	38	25	13	20	23	15	5	8	5		5	5
Laneige	21	13	26	18	13	10	10	8	3	5		3
Clarins	32	16	30	22	30	11	11	5	**16**	5	3	
Average	**26**	**20**	**22**	**21**	**15**	**13**	**7**	**6**	**6**	**5**	**5**	**5**

Source: Ehrenberg-Bass Data collection

Durables—looking over time

With durable categories, it is necessary to expand the time frame to see the duplication of purchase competition patterns. Table 3.7 contains an example from fitness trackers in the UK. This is a relatively new category, so we asked people which fitness tracker they have now, and which others, if any, they had ever owned. While 62% had only ever owned one brand, due to a combination of once-only buying and repeat buying the same brand, 38% had owned multiple brands of fitness tracker, including the Apple Watch, which had promoted this function. The data shows that every brand of fitness tracker (including Apple Watch) has 40% of its customer base who have currently or previously owned a Fitbit, while only 13% have or had a Goji. You can see the excess sharing between Honor and Goji: this is due to small brands having many more heavy category buyers in their customer base. This means they attract customers who have had larger repertoires and so are more likely to have also owned other small brands.

Table 3.7: Duplication of purchase table for fitness trackers in the UK (2019)

Buyers of	Buyers buying brand (%)	Buyers who also owned (%)				
		Fitbit	Apple Watch	Garmin	Honor	Goji
Fitbit	37		16	13	5	4
Apple Watch	14	43		21	13	7
Garmin	12	42	25		18	17
Honor	5	39	37	41		22
Goji	4	45	28	55	31	
Average	14	42	26	33	17	13

Take the McDonald's challenge

Let us take a look at how brands compete within a category with quite a number of functional differences: fast food. Before you look at Table 3.8, think about the major brands you know, and how they might share customers. Where might partitions lie? Would you expect McDonald's and Burger King to attract people who like burgers, and so share customers more than expected? Or perhaps because these brands offer a similar product range, a consumer only needs one in their repertoire to satisfy that feel-like-a-burger moment? What about Pizza Hut and Domino's? Would you expect them to share more or fewer customers than expected?

It would be easy to craft a credible story to support possibilities of both higher and lower sharing between brands. But the data tells us we would be wrong in both cases. Actually McDonald's and Burger King share customers in line with the duplication of purchase law predictions, and so do Pizza Hut and Domino's. Indeed McDonald's and Domino's also share customers in line with expectations, as do Pizza Hut and Burger King (see Table 3.8). The major partition (highlighted) is between Vips and Sanborns, who both only offer cafeteria-style local cuisine.

Apart from this exception, fast food retailers in Mexico share customers with other retailers in line with the competitors' penetration. Everyone shares more customers with Burger King (a big brand) and fewer customers with Gorditas Dona Tota (a much smaller brand), irrespective of the specific food they sell. This is how we expect a normal competitive market to look.

Before we get too involved with the exceptions, let's remember what this law-like pattern in competition means for growth. If Chili's wants to grow to double in size in Mexico, it will have to look like Pizza Hut in Mexico. We don't mean it will start selling pizzas but it will have many more people buying it, and the sales it will steal will come mainly from the larger competitors (Burger King, Domino's) and to a lesser degree from the smaller brands (Sanborns, Gorditas Dona Tota). It is not about targeting a specific competitor but drawing customers from all brands in proportion to their share.

Table 3.8: Duplication of purchase table for fast food in Mexico (2014)

Customers of	Customers buying brand (%)	Customers also buying in six-month period (%)									
		Burger King	Domino's	KFC	McDonald's	Subway	Pizza Hut	Vips	Sanborns	Chili's	Gorditas Dona Tota
Burger King	56		65	63	62	61	52	46	42	28	16
Domino's	54	66		64	66	59	58	46	40	27	16
KFC	52	67	67		63	57	56	44	38	28	17
McDonald's	51	68	70	64		60	55	44	37	30	15
Subway	46	74	69	65	66		55	49	43	32	17
Pizza Hut	42	69	75	70	67	61		47	44	29	14
Vips	35	74	71	66	65	65	57		61	37	18
Sanborns	30	78	72	66	63	65	61	70		40	19
Chili's	20	76	72	72	75	73	59	63	59		20
Gorditas Dona Tota	13	72	71	70	60	63	48	49	45	33	
Average	40	72	70	67	65	63	56	51	45	32	17

Insights from partitions

The duplication of purchase law gives us the benchmarks to identify when brands share more or fewer customers than they should. Clusters of over-sharing and under-sharing partitions are usually easy to spot. As a rule of thumb we look for 10 percentage points difference from average, but this is just a guide. The first partitions to note are those with deviations on both sides of the diagonal (such as in the case of Sanborns and Vips in Table 3.8). But the occasional, one-sided deviations are also worth noting as they can suggest marketing shortfalls.

Finding explanations for these partitions can help identify what features are important to consumers, highlight problems to correct or uncover market opportunities. Let's look at the soft drink category in Turkey. Again, this is a category with a number of functional differences (diet drinks, fruit flavoured, colas), some positioning differences (Cola-Turka marketing itself as the brand that makes you more Turkish), plus a combination of local (Uludag, Yedigün) and global brands (Coca-Cola, Pepsi, Sprite).

With many possibilities for slicing and dicing the market, let's first use a duplication of purchase table (Table 3.9) to find the excess or deficits in sharing—and uncover what brand characteristics really make a demonstrative difference to the behaviour of buyers.

First, does nationalism matter? Looking at Table 3.9, it would seem a little bit, but not much. Cola-Turka and Coca-Cola share slightly fewer customers than average, but still 72% of Cola-Turka's drinkers also drank Coca-Cola in the last three months—not really that different from the average of 80%.

Second, does diet matter? We can see that the diet soft drinks (Coca-Cola light, Coke Zero, Pepsi Light) all share customers more than expected, so it seems this is an important functional difference. Therefore it might be prudent for all companies to ensure they have a diet version to compete in that partition. Not doing so would restrict penetration a little, as the brand would fail to tap into some buying situations.

Third, does brand name matter? We see that Pepsi Light shares more customers than it should with Pepsi (73% versus an average of 59%) but the reverse is not the case, whereby 16% of Pepsi customers also buy

Table 3.9: Duplication of purchase table for soft drinks in Turkey (2014)

Buyers of	Buyers buying brand (%)	Buyers also buying in last three months (%)												
		Coca-Cola	Fanta	Uludag	Pepsi	Yedigün	Sprite	Çamlıca	Sirma	Cola-Turka	Coca-Cola light	Coke Zero	7up	Pepsi Light
Coca-Cola	70		59	48	52	40	43	38	29	17	19	16	12	11
Fanta	52	79		55	55	57	47	45	35	23	20	14	14	12
Uludag	45	75	64		53	55	48	58	37	24	20	15	14	12
Pepsi	44	83	65	54		54	47	45	34	25	22	15	15	16
Yedigün	38	75	79	65	63		50	55	36	28	21	15	18	14
Sprite	37	82	66	59	56	51		53	41	23	25	19	21	14
Çamlıca	36	74	65	73	55	58	55		44	31	20	15	18	14
Sirma	26	76	69	62	56	51	57	59		28	28	21	19	16
Cola-Turka	17	72	73	65	66	63	50	67	44		30	17	18	23
Coca-Cola light	16	83	65	57	61	50	57	44	46	31		41	19	41
Coke Zero	14	83	53	50	48	41	50	39	41	20	47		18	32
7up	10	82	75	63	65	67	80	63	52	30	30	25		20
Pepsi Light	10	83	68	56	73	56	55	53	44	40	68	47	21	
Average	**26**	**80**	**66**	**60**	**59**	**54**	**55**	**54**	**42**	**28**	**26**	**18**	**18**	**16**

Pepsi Light, which is as expected. This is most likely due to an issue with physical availability. Pepsi Light, being a small brand, probably has incomplete distribution. Where it is distributed, it will usually sit right by Pepsi, thereby causing what looks like excess cannibalisation. PepsiCo should aim to fix the distribution shortfall, and then the sharing should revert to normal (similar to Coca-Cola, Coca-Cola light and Coke Zero). Shared brand names rarely result in a deviation from the duplication of purchase law except in the case of a small, poorly distributed sibling brand. This is something to be rectified rather than celebrated.

Are local brands a separate sub-market?

Throughout the history of globalisation research, local brands have been a source of intense interest. Initially, it was thought they would suffer, and be perceived as poorer quality than their global counterparts. Now people, given the success of some local brands in emerging markets, have performed a 180-degree turn, and speculate that local brands will command higher brand loyalty because of nationalistic sentiments.

As illustrated by the two examples here (fast food in Mexico and soft drinks in Turkey—Tables 3.8 and 3.9) where both local and global brands are present, no local or global brand partition exists. Nor, from earlier in the chapter, do we see evidence that local brands sell to a different profile of buyer. That is, no one specifically buys (or doesn't buy) local brands. Local brands compete in the same market as every other brand. Whether you should fear or ignore them is directly related to their current market share.

On occasion we see deviations for local brands but, as previously mentioned, these tend to be a by-products of patchy (often regional) distribution. In countries as large and diverse as China and India, where economies have been relatively sheltered from global markets historically, the presence of strong regional players is unsurprising. Whether these regional brands can become strong national brands is a different issue. Our advice would be always when you see a brand acting differently, first look for explanations in incomplete distribution or functional differences. Only after these two explanations have been excluded should you explore more esoteric explanations such as brand positioning or differentiation.

Conclusion

To grow, your brand needs to attract new customers. This means gaining customers from competitors, and this chapter sheds light as to which ones. Understanding how brands compete, so you don't get distracted by less important competition, need not be complicated. We have some simple empirical laws that hold in a wide range of markets to help us make sense of even complex, many layered, categories. Remember these key facts:

- The profile of your brand's customer base should follow that of the category profile. If it doesn't, find out why your market is restricted, and fix it if you can.

- Expect that your brand's major competition will be larger-share brands, unless you have empirical evidence to tell you otherwise.

- If you grow, you most likely will take sales from all brands, in proportion to their current share, so don't be distracted by positioning claims or even functional differences on the path to growth—sometimes these matter, but often less than you imagine.

- Use partition analysis to make sure you are playing in the whole market, and not locking the brand out of key subcategories because you don't offer a suitable variant. Look for and, if possible, eradicate these barriers to penetration growth.

4

Building Mental Availability

Jenni Romaniuk

In prior chapters we explained why brands, even in complex, high-involvement or intangible categories, compete largely for mental and physical availability. Growth depends on building these two market-based assets at a faster rate than competitors. This chapter takes an in-depth look at mental availability and explains why category entry points are useful memory structures to prioritise. It also highlights the importance of refreshing existing memories, in addition to building new ones.

Marketers should also reconsider long-held ideas, such as the consideration set, brand positioning and concerns about brand love/rejection, in light of current knowledge about buyer memory and behaviour.

The brand = our memories

Appearances can be deceiving. Even when we look vacant to observers, a lot is going on in our brains. Unfortunately, not all of that activity is helpful. Your brain can be like an unreliable friend, who forgets anniversaries or to pick up milk and tells you another beer is the best cure for a hangover. Our brain notices what it notices, and then thinks what it thinks.

Encountering a brand *may* stimulate thoughts and feelings. When we do, brand memory structures develop (if new) or are refreshed (if known). If useful, these memories contribute to the brand's customer-based brand equity, which is the buyer's mental construction of the brand (for example, Keller, 1993). Brands pop into our daily lives in many ways:

- using, consuming or buying
- seeing other people use or buy, such as friends or celebrities
- seeing or hearing advertising, sponsorships or posts on social media
- interacting with the brand on social media
- reading or hearing about it from someone—a friend or family member.

Each such encounter *can* build the brand's network in a buyer's memory. New memories add to the network, and refreshment of existing memories staves off their decay.[1]

We all have similar brains

One human brain works largely in the same way as another (just as human eyes, ears and feet work in much the same way). Yes, some of us are better at maths and others at dancing but, in the absence of a cognitive impairment, our brains are similar. Neurosurgeons don't need to know your nationality or race in order to perform brain surgery.

While our brains are very similar, our life experiences create our memories, which means different brains hold different stuff (memories). Neuroscientist Susan Greenfield calls memory the 'personalisation' of our brains (Greenfield, 2000). *How* a brand is encoded, stored and retrieved from memory is similar across buyers, but *what* our memories contain

---

1   Therefore, to build mental availability, the first step is to expose the category buyer to the marketing activity. This is why reaching as many category buyers as possible is a primary objective in media planning (see Chapter 6)—it is an essential part of building mental availability.

varies, as it reflects our personal encounters with categories and brands. A key role of marketing activity is to shape buyer memories to the brand's advantage. To do this, we need to understand why and how memories are formed and used.

Memory affects buying; buying affects memory

A stark empirical fact is that we know more about brands we buy, and the act of buying refreshes and builds our brand memories. We rarely buy brands we don't know, and rarely think about brands we don't buy. One of the best-established empirical laws about brand associations reflects this: a brand is more likely to evoke associations in its users than in its non-users.

This pattern was documented in the 1960s by Andrew Ehrenberg and colleagues (Bird & Channon, 1969; Bird, Channon & Ehrenberg, 1970). Forty years later, Romaniuk, Bogomolova and Dall'Olmo Riley (2012) showed this law continues to hold in a wide range of categories and countries, including services, emerging markets and durables (see Table 4.1). Indeed, the effect of buying a brand on brand memories lingers long after ceasing the behaviour, as we can see that former buyers are more likely to give associations than those who have never bought the brand.

Table 4.1: Brand associations for buyers and non-buyers across different countries and categories, selected from Romaniuk, Bogomolova and Dall'Olmo Riley (2012)

Countries	Current buyers (%)	Former buyer (%)	Never bought (%)
South Korea	36	31	23
India	77	28	16
Brazil	44	13	7
Russia	50	20	9
Turkey	39	10	5
China	30	15	4
Services categories			
Personal banking	52	15	10
Financial advisers	43	33	11
Supermarket retailers	37	18	8

Countries	Current buyers (%)	Former buyer (%)	Never bought (%)
Fast food retail	34	22	8
Average (all)	48	19	10
Average (Bird, Channon & Ehrenberg, 1970)	50	20	10

This tendency for buyers to give more responses translates to bigger brands (with more buyers) usually scoring higher on attributes than small brands. For example, Table 4.2 shows responses to 'good as a gift' for buyers and non-buyers for whisky brands in a mature (the UK) and an emerging (South Africa) whisky market. Buyers of each brand consistently give more associations than non-buyers: a rule of thumb is about two to three times in favour of buyers.

Table 4.2: Percentage response to 'good as a gift' for the same whisky brands across two markets (2010)

Brands	South Africa		United Kingdom	
	Buyer %	Non-buyer %	Buyer %	Non-buyer %
Jack Daniels	53	31	61	24
Bells	28	20	40	15
Grants	23	10	33	15
Average	35	20	45	18

Our brain when thinking about brands and buying

Let's now look at the basic architecture of the brand in the brain, and how we encode, store and access the memories it contains. If we know how this cognitive engine works, we can get better mileage out of our efforts to influence the brain on our brand's behalf.

Types of memory

We often equate our memory to a library. When we need to recall something, like the brand of shiraz we drank last time we ate at that Greek restaurant, we metaphorically trundle off to the library (search our brains for when we last drank that wine) and retrieve the book (the memory of being at that Greek restaurant) we are looking for. This metaphor distracts us from the fact that we are accessing memories continuously, in real time, at lightning speed from all parts of our brains. These are some of the most common types of memory we use every waking second, often without paying any conscious attention (see also Figure 4.1):

- *Semantic memory* is our memory for words and their meaning, such as knowledge that Singapore is a place, that noodles are a food and that Koka is a brand of instant noodle. We draw on this knowledge for reasoning and solving problems.

- *Episodic memory* is our memory for specific events, such as that time we went out to celebrate my dad's 70th birthday (the event) at The Greek on Halifax (a restaurant). Many events start out as episodic memories and then get integrated into semantic memory over time as the components of each event become part of our general memory structure.

- *Implicit memory* includes our memory for processes. Implicit memory often directs our behaviour when we are on autopilot, such as using a knife and fork while eating at the Greek restaurant. This part of our memory can underpin many everyday brand choices in locations where we often shop, such as when we instinctively reach for something on shelf, while at the same time thinking about that unfinished project at work.

- *Sensory memory* is our memory for smells, sounds, sights and touch, such as the smell of a sun-kissed tomato or the al dente texture of a well-cooked pasta. Sensory memories, while powerful recall triggers in the moment, fade quickly.

Figure 4.1: Types of memory

Semantic	Episodic	Implicit	Sensory
Words and meanings—for example, definition of 'plethora', the difference between 'right' and 'write'	Events and occasions—for example, your niece's birthday, your last workout	Processes and the subconscious—for example, typing, driving a car	Anything to do with the senses—for example, smell, touch, hearing experiences

Our memories help us navigate the day. They helped me to physically type this paragraph, without having to consciously think about every keystroke (implicit), to recall past events for examples (episodic) and to make sure the right words were used in the right places (semantic).

Building brand memories

Associative network theories (ANT) are a widely accepted group of theories of memory that share common foundations (for more detail, see Anderson & Bower, 1979). These theoretical foundations explain how human memories are created, stored and used.

The first foundation is about memory storage, namely that memories consist of nodes, each of which represents a different idea/concept previously encountered. When something new is added to your memory it is stored as a node, and the meaning of this node is defined by the links it uses to join your existing memory network. For example, recently I learnt a new word, 'extruded', in the context of snacks. It was explained to me as meaning 'a snack that comes out through a pipe'. This means that the word 'extruded' (for better or worse) is attached to the 'snack' part of my brain that also stores information about corn chips, potato chips, M&Ms and whether those lentil snacks are yummy or taste like cardboard. Had I learnt that word in a different context, such as in metallurgy, it would be in a different part of my brain.

When encountered together or co-presented, these nodes can form links (become *associated*). Co-presentation means two items experienced in close proximity to each other (ideally at the same time). The quality of co-presentation with the brand influences whether any exposure registers as a brand-building activity. It also influences the building of distinctive assets, which require co-presentation between the asset and the brand name (Romaniuk, 2018a).

Using brand memories

For a small part of any day, we are audiences for marketing activities, and for an even smaller part of any day, we are buyers of brands. It's easy to forget that for most buyers on most days, buying (including thinking about buying) takes up very little time and (ideally) very little effort. When we buy, we draw on a relevant subset of our memory to help make each choice. The thoughts and actions of buying typically have the following characteristics; they are:

- instantaneous, without (much) conscious deliberation
- influenced by context, which defines what makes a triggered memory relevant
- inconsistent, in that today's retrieved thoughts are not necessarily retrieved tomorrow.

When buying, our search of memory has a purpose: to identify something to buy for *that* situation. This is quite different from, say, accessing memory to complete a school test; buyers are not seeking to generate a list of brands in a category. Buyers use specific thoughts, also called *cues*, to access (hopefully) relevant answers. This process is referred to as *cued retrieval* (for example, Tulving & Craik, 2000).

Cued retrieval

What we (easily) think of largely determines what we buy. The key question is: what determines what we (easily) think of? A key factor is the cue used to access memory, as this 'doorway' determines the possible paths your thoughts can travel down. Open the green door and your mind can travel down one set of paths in memory; open the red door and you can access a different set of retrieval paths. The retrieval cue first activates brands *directly linked* in memory. For successfully managing brands, this means:

- knowing what cues buyers use to generate options to buy; and
- building/freshening links to these cues.

If your brand's links are absent or stale, then a buyer can retrieve other options (usually competitor brands). If a salient competitor can do the job, it usually gets bought. Buyers rarely want to expend more cognitive or physical effort to go searching for alternatives if a *good enough* one is easily available.

Let's work through an example. If you feel *tired*, you might then look for (cue) *something to pick me up*, and so options (Coke, Red Bull, Starbucks) will then pop into your brain, based on what you have mentally available as a *pick-me-up*. If one of these options easily works (you know of a Coke vending machine close by), then you seek that out. Expending extra energy to think of Pepsi or other alternatives is unnecessary.

If none of the options work (perhaps the vending machine only takes coins and you don't have any cash handy), then you can dredge your memory further for alternatives or ask others for advice. But, in most cases, a quick search of memory can provide more than enough easily buyable options.

An often-forgotten point is that the *direction* (of retrieval) also matters. Just because the brand easily cues something from memory, it doesn't mean that same something can cue the brand just as easily (Holden & Lutz 1992). For example, you might know that Moroccan-born French brothers started Guess, the clothing brand, but it's unlikely that the cue *French fashion* will ever evoke the brand Guess. With mental availability we are interested in what cues buyers use when we want our brand to be retrieved (when people are thinking of *something to wear to work*, do they think of Guess?), rather than what people think of when the brand is the cue (what does the brand *Guess* evoke?).

Category entry points

The retrieval cues buyers use to access their memories come from the experiences that buyers in the category share. For example, we all have birthdays, times we want to treat ourselves, and days when we don't have any energy, or need to cool down in weather when it is too hot to move. We refer to these thoughts category buyers use (cues) to locate options to buy as *category entry points* (CEPs) because they signal when someone *mentally enters the category buying process* at that time, and therefore becomes a potential brand buyer.

You can think of these CEPs as 'mental distribution outlets' (Romaniuk, 2003). When building physical availability, you want your brand to be present in as many shopping channels as possible—on the shelf of every supermarket, in every pharmacy, on each retailer website and in every shopping mall. The widespread distribution maximises the chance that when a shopper is ready to buy in the category, and your brand has made the cut as an option in that context, your brand is there ready to be bought: CEPs are the cognitive equivalent of channels that build mental availability, whereby the aim is to maximise the chance the brand is thought of, no matter what CEP pathway a buyer might go down.

Therefore, when building mental availability, the aim is to create wider, fresher networks of CEPs.

CEPs are pre-brand. They represent the buyer's thoughts or influences before brands are thought about. Both internal motivations (for example, feeling hungry) and external situations (for example, to share with the kids) can play a part. Figure 4.2 illustrates the Ws framework we developed for generating a category's CEPs and examples from the coffee category.

Figure 4.2: Ws framework for CEP generation

It is a useful practice to get marketers to use this framework to generate their own list of CEPs, and then compare those results from that generated from category buyers. This will help understand how much the marketing team is in tune with the tools to build mental availability. I find that often, marketer CEP lists contain many brand qualities they think consumers like (our brand is *friendly* and *approachable*, *open on Sundays*, has *Ru Paul* as an endorser), rather than CEPs, highlighting the need for more learning in this area.

Building linkages to CEPs

Buyers naturally build links between brands and CEPs as they use a category in different contexts over time. Experiences become established and refreshed in memory, available to be retrieved later on. However, we can use marketing activity to influence and accelerate this process on the brand's behalf, through building links between brands and CEPs outside of normal buying/using patterns. An example of this is McDonald's and coffee. Thinking back a decade ago, how long would it have taken you to go to McDonald's for a decent coffee if there had not been extensive advertising of its McCafé and fancier coffee offerings? You might have passed a McDonald's in the morning, seen the word McCafé, and noticed a smell of coffee. If you looked in and saw the actual coffee machines, it might have 'clicked' that McDonald's offers 'good' coffee (though you probably forgot soon after). Then one day, you might have thought, 'I'll grab a coffee at McDonald's' on your way to a meeting.

For the many millions of McDonald's buyers, this building of links between McDonald's and coffee-buying contexts would have taken a considerable time to develop—probably much longer than financially desirable for McDonald's. Advertising CEPs around coffee usage in the context of the brand got more people through the doors more quickly and informed potential buyers of the many different contexts where McDonald's coffee is a possible option.[2] Now McCafé[3] is one of the leading brands in coffee in the USA (USA Today, 2020).

Different countries = different CEPs?

As CEPs reflect brand buying or usage experiences, common ones can vary across countries. Lifestyles differ because of culture, climate, wealth, religion and infrastructure, so there is some customisation to the local environment. However, typically the differences in CEPs between countries are fewer than marketers expect. CEPs across countries can vary in two ways that are important for messaging. First are differences in substance of the CEPs, where a CEP is present in one country but not in another; for example, in Southern Europe there is *merenda*, which is a small snack/meal given to children around 5 p.m. to tide them over between lunch and the later dinner; this is not present in many other locations. Second are differences in CEP incidence, where a CEP is much more commonly encountered in one country than in another. For example, having an after-work drink with workmates at the pub is more common in the UK than in most other countries.

---

2   Alongside McDonald's altering their physical availability by changing their opening hours as well.
3   Fun fact: McCafé actually started in Melbourne, Australia!

Those differences notwithstanding, I find around 70% of the results for CEPs are the same, even when marketers initially thought the buyers in each country to be very different for that category. More commonly relevant CEPs can be used in global campaigns to avoid the costly tailoring of messages, while CEPs with a substantially higher relevance in a particular country or region can be incorporated into local initiatives.

Psst ... a secret about big brands

Traditional notions about brand differentiation and positioning can easily lead to the conclusion that brands need to be strong on one or two CEPs to be successful. This ignores an important (empirical) fact: *large share brands are linked to a broader range of CEPs than smaller brands.* This breadth of memory structures is a key part of their equity. If you want to create a big brand, you need the brand to be linked to many different CEPs in the category—not just one or two.

For example, let's look at an example from social media in the USA. We identified 38 CEPs from a Stage 1 CEP elicitation questionnaire administered to 61 social media users in the USA in 2019. We calculated how many of these CEPs are linked to each brand, and compared the distributions for Facebook, Snapchat and TikTok. Facebook, the most popular social media site, has more people with more CEPs than the less popular social media sites. TikTok has more people with zero CEPs, and fewer people with four or more CEPs than the other sites (see Figure 4.3). Big brands have fresher memory structures for more category buyers across more CEPs—which is one of the biggest (mental) differences between big and small brands.

Figure 4.3: Number of CEPs for social media sites in the USA (2019)

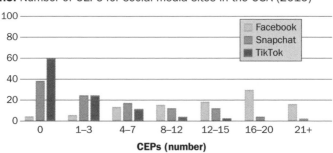

Not one 'consideration set': many context-specific evoked sets

The term *consideration set* usually refers to the (one) subset of brands that is actively considered for purchase (in line with Howard & Sheth, 1969). Traditional texts refer to a brand establishing itself as part of the consideration set and, even today, many brand-health trackers include a question along the lines of 'Which of the following brands would you consider for purchase?'

This idea of a 'one consideration set fits all purchase occasions' is an outdated model, created without modern knowledge about how buyers retain, process and access brand memories. Buyers don't have a single consideration set: this would be a very inefficient use of memory, as at every purchase occasion people would have to retrieve many more, often irrelevant, options than they need. Table 4.3 shows the variation across buyers and CEPs for four social media users. Brands vary, and the number of brands also varies. This is normal—vary the retrieval cue, vary the responses. There is no static consideration set that buyers go to for all of a category's buying contexts. This means there is no real benefit in asking people directly what brands they consider. The (real) answer will always be: 'It depends …'.

Table 4.3: Example of how CEPs vary across category buyers for social media in the USA (2019)

CEP	Female, 55–70 years, Arizona	Female, 16–24 years, New York	Male, 25–34 years, West Virginia	Male, 45–54 years, Florida
Good to use in the evening before bed	Facebook Messenger Instagram YouTube	Facebook YouTube	None	WhatsApp
When someone wants quick and instant response	Facebook Messenger Instagram YouTube	Messenger WhatsApp	Twitter	Twitter

CEP	Female, 55–70 years, Arizona	Female, 16–24 years, New York	Male, 25–34 years, West Virginia	Male, 45–54 years, Florida
Something to do while watching TV or eating	Facebook Instagram YouTube	Instagram	Pinterest YouTube	Instagram Snapchat Twitter WhatsApp
For someone who wants to keep up with news/current events	Facebook Messenger YouTube	Facebook Messenger Instagram WhatsApp	LinkedIn Twitter	Twitter YouTube

Remember CEPs are not just about internal needs—external factors also shape what buyers retrieve. In the morning, hot coffee brands might be more salient as options to *pick me up*, while in the afternoon on a hot day, it's more likely to be cold beverages. This contextual influence on retrieval also largely happens without conscious thought. It creates (more efficient) sets with brands *relevant* to the immediate situation. We don't want to waste cognitive energy thinking of things we then have to spend more cognitive energy evaluating and rejecting. Our brands are smarter (lazier) than that—they just try to go straight to getting us the useful stuff.

Category buying and CEP experiences

Those who buy a category more experience a wider range of CEPs. It is unusual to find a heavy category buyer who only accesses the category by one or two CEPs. This relationship is illustrated in Figure 4.4 with data from a durable retail category, with purchases in the hundreds and even thousands of dollars. Buyers who bought from the category 11+ times experienced on average three times the CEPs of someone who bought from the category one to three times. Therefore, not only do heavy category buyers have a larger repertoire of brands, but they also draw on a wider range of CEPs. *More frequent category buying = more variety in CEP contexts and brands.* This again reinforces the idea of goal of wider, fresher networks of CEPs.

Figure 4.4: The relationship between number of purchases and number of CEPs experienced for a durable product

Categories often have a range of CEPs and a cornucopia of brands that consumers can think of for each. To be bought, a brand must first be thought of—the breadth (how many) and strength (how strong) of the brand's links to relevant cues determine the chance of this happening (Romaniuk & Sharp, 2004). This means a brand's mental availability is its accessibility from memory across the range of category contexts that buyers encounter (Romaniuk, 2013). We initially referred to this as 'brand salience', but this led to confusion between the longer-term propensity for the brand to be thought of (which we now call 'mental availability'), and the in-the-moment salience of a brand. The difference is that salience is situation-specific retrieval performance, while mental availability captures the brand's longer-term retrieval potential. For example, how easily did you think of Costa Coffee this morning on your way to work (brand salience), compared to how often do you think of Costa Coffee when you are in coffee-buying situations over the week, month or year (mental availability).

A focus on the longer-term propensity to think of the brand is important for building mental availability, as highlighting the brand's performance for a single cue is both strategically and tactically misleading. The strategic aim is for wider, fresher memory networks. The tactical aim is to, over time, build strong links between different CEPs and the brand. This means that a brand's mental availability needs to be assessed across a wide range of CEPs, relative to its competitors for buyer memory.

Mental availability measurement

The more links to CEPs a brand has, relative to competitors, the greater the chance is that it will be salient in any buying situation. To reflect this, Romaniuk (2013) draws on results from a representative set of CEPs across key brands in a category to calculate a brand's *mental market share and underlying metrics*. This approach focuses on the brand's performance across the whole CEP network rather than the brand's performance on any specific CEP.[4] The key ingredients for a good mental availability measure are:

- *CEPs*—the CEPs more commonly encountered by buyers in the category.
- *Brands*—the bigger brands in the category and a representative set of smaller ones. Even if you are a small brand, remember your biggest competition is the larger brands (as per the duplication of purchase law, explained in Chapter 3). Including major competitors ensures you get a realistic assessment of the brand's mental availability.
- *Free choice; pick any linkage measurement approach with brands prompted*—this approach is where you have the CEP and ask which brands, from a list, are linked to the CEP. It works for measuring mental availability because its binary nature (link or no response) replicates the retrieval process, but the prompted nature of the measurement avoids the inhibition/priming effects that accompany repeated brand unprompted measurement.

To explain further, our early R&D testing showed that brand unprompted measures elicit fewer brand responses than are present in memory, particularly from non-brand users. And over multiple attributes, a brand not initially retrieved has a much lower chance to be thought of for a latter attribute (as working memory fills up and respondents have easily accessible brands to mention). These issues were exacerbated for service categories compared to packaged goods categories (for full testing results see Romaniuk, 2006). Using a 'free choice; pick any' approach (as described in Barnard & Ehrenberg, 1990)

---

4   See Romaniuk and Sharp (2000) for a method for determining a brand's performance on any one specific CEP for brand image analysis.

might appear to disproportionately advantage small brands; however, the empirical results show us category buyers are perfectly happy ignoring brands they don't know or don't link to that attribute/CEP. Therefore, this prompted, 'free choice; pick any' approach is the recommended way to capture CEP–brand linkages when measuring mental availability.

Mental availability metrics

Measurement needs to turn into metrics to assess brand performance and monitor it over time. The key metrics to assess the mental availability are:

- *mental market share*—the brand's percentage of CEP associations, of the total CEP associations for the brand and competitors. It reflects the brand's relative retrieval competitiveness in the whole category.
- *mental penetration*—the percentage of category buyers who link the brand with at least one CEP. This measures brand awareness more in line with associative network theories of memory, as it calculates the possibility of retrieval across the multiple potential pathways to retrieve the brand. The higher the mental penetration, the more category buyers have the brand mentally available.
- *network size*—how many CEPs the brand is linked to in the minds of those aware: the wider the network, the more potential pathways for brand retrieval. This metric is useful for assessing if advertising is maintaining or building the CEP network.

While these metrics often correlate with their sales equivalents at a single point in time—this is normal for brand-health metrics—disparities between mental and sales market share can highlight issues with physical availability (for example, is the price too high? Or is the product not prominent on the shelf?). You should expect a double jeopardy between mental penetration and network size. A deviation from double jeopardy could indicate a reach issue in the brand's media plan (for example, are we missing light buyers?) or messaging (for example, has our message been too narrow?).[5]

---

5   Romaniuk (2013) shows how the NBD Dirichlet model identifies deviations in the absence of sales data or in categories such as services where repeat buying data is not easily available.

Importantly, these metrics can help track the performance of marketing activity in building long-term memory structures, particularly amongst light and non-buyers of the brand, from whom growth will come (for example, Vaughan et al., 2020). For example, a campaign highlighting a new CEP should grow network size; a media schedule that has wider reach should build mental penetration; and a better correct branding score for a campaign should build both metrics.

Table 4.4 is an example of these metrics for phone handsets in India. We identified CEPs to cover a wide range of aspects of mobile phone handsets: for example, *want something easy to use, need a battery would last a long time, offers a design I would be proud to show others, works well for online shopping*, or *would be good for social media*.

Table 4.4: Example of mental availability metrics for phone handsets in India (2014)

Brand	Mental market share (%)	Mental penetration (%)	Network size (mean)
Samsung	21	90	10.8
Nokia	17	85	9.3
Apple iPhone	15	80	8.3
Micromax	9	69	5.8
HTC	8	53	6.8
BlackBerry	7	60	5.6
LG	5	48	4.5
Motorola	4	44	4.1
Karbonn	4	54	3.1
Lava	3	45	2.7
XOLO	2	33	3.4
Videocon	2	38	2.2
Huawei	2	32	2.4
Celkon	2	37	2.1

The metrics show again the difference between bigger and smaller brands. Bigger brands have higher mental penetration (more category buyers with a chance of thinking of the brand) and higher network size (more CEPs even amongst those category buyers). For example, Samsung has a chance of being accessible for 90% of category buyers, for 10.8 CEPs (out of 16). In contrast, HTC has a chance of being accessible for only 53% of buyers, for only 6.8 CEPs. We can also see some exceptions: for example, Micromax has a higher mental penetration and lower network size for its rank order. This suggests the brand has spent too long on a single message, and needs to broaden its links to CEPs to make it fresh in a wider range of phone-buying situations.

The correlation between mental market share and market share (value) (figures from Press Trust of India, 2013) for a subset of brands in the Indian market is shown in Figure 4.5. We can see the brands generally appear in the same rank order, with a notable exception being Apple iPhones—which have higher mental market share than sales. This disparity is likely due to its higher price creating a barrier to purchase. In contrast Lava and Karbonn, which are cheaper local brands, have lower mental availability than their sales would suggest. These brands might not be as mentally available, but attract buyers in-store due to their strong physical availability advantage of being low in price.

Figure 4.5: Comparison between mental market share and market share (value sales) for the phone handset market in India (where data was available)

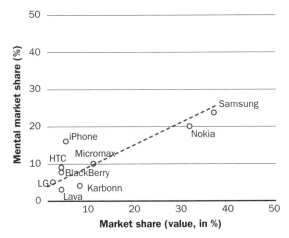

Why not use top-of-mind awareness?

It's a reasonable question to ask why not just use the brand's top-of-mind awareness (TOMA), or first brand recalled with the category prompt, to measure mental availability? The combination of the characteristics of the measure—unprompted, first response only—that make it cognitively more difficult for category buyers (Romaniuk, Wight & Faulkner, 2017) and the use of the single category cue mean that TOMA is unable to capture the brand linkages from the non and very light buyers the brand needs to grow (for a more detailed argument on this, see Romaniuk & Sharp, 2004).

Figure 4.6, which plots TOMA against brand buying for the quick service food category, shows why this is the case. Small brands get very little TOMA and show little variance even with quite large differences in brand penetration, but TOMA skyrockets for big brands, with more past frequent buyers and more recent buyers. However, TOMA awareness might be useful if your primary concern is heavy brand buyers/large share brands (see Wight, 2010; Romaniuk, Wight & Faulkner, 2017). To date there is no convincing evidence that this is the case, but it also has not been well tested, so remains possible.

Figure 4.6: Top-of-mind awareness plotted against brand buying for quick service food

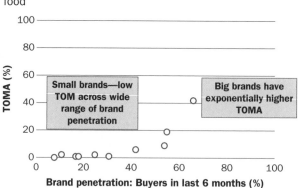

Building and freshening brand memories

Mental availability is an ongoing battle for memory freshness. Advertising of CEPs isn't just helpful when developing new links to new CEPs: remember, everything category buyers know about a brand is a memory that is prone to decay. As time moves on from each encounter with a brand, buyer memories fade, and therefore links to rarely used CEPs need to be refreshed to avoid future retrieval failure. Many of your brand's customers also buy your competitors' brands (see Chapter 3), and so will notice their advertising. Seeing competitors' brands also make the brand's memories relatively harder to retrieve. Therefore, links to commonly used CEPs need to be refreshed to counteract/overcome exposure to competitor activity and usage.

Even the biggest brands have many buyers with very few fresh, accessible brand associations. For example, if we examine the CEP distribution across Coca-Cola and Jarritos (a local soft drink with cola and fruit variants) in Mexico we find 56% of Jarritos buyers (the smaller brand) have fewer than five CEP linkages, compared to 23% of Coca-Cola buyers (see Figure 4.7). With many current buyers holding few CEPs about the brand, refreshing their few accessible CEPs is important just to maintain market share. To grow, you need to build freshness across category buyers *and* CEPs.

Figure 4.7: Distribution of CEPs for Coca-Cola and Jarritos in Mexico (2014)

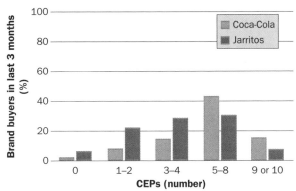

Brand positioning = your advertised messages

It's time to reposition brand positioning.

Traditional texts tell us that a strong brand equals a strongly positioned brand, ideally with unique associations. We have shown this to be misguided—strong brands don't rely on a single proposition but are mentally available, and compete successfully against other brands across a wide range of category needs. A brand's position is seldom mysterious—your marketing efforts create it, particularly advertising because of its potential for wide reach.[6] The strength of any position is a function of how well these messages have cut through and become linked to the brand in buyer memory, particularly amongst the brand's very light or non-buyers.

When well-branded advertising builds memory structures, the brand gets a higher than expected response on that attribute. But competitor interference and the fading of memories over time mean that this heightened response is a temporary rather than permanent state—if the reinforcement ceases (through a change of message or use of poor-quality creativity), this excess response reverts to normal (Romaniuk & Nicholls, 2006; Romaniuk & Sharp 2000).

A valuable test of the effectiveness of specific advertised message is to see whether the brand is better known for a specific attribute (including CEPs) than it should be for its size. However, over time the advertised messages should change, and with it the 'positioning' attributes. It is also important to separate out specific execution objectives from that of a total campaign. A single execution needs a single clear message, but building mental availability requires spotlighting different parts of the broader CEP network over different executions and over time.

When designing a message strategy, ask the following questions:

- Which CEP will exposure to this execution build? Will this be obvious, even for the lightest category and brand buyer?[7] If the link between the message take-out and the CEP is not obvious, then rethink the creative.
- Is this CEP often useful for a large number of people? The more common the CEP, the more impact the advertising can have. The more obscure the CEP, the fewer opportunities the advertising will have to have maximum effect.
- When was the last time you promoted this CEP? If it featured in a recent campaign, perhaps use this opportunity to spotlight

---

6   Unless it is a functional quality of the brand that non-users can infer from the name such as Royal Bank of Scotland and 'Scottish'.
7   Note: This test should be applied to all marketing activities, not just advertising.

neglected CEPs instead, as freshening these memories might benefit the brand more than reminding potential buyers of recently featured CEPs.

Use the measurement of the brand's 'position' to test whether your advertising has been successful in building links to that CEP. If your advertising is working, as the message changes, so too should what the brand is known for. This change in position reflects the success of the newer campaign.

Love, hate and the wide chasm between them

Over many decades, the idea of emotional attachments has been dressed up with different names. More recently it has been called 'brand love', but let's not get fooled by old concepts with new labels; previous incarnations such as brand attitude, brand relationships and brand engagement all touted the same idea.

People can develop feelings about brands. It's just that these feelings are typically weak (it's fine/okay/does the job) and reflect, rather than predict, their own buying behaviour (I buy it so therefore I like it). We should be wary of giving these feelings too much weight in the buying process, simply because very little evidence supports any disproportionate attention, including for emerging markets and higher-involvement categories such as services and durables.

Two common mistakes inflate the importance of strong emotions about brands.

Mistake 1: Assuming non-buying equals brand rejection

One mistaken assumption is that most non-brand users have actively rejected the brand. Testing by the Ehrenberg–Bass Institute across more than 500 brands in twenty-four product categories and twenty-three countries reveals that explicit brand rejection is low, even in emerging markets (see Figure 4.8). Lack of mental availability is a far more important challenge to overcome than buyer rejection.

Figure 4.8: Rejection levels in different markets (taken from Romaniuk, Nenycz-Thiel & Truong, 2011)

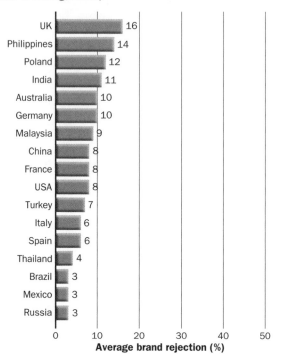

Mistake 2: Assuming everyone has an 'attitude'

It is easy to inflate the importance of attitudes to brands by forcing people to create an on-the-spot opinion, with limited response options. In the absence of a 'don't know' or 'no opinion' option on a scale, non-users usually default to the mid-point response (say four out of seven, or three out of five). This assigns a large value to 'no attitude', particularly for small brands that will have more non-users without an opinion. This gives the impression of a stronger attitude than is really present (Romaniuk 2008).

Having a full spectrum of evaluations in the response set, including no attitude at all, will give you a more realistic picture of the strength and dispersion of attitudes to the brand. A non-response is sometimes just that—don't know/don't think about it/don't care!

All you need is love?

One extreme emotion that has captured the attention of marketers is brand love ('the strongest emotion of all' says advertising guru Kevin Roberts, 2004). The claim is building brand love will lead to brand growth, but the weight of evidence does not support this assertion. This paragraph was originally written in 2014. Now, upon rewriting in 2020, the passion for brand love does appear to have been abated and I did consider cutting this section. However, given the cyclical nature of these fads, this type of idea, that relies on buyers feeling a strong emotion, is likely to pop up again before the next revision. Call it what you may, the general caveat to this type of 'extremely positive brand attitude' metric remains. Investigations into deep emotions/attitudes/behaviours towards brands show these deep feelings and behaviours are rare, and of little consequence to a brand's market share or growth. These measures (whether via actual behaviour or in surveys) are simply unable to pick up (often small) changes in non and very light buyers. Perhaps they might be useful in detecting potential decline for a very large share brand (similar to TOMA), but again more testing and evidence is needed here.

A more typical brand attitude profile is a few people loving the brand, a few people hating the brand, and the vast majority thinking it is a perfectly okay brand to possibly or occasionally buy. It doesn't matter if the category is packaged goods, durables, services or luxury, and whether it's in the developed world or emerging markets. All these markets and categories have many buyers that are inexperienced, but this does not make them besotted fools for brands.

Conclusion

Building mental availability requires attaching the brand to memory structures that are useful for buyers when they are thinking about buying. In this chapter we introduced the concept of category entry points (CEPs) — which represent the possible retrieval cues buyers use to think of options to buy. CEPs underpin mental availability: the wider and fresher the network of CEPs, the more likely the brand will be salient in buying situations across both *time* and *buyers*. These are, therefore, important memory linkages for a brand to create and refresh over time to combat decay.

Creating a list of priority CEPs for each of your markets will help you identify opportunities for messaging in global and local campaigns. But don't assume large differences in CEPs across countries, even if the countries have quite different cultures. Often similarities in how people interact with a category can dwarf any differences in culture. For example, there are many different countries in which people drink coffee and each of those countries has its own culture and lifestyle, but all coffee buyers, from the UK to Uzbekistan, drink coffee to wake up, get some energy, catch up with friends, and while at work, to some degree.

Instead of one consideration set, we refer to many different context-specific evoked sets. And instead of narrowcasting a brand by positioning it strongly, we now think of positioning as a transient reflection of the successful processing of current advertised messages. This ensures our marketing concepts keep pace with advances in our understanding about how the brain works and that we can draw on and use information in people's memories to help make choices.

To measure mental availability, a 'free choice; pick any' approach that captures as many brand–CEP linkages as possible is the most effective approach, particularly when the goal is to capture the presence of the brand in the memories of non and very light brand buyers.

5

Leveraging Distinctive Assets

Jenni Romaniuk

Distinctive assets are non-brand name elements, such as colours, logos, characters and fonts that can trigger the brand for category buyers. This chapter discusses the difference between building and using an asset; how to select assets for investment and avoid assets that will be difficult to build; and how to execute assets to improve branding quality.

The chapter also explains useful metrics for assessing distinctive asset current strength and future potential, the tool of the Distinctive Asset Grid, as well as what it means to build a distinctive asset palette. Finally, there is a brief outline of the role of distinctive assets in building mental and physical availability.

Meet our owl

This chapter is about how to identify, select and develop distinctive assets, as well as how to avoid common traps, particularly for big, established brands. To kick off this conversation, I'd like to introduce you to the Ehrenberg–Bass Institute's owl.[1] You will see her throughout the book. Our corporate sponsors might also recognise her from corporate reports and email updates. She gives the Ehrenberg–Bass Institute brand name a visually rich image to signal and remind you about the brand in different contexts, such as in the middle of a page, where a big 'Ehrenberg–Bass Institute' would distract from the text! This chapter is about her, and other brand assets, and the tasks they perform.

What's in a (brand) name?

Every brand has a name that distinguishes it from other brands. This name creates an anchor for the brand in the memory of category buyers and connects the brand to other memories. The brand, in the form of a word, becomes part of our semantic memory. Our understanding of the brand develops as we encounter different facets of the brand, such as its appearance and when it is useful.

Over time, other memory structures can become brand 'proxies', in that their primary role is to trigger the brand name in buyers' memories. These brand proxies, or distinctive assets, include colours, logos, sounds, characters, taglines—anything that is sensory where the primary meaning is a brand name. Let's look at the different types of distinctive assets available to a brand.

---

1   Her name is now Andie; thanks to Mark Schulz for the suggestion

The (many) types of distinctive assets

The opportunity (and challenge) of distinctive assets is the wide range of potential assets to choose from (see Figure 5.1). Listed are seven types of visual and audio assets, each with several sub-types. For example, colour-based assets can be single colours, colour combinations or colour + design assets, while word-based assets comprise fonts (how words are visually shown), single words and taglines/phrases. Each of these asset types have properties that can be harnessed or might be a liability depending on the operating environment. For example, there are some environments, such as on a text-heavy news site, where being a word-based asset such as a tagline can be a liability and a face asset could be more effective to draw attention to the brand. However, on a 'people-heavy' Instagram site, the reverse might be the case.

Figure 5.1: Types of distinctive assets (based on the list in Romaniuk, 2018a)

Visual assets					Audio assets		Other
Colours	**Word-based**	**Story**	**Shapes**	**Faces**	**Music**	**Sounds**	**Other senses**
Single colours	Taglines	Components	Logos/symbols	Celebrities	Jingles	Non-vocal	Touch
Colour combinations	Words	Moments	Product forms	Spokes-people	Background instrumental	Vocal	Smell
Colour + design	Fonts	Styles	Pack shapes	Characters	Popular songs	Styles	Taste

Our history of testing distinctive assets in many categories has taught us that any of these visual or audio asset types can become strong distinctive assets. To get there, however, requires two steps. The first is to select the right raw ingredients for asset building. The second is the quality of execution when building or using the asset.

Building an asset

When we release a distinctive asset into the wild, there are two possible objectives: to *build* the asset or to *use* it as a branding device. When an asset is new/weak, the primary objective is asset building, but as an asset grows in strength, the primary objective shifts to using the asset as a replacement for the brand. Both building and using an asset require prominent, attention-grabbing execution of that asset, but the role of the brand name differs. When the primary objective is asset building, co-presentation with the brand name is crucial as the aim is to link the asset and the brand name. When the primary objective is to use the asset, the brand name takes a back seat as the distinctive asset steps into the branding role.

In practice, all executions using an asset will have a mix of building and using objectives, as even the strongest assets need to be taught to the next generation of category buyers. However, understanding whether the primary objective is building or using the asset helps to make sure the brand name is appropriately incorporated when needed. Neglect of the brand name when the primary objective is asset building is one of the reasons distinctive assets languish.

Step 1: Selection—choose your brand's assets wisely

When deciding which assets to build, there are a few areas to consider before making your choice. These are the intended branding environments, the history of the brand and the metrics for potential assets.

Consider the environment—where are you going to be using the assets?

Start at the end—build assets that can be widely used. Distinctive assets are a tool to improve branding quality in two broad types of environments: media and sales. Media environments include all forms of advertising, social media and sponsorship environments (sporting stadiums, music venues, player uniforms), anywhere outside of places where you actually sell the product. Sales environments are places where the brand is sold. Examples include bricks-and-mortar stores, online, owned channels, via an intermediary (retailer, broker), and vending machines. Sometimes a location can function as both. For example, a brand could have signage on the sporting ground and sell the product at the concession stands. It is useful to separate these two environments as the assets that help a brand be noticed on a billboard can be very different from those that help it stand out in a fridge at the concession stand. Mapping the properties of the branding environments helps you understand the range of assets useful to the brand. Here are some useful questions to ask:

- Are there words or pictures in the environment? Does one form dominate?
- How is colour used? Is there a wide variety of colours or do certain ones dominate? Are colour blocks present (or can they be)?
- What (if any) role does audio play?
- How much control do you have over the brand's immediate surroundings? If little or no control, what are the properties (colour, form, shape, size) of items close by?

The aim is to understand the branding environments to ensure assets have a good chance of standing out and attracting attention in these environments, and so be widely and effectively used.

Consider the brand's history—what has the brand built in the past?

Brands with a long history have typically had many brand managers, each of whom have put their own stamp on the brand's identity. Past iterations of creative advertising and packaging may contain distinctive assets that could be resurrected. This can accelerate asset building as it is much easier to refresh an existing memory than to develop a new one. Harnessing history can be a way of quickly (re)creating a strong distinctive asset.

A review of the brand's history can also identify implementation improvements. Perhaps past management lacked the commitment to build a strong asset? If the brand has been switching between two or three taglines, the lack of focus on one single tagline may be a key driver of poor past distinctive asset performance, rather than any issue with the taglines themselves.

Consider the metrics to make your choices evidence based

When you live and breathe a brand it is easy to overestimate the strength of its distinctive assets, to the point of assuming everyone is bored with an asset—just because you might be.

Therefore, before you make any decisions on distinctive assets, get objective metrics on distinctive assets you are currently using, as well as any assets you are looking to build, change or drop. This makes sure you are judging distinctive asset strength through the eyes of the most important audience—the category buyer.

The two components any valuable distinctive asset needs are:

- *uniqueness*—it only evokes your brand, and not competitors' brands
- *fame*—amongst category buyers, the knowledge that your brand is linked to the asset is widespread.

Benchmark metrics

Uniqueness scores depend at least partially on what other brands have done/are doing. This means you have less control over this metric and uniqueness, once lost, is difficult to regain as you can't tell category buyers what *not* to think. Therefore, identifying low uniqueness at the benchmarking stage can help work out which assets to cull and avoid wasting time and effort on assets with little chance of success. The main purposes of identifying fame at benchmarking are to assess past asset-building activities and find out if there are category buyer segments that have been neglected. Over time, fame becomes a valuable tool to assess the efficacy of asset-building activities.

Measuring distinctive asset strength

We tested four different options for measuring distinctive asset strength, with two options for cuing (brand or asset) and two options for responses (prompted or unprompted). The best approach out of those tested is the asset-cued, brand-unprompted method. This approach elicited more competitor responses and had the lowest scores for guessing,[2] both of which are important facets of a distinctive asset measure (Romaniuk & Nencyz-Thiel, 2014).

The metrics of fame and uniqueness capture the likelihood that the asset will trigger the brand name, and only the brand name, amongst category buyers (Romaniuk & Nenycz-Thiel, 2014). This approach also replicates what we want an asset to do in the real world, which is to trigger the brand in its absence.[3] It is also context-free, which means the results are not affected (positively or negatively) by the testing environment.

Fame and uniqueness metrics are calculated in the following way:

- *fame*—the proportion of category buyers that links the brand name to the asset; 45% fame means 45% of category buyers link the target brand with the asset.

- *uniqueness*—the share of responses for that asset that goes to the brand (versus competitors' brands); 60% uniqueness means of all the brand linkages to the asset, 60% are for the target brand, and 40% of responses are for competitor brands.

There are some asset types with systematically higher uniqueness. Testing of over 1200 potential assets across thirteen categories finds characters, logos and fonts have the highest potential for ownership. Colour, on the other hand, is the most challenging, with significantly lower uniqueness than other asset types (Ward et al., 2020; Major, Tanaka & Romaniuk, 2014). However, within asset types, results show instances of poor and exemplar performance, which means any asset type can be strong, and quality of execution is an important ingredient in achieving this goal (Romaniuk, 2018b; Ward et al., 2020).

---

2   Approaches where the brand name is prompted were prone to an average of 20 percentage points guessing inflation.

3   This is partially why response latency measures were rejected early in our distinctive asset Measurement R&D. The challenge the brand faces is not being the first or quickest retrieved, but rather being retrieved at all. Once retrieved, a brand competes with other options in memory. Being a few milliseconds earlier is not of great advantage and should not be the primary basis for selecting an asset for investment.

Interpreting distinctive asset metrics

Fame

High levels of fame mean any category buyer is highly likely to think of the brand when exposed to the asset. Low levels of fame mean that the asset is not (yet) strong enough to be a replacement for the brand name. An asset identified as having low fame when initially benchmarking asset strength could still be a candidate for investment, particularly if it hits a sense or part of the brain that other assets don't, and/or can work in a commonly used environment better than other assets.

The two primary ways to increase fame are wider reaching asset-building activities and improvements in asset–brand name execution. For any asset, fame declines when asset use is not sufficiently widespread to refresh existing memories (or build new ones). For assets in the building stage, fame can also decline if the quality of asset–brand name execution declines.

Uniqueness

High uniqueness means the brand is highly likely to be the only brand evoked when category buyers are exposed to the asset. It is wise to select assets with initially high uniqueness. The challenge is to keep uniqueness high while building fame through well-branded executions, as any lulls in branding quality could be opportunities for competitor links to form. It is also useful to monitor competitor activity to quickly identify any encroachment on the asset.

If you choose to build an asset that has low uniqueness, you will have a battle on your hands. Competitors have already made inroads in building their own fame with the asset, which means any use of that asset risks triggering competitors also linked (in line with the associative network theories of memory discussed in Chapter 4). Therefore, investment in this asset will struggle to gain return, due to a high risk of the misattribution to other brands. Reclaiming an asset that lacks uniqueness will require a very strong direct reference to the brand name, and it will also need to be pre-tested to ensure any competitor brands are not inadvertently triggered.

The Distinctive Asset Grid

The potential of an asset can be identified via its position on the Distinctive Asset Grid (see Figure 5.2). The grid has four quadrants with a cut-off at the 50% level to represent the two tipping points in the brand's favour. If an asset has 50% or more fame, then assets are more likely than not to trigger the brand for category buyers; if an asset has 50% or more uniqueness, then it is the dominant brand retrieved. However, all assets should aim for 100% fame and 100% uniqueness (the target). Don't be distracted by industry norms or averages. These assets are to take the place of the brand name, and remember, both mental and physical availability only get built if the brand is easily recognisable.

Figure 5.2: The Distinctive Asset Grid[4] (developed by Jenni Romaniuk)

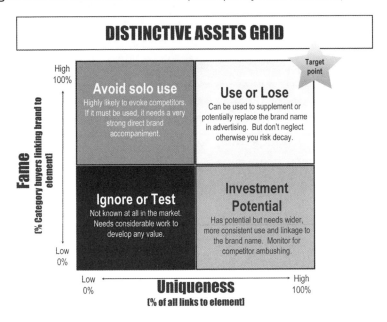

Plotting all the assets on a single grid can give a nice pictorial representation of the brand's current performance in building an overall strong brand identity (see Chapter 11 in *Building Distinctive Brand Assets*; Romaniuk, 2018b) for more detail about interpreting common grid

---

4 If you would like to use this grid, please be in contact and I will send you a colour copy.

structures). Placement of each asset in a quadrant reveals the strategic potential of that specific asset:

- *Use or lose* (over 50% fame *and* uniqueness)—this quadrant is called 'Use or lose' or 'usable', as it identifies the strongest distinctive assets that can be *used* as stand-alone branding devices, and reminds us that without reinforcement, the assets are likely to be *lost*. Even the strongest asset needs to be executed prominently to keep buyers' memory structures fresh. Assets that just cross the 50% threshold still need more building activity, but the shift from asset building to asset using can increase in line with fame increases.

- *Investment potential* (over 50% uniqueness but less than 50% fame)— this quadrant, also called 'investable', is the next most interesting quadrant as it reveals assets with a head start on the metric that is most difficult to fix. Wider-reaching asset-building activities can shift the asset to Use or lose status. In the benchmarking stage this quadrant usually reveals asset types where marketers have tinkered with assets, often unnecessarily. It's not unusual to see multiple taglines, advertising styles or pack styles in this quadrant—many assets of the same type with potential, but none with sufficient investment to become a strong asset. Benchmarking your distinctive assets is a good opportunity to identify and stop this chop-and-change mentality that fragments valuable asset-building resources and holds back the building of strong assets.

- *Avoid solo use* (over 50% fame but less than 50% uniqueness)—this is a tricky quadrant as the asset has fame, but for your competitors as well. These assets are, or are becoming, generic category (for example, red in tomato sauce) or sub-category (for example, yellow for lemon scent) signals. A cause can be new entrants mirroring the cues of the established brands. While it is hard to give up an asset when fame is high, without strong direct branding you risk giving valuable mental real estate to competitors' brands.

- *Ignore or test* (less than 50% fame *and* uniqueness)—these assets have nothing that gives them a head start over other options. Primary causes are being new to the brand, lacking cut-through or being much stronger for competitors. Delving more deeply into past efforts and current competitive links can help reveal which of these is the case and whether there are any barriers to building the asset. While all asset *types* can be strong assets, not all assets can be strong: some simply lack the form or structure to be noticeable in a cluttered environment. If you have been trying to build an asset, following all the right execution processes and it stubbornly remains in the Ignore or test quadrant, maybe it's not you, maybe it's the asset—and it's time to move on to something with more potential.

Distinctiveness measurement in action

To illustrate the grid, and how results can vary across countries, we tested the strength of assets from well-known brands in the USA and China. The assets and brands tested included the following:

- logos from car brands such as BMW, Volkswagen, Hyundai and Chevrolet
- logos from Apple and HTC and the font from IBM
- logos from sportswear brands such Nike, Puma and Adidas
- images and logos from soft drink brands such as Coca-Cola and Pepsi
- logos from fast-food brands such as KFC and Domino's
- the character of Ronald McDonald from McDonald's.

For each country, we calculated each asset's fame and uniqueness metrics.[5] Here are highlights of the results.

- The KFC logo is highly usable in both countries, while Ronald McDonald (character) is usable in the USA and borderline investable–usable in China. Domino's and Burger King have lower fame in China.
- Four of the car logos (BMW, Volkswagen, Hyundai and Chevrolet) are usable in both countries. Hyundai is stronger in China than in the USA.

---

5   Samples of n = 300 online survey in each country, conducted March 2015.

- Apple has the strongest overall performance for technology brands, with fame scores of 90% or higher and uniqueness 100% in both countries, while IBM's font is investable in both countries. In contrast the HTC logo is in the Ignore or test quadrant in both countries.

- Of the sportswear brands, unsurprisingly given the publicity it receives, the Nike swoosh is strong in both countries but it has strong competition. Logos from Adidas and Puma also achieve usable status in both countries, although not quite at Nike's level. Results are lower for Asics and Reebok logos.

- In the battle of the drink logos, we found Pepsi at usable level in both countries. Coca-Cola's red-and-white wave image is usable the USA, but only investable in China. This might be due to Coca-Cola's lack of emphasis on the colour red at the time of the survey, with Coke Zero still black and Coca-Cola Life still present in the category and in a green can.

Figures 5.3 and 5.4 show the grids for each country.

Figure 5.3: Distinctive asset results for key brand assets in the USA (2015)

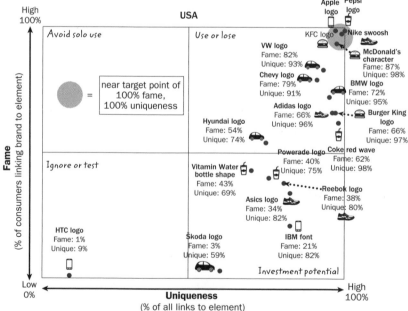

Figure 5.4: Distinctive asset results for key brand assets in China (2015)

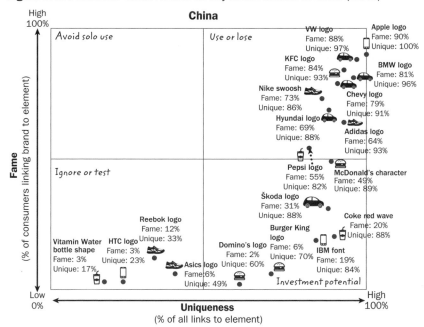

Don't get caught up in the meaning of it all

Marketing and advertising have great storytellers, and it is easy to get caught up in the mythology and romanticism of it all. But buyers rarely know (or care) about this rich allegory. For example, when you see Johnnie Walker's striding man, do you realise that he was reversed from walking left to walking right to be seen as moving forward and progressing towards fulfilling his personal goals (Epstein, 2014)? Neither did I.

When selecting distinctive assets, the number of options can be overwhelming. This can lead marketers to draw on the brand's current products, values or purpose to inspire or select assets for investment. The brand wants to be perceived by category buyers as having a certain quality, therefore you aim to select the assets based on the criterion of how well they help build this image around that quality. This short-term strategy can backfire in the long term.

Think about some of the biggest brands today and how they have evolved in terms of their product mix and business models: remember Apple used to be a computer company, Starbucks was all about coffee,

McDonald's talked only about hamburgers and Amazon once just sold books. Having a distinctive asset closely linked to what the company offers or stands for *now* means you're likely to have to modify or abandon that asset in the future.

Other strong meanings for an asset also create mental competition for the brand when trying to build an asset. If when I see a dachshund in an ad I think of my own pup Alfie, that brand has to compete with all my memories of Alfie that will dominate for retrieval (I see him more often than any advertising!). In the context of the category, the brand name should be the strongest meaning for any distinctive asset. Other meanings only serve to make asset building difficult, narrow the potential uses of the asset and put asset longevity at risk.

Step 2: Execute well

A common question is how long it takes to build a distinctive asset to usable status. The answer depends on how well you implement the following three steps:

Reach all category buyers. Only those buyers exposed to the brand with the distinctive asset can build memory linkages. If your asset-building activity reaches 50% of category buyers, then 50% have a chance of learning that the asset is linked to the brand. Put simply, a reach of 50% builds distinctive assets quicker than a reach of 30%, but not as quickly as if you reach 80% of category buyers.

Create prominent (co-presentation) moments. To work, the asset needs to be noticed, and so needs to have a prominent place in the execution. If the primary objective of the execution is to build an asset with low fame, then category buyers need exposure to moments where the asset and the brand name are together (called co-presentation). This exposure builds links between the two items in memory. The more prominent these co-presentation moments are, the quicker you will establish distinctive assets amongst those who are exposed.

Ensure consistency. Every exposure is a 'do or decay' branding moment. The window to insert the brand into people's lives is small and short-lived. Consistency is key to making every exposure count. Inconsistency is more than just a missed opportunity to strengthen a distinctive asset; it can set the brand's identity backwards by creating associations that interfere with future retrieval. This is a mistake often made when creating a brand identity for new variants.

TAKE THE TEST

A useful exercise is to lay out, on one big table, all of the brand collateral that a category buyer is likely to see. Don't just confine it to printed material; print out web pages, presence in online stores, any variants that draw on the brand name—indeed, anything that the category buyer might see.

What jumps out at you as you look across the table? Is it a sea of red? Or a mix of colours? Does a character continually jump out? An expression? A shape?

Do all of the items look like they have come from the same family? Or do a few oddities look like they belong somewhere else?

This is the first step to check your past execution and eliminate inconsistencies.

Setting the long-term strategy to create a distinctive asset palette

A distinctive asset palette is the set of distinctive assets that can be used as branding devices across media and sales environments. Having diversity within the set means you can select the asset(s) that work better within each branding environment. A diverse palette of distinctive assets could include the following elements:

- a colour-based asset—to help the branding in wide environments with lots of visual clutter
- a shape-based asset—a logo, symbol or product form—to help branding in text-rich environments
- something with a face (a character or spokesperson)—to help the brand gain attention in creative settings
- a sound—to help branding in audio environments or when eyes are not on screen
- a phrase—to use in image-rich environments.

Set up the distinctive asset palette as a long-term goal but start by building in waves of one or two at a time. Move to the next wave of assets once the initial wave has reached close to 100% fame and 100% uniqueness. Assets that can also be used in shopping environments or at the start of an advertisement can be prioritised as they provide additional benefits to the buyer and brand.

Distinctive assets and mental availability

To build mental availability, a brand needs to have fresh links to a wide range of category entry points (CEPs; refer to Chapter 4). Category buyers build links to CEPs when they are exposed to the brand alongside the CEP. Distinctive assets help the branding side of the equation to build mental availability (having a relevant message is the other side). Remember: the easier it is to process the brand, the more attention a viewer can give to the message.

Different touch-points help us insert our brand into a buyer's life, and freshen the brand's memory structures: *if the brand is a noticeable part of the marketing communications activity*. Distinctive assets can help the brand gain attention in the following ways:

- *Increase the amount of branding within any marketing activity*. Distinctive assets provide additional branding devices. Advertisers (often misguidedly) fear boring buyers if too much of the advertisement's real estate is devoted to the brand name. The brand name is therefore typically a small part of any advertisement, with more time and space spent on creative and messaging elements (Romaniuk, 2009). Branding via distinctive assets can mitigate this fear, and increase branding content (Hartnett, Romaniuk & Kennedy, 2016).

- *Broaden the audience for the brand exposure*. People with low literacy can use shapes, colours or characters as brand identifiers. This allows the branding to reach more category buyers. This is particularly important in emerging markets, where education levels vary considerably, including amongst owners of traditional small and nano retail outlets. But even in developed markets, literacy is an issue; for example, 21% of the US population is classed as having low English literacy (NCES, 2019).

- *Provide script-independent branding.* Written language in countries such as China, Thailand, Greece and Russia use different scripts for letters. Representing the brand in non-word forms, such as logos or characters, can create consistency for campaigns that involve countries with different language types.

- *Improve the quality of brand execution.* Branding execution is not just about the quantity of branding—quality also matters (Romaniuk, 2009). Distinctive assets improve the quality of brand execution by paving the way for smarter execution tactics that often face resistance when directly involving the brand name. For example, early brand exposure in television advertising is a proven tactic to increase correct branding, but advertisers often worry that buyers will switch off once they see the brand name and miss the rest of the advertisement. Drawing on a distinctive asset, such as music or a character, can overcome this resistance to early branding.[6]

- *Increase the competitiveness of the brand versus other creative distractions.* Within an execution, using distinctive assets such as colours, sounds, faces, ad moments or styles can help the brand compete for viewer attention in the face of competition from traditionally more interesting aspects of the creative execution, such as a celebrity, puppy or a baby.

- *Act as a bridge to link executions across media platforms.* Operating in today's media environment requires a flexible approach to media choices. To reach a large, diverse, potential buyer population, campaigns might need to stretch from sophisticated digital technology to catch the young to more traditional radio to reach commuters to posters on neighbourhood streets to reach homemakers on their way to do the household shopping. Distinctive assets can connect executions across media in a multi-platform campaign, providing a linchpin that still allows for variation in creative elements to maximise the strengths of different media formats.

---

6   The use of effective brand execution, rather than just adding more branding, becomes even more important as video advertising is getting shorter, with five-second ads and six-second videos gaining popularity—these mean less time for everything, including branding.

- *Act as a bridge to past campaigns, and link them with current executions.* When launching a new campaign, everyone's attention is on the new: new message, new look and feel, new talent and new media (understandably—it's exciting!). But we need to also be confident that category buyers who see the new campaign know which brand it is for. Distinctive assets provide a brand-consistent look and feel to any execution, so the buyer files it away quickly and correctly. Current campaigns can then capitalise on past campaigns, rather than the viewer needing to start afresh each time.

Distinctive assets and physical availability

Most sales environments are rife with competitive clutter. Buyers are distracted; anything that is hard to find is likely to stay lost. Distinctive assets help the brand's *prominence* in its shopping environment, making it easy to find. Shopping environments can vary from a mall to an online broker, phone app, supermarket, hypermarket, convenience store, vending machine, car yard or website. Imagine if I wanted to book a flight right here and now—what are the different options I have? Airline websites, online travel websites (Expedia, Webjet), travel company websites, travel agents, my Qantas app, my American Airlines app. Plus with anything online I have three devices I can use: this computer, a tablet or my phone. An airline needs to stand out in all of these different environments (even my Qantas app offers me flights on Emirates, Qatar and other Oneworld airlines).

If I wanted to buy a television tomorrow, I also have a large number of options, involving both physical and online outlets, computer and app options, specialty retailers, direct manufacturer options or department stores. It can be overwhelming navigating channels, retailers, brands and product options such as screen size and type of resolution (I know, at the time of writing this I had just bought a television after my previous one stopped working!). The brand needs to try to stand out in all of the sales environments where it is present, which means having the diverse set of assets that help do this. Chapter 9 further discusses 'shopping assets', which are the assets that category buyers use when trying to find the brand in different shopping environments.

Conclusion

This chapter provided guidance for building a strong brand identity. Distilled from this chapter are the following tactical dos and don'ts to help you build a strong brand identity:

- *Do* select a palette that taps into different parts of the brain to give the brand identity diversity.
- *Do* measure the strength of the brand's distinctive assets—your judgement (and that of the marketing team) is likely to be overly optimistic.
- *Do* make sure distinctive assets are used consistently to capitalise on any opportunity to build distinctive assets. Inconsistency is at best an opportunity cost and at worst self-sabotage.
- *Don't* choose a distinctive asset based on what it means to buyers; select assets where the strongest meaning can be the brand name.
- *Don't* stop using the strong assets—remember that non-use has a price, and that price is buyers' memory decay.

With a strategy in place to build a strong, neurologically diverse palette, distinctive assets can help accelerate a brand's mental and physical availability–building activities. For those who want to deeply delve into distinctive assets, the book *Building Distinctive Brand Assets* (Romaniuk, 2018a) goes into much greater detail about the topics covered here, including expanded evidence on the use of different asset types, branding for variants and setting up a distinctive asset management system to build and protect distinctive assets.

6

Achieving Reach

Jenni Romaniuk

Marketing activities need reach. Why? Because brand growth depends on the brand increasing its penetration (double jeopardy law, discussed in Chapter 1) and recruiting light/infrequent category buyers (natural monopoly law, discussed in Chapter 2). It's difficult to recruit category buyers you don't reach, which means you need to scale the reach in your marketing activities to move the needle on the brand's sales. It is surprising that mainstream acceptance of this media-planning goal has taken so long, and that when companies like P&G highlight reach's importance (Hammett, 2019), this makes news!

Another important aim of media strategy is to minimise the time gap between each purchase occasion and the last advertising exposure (for your brand). This means reaching as many category buyers as regularly as you can afford. Media fragmentation and the sheer number of media options makes achieving something as simple as reach something that requires planning to accomplish. It is easy to get distracted from this goal of achieving reach by claims of exclusive audiences, engagement and proprietary metrics to assess effectiveness.

This chapter covers some broad fundamentals of media selection and scheduling to achieve reach in a fragmented environment. It contains knowledge to make it easier to choose between the many different options available, even when the data on category buyer media consumption is poor or lacks standardisation.

Living in a fragmented media world

Marketing activities only build mental availability in the audience they reach. This makes planning for reach the foundation of any sound media strategy. The digital revolution ushered in more ways of reaching buyers, offering tantalising prospects of lower overall costs, better timing of exposure and even lower advertising avoidance. But achieving such outcomes is hardly straightforward. Every media opportunity has attractive and unattractive features. Before we go into some guidelines for selecting media to achieve reach, let's first clarify what we mean by 'reach' and dismantle some of the persistent arguments against reach-based planning.

What does *reach* really mean?

The media-planning industry has its own jargon, which surprisingly is seldom taught in marketing degrees. *Reach* refers to the size of the audience exposed to your marketing activity in a specific time period: for example, '40% 1+ reach' means that 40% of a particular population (say, 18–48-year-olds) in a specific time period in a particular geographic area receiving one or more (potential[1]) advertising exposures.

This is a simple metric but one unfortunately difficult to calculate across multiple media, as each tends to have its own measurement system.

---

1   With most media, it is never possible to guarantee that a person has really received an exposure, due to advertising avoidance (for example, switching channels or using web ad-blockers) and lack of noticing of some exposures. Advertising 'exposures' are therefore often called 'opportunities to see' (OTS).

Most marketers live with knowing that, say, their television advertising achieved 65% reach while their Facebook advertising achieved 20% reach in the same period, with only a rough estimate of how much unduplicated reach they achieved by advertising in both media.

To reiterate, the importance of reach should be very obvious: a brand's marketing activity can only influence the category buyers[2] it reaches. Marketing activity that reaches a large proportion of category buyers *can* have a large sales impact, while an activity that reaches only a small group of people can, even if it achieves its best result, only have a small sales impact.

Some basic maths reveals that if you lose (or plan for lower) reach, the extra response needed to achieve the same sales quickly becomes unachievable. For example, let's take the case of achieving 60% reach and having a 5% behavioural impact (this might be clicking or making an enquiry but, in this case, let's say it is placing an order). If the population is 1000 people, this combination will generate 30 sales (600 people × 0.05):

- if your reach is reduced to 40%, then you need 7.5% behavioural impact (that is, an extra 50% response) to achieve the same 30 sales (400 × 0.075)
- if your reach is halved, at 30%, then you need 10% behavioural impact (or 200% increase in response) to achieve the same 30 sales (300 × 0.1)
- if you focus on a low-reach activity, and only reach 10% of category buyers, then you need six times the baseline response (or a whopping 600% increase!) to achieve the same 30 sales (100 × 0.3).

Lower reach makes it harder to maintain the same sales level, let alone grow. While media plans can vary enormously in terms of the reach they generate—that is, you can buy more reach—rarely can they guarantee greater impact.

Reach versus spend

It has become a recurring fashion to focus volume metrics to assess the performance of the media budget. Volume metrics focus on how much

---

2   Sometimes word of mouth is put forward as a way to reach more people than planned for in the media schedule (this is discussed in Chapter 7).

of something is done, such as share of voice, share of spend and total media budget. These volume metrics are plotted against market share or some other outcome to determine the effectiveness of past spend, or the future trajectory of the brand (Jones, 1990; Danenberg et al., 2016). The danger with this approach is that it makes the assumption that two brands spending the same amount of money (even relative to share) should get the same performance. Budgets can be spent wisely, foolishly or somewhere in between. Even reach alone is not a suitable metric, as short-term reach can be achieved with a great deal of wastage with a burst strategy (Sharp, Newstead & Danenberg, 2011). Reach is a measure of the distribution of that advertising spend, and its ability to reach as many category buyer 'brains' as possible. While overall spend might be a rough-and-ready proxy, it's not very useful over time when assessing the performance of your media plans.

Concentrating on metrics that focus on the volume of media spend is like assessing the efficacy of an athlete's training solely on how long they train. A better athlete doesn't train more. They train across the range of activities needed to achieve the best performance on the day and don't just spend all their time doing bicep curls. Don't get distracted by these volume approaches—work to get the data needed to properly assess the use of your media budget.

But I can't plan for reach because …

We still hear excuses to justify *not* having reach as the primary media objective. Here is the faulty logic underpinning some of the most persistent reasons we hear. You can draw on these arguments if someone presents these reasons to you.

But the market is big and my budget is small

Regardless of how large or small your budget is, you always want as much reach as your money will buy. Having a small budget means you can ill afford to waste it. Brands with (perceived) small budgets routinely do themselves harm by assuming that they cannot afford reach and therefore move towards high cost-per-contact media: that is, trading reach for 'engagement'. This tendency (unnecessarily) means you reach fewer category buyers and gives bigger brands, able to reach them instead, another advantage.

The real challenge for small brands is not that they can't afford reach; rather it's that their physical availability may be restricted. This means much of their advertising may reach buyers for whom the brand isn't easy to buy. Sometimes tinkering with the media or advertising is not the solution to getting more from advertising spend, but rather focusing instead on building physical availability.

But don't I need a frequency of at least three?

This is an old myth. Advertising isn't like a theoretical physics lecture; it doesn't need repeated viewings and much contemplation before it finally sinks in. Good advertising works straight out of the gate and bad advertising,[3] even if repeated, has little effect. Not planning for reach and instead ending up with a small group of category buyers being hit by marketing activities two, three and more times is an inefficient use of the media budget.

Nearby repeat exposures to the same person don't have as much effect as the first one. This is intuitively obvious (once you know) and shows up in real-world single-source data: the first exposure within a time period has the greatest sales effect (Taylor, Kennedy & Sharp, 2009). Further support for scheduling to space out exposures to the same person comes from a meta-analysis of laboratory experiments into learning from fields of cognitive psychology and marketing (Sawyer, Noel & Janiszewski, 2009). Spaced exposures cumulate in stronger memories than exposures that are experienced close together. You need to give people time to 'forget', so they can re-remember. Seeing the same thing again in a short period of time is a recipe for boredom and inattention.

Just because you can't reach all category buyers don't mean you shouldn't try. Studies into media consumption behaviour reveal why planning to reach as many category buyers as possible achieves better

---

3   Much bad advertising doesn't cause sales for a brand because it is working for other brands. Increasing the media weight is a dangerous way to attempt to fix this.

coverage (for example, Sharp, Beal & Collins, 2009). Exposure patterns within and across media mean some people are simply easier to reach than others: they watch television/are on Instagram more often and so wherever you schedule your marketing activity within that media platform, they are easier to hit.

These media consumption patterns highlight why planning for reach is vitally important. If you don't plan to reach out to new buyers, excess frequency is the more likely natural outcome. This build-up of (less valuable) frequency reduces the return from your media budget as the second exposure costs the same as the first, but the return from two or more exposures is much lower.

My advertising message is so sophisticated people need to see it several times to get it

It is risky to draw on a multi-exposure advertising approach. For every lauded complex storyline campaign, there is a raft of quickly buried failures. Media consumption patterns make it difficult to schedule accurately for multiple, sequentially timed exposures to the same person. But even if we could, why would we want to? Why take two or three exposures to achieve what could be achieved in one? This only makes sense if you are expecting at least two or three times the response level from those who do see it several times. Can your campaign guarantee this?

Successful advertising has a lingering effect on the category buyer brain, so any repeat exposure within a short time frame is less efficient than reaching out to a new brain. The principle of one-exposure media planning affects creativity—it means designing advertising that works first time, every time.

I need to match my competitors' burst

Matching bad spending with similar bad spending is a recipe for both brands to be undercut by a smarter competitor. While bursts deliver reach in a short period of time, they also repeatedly hit heavier media consumers, which makes them an inefficient and ineffective way to reach light media consumers (Ceber, 2009). No brand can sustain a burst (by definition), and only people who are in the market at the time of or shortly after the burst can contribute to sales. Unless you have a highly seasonal product (for example, 80% sold in a short period of time), even a successful in-the-moment burst will mean the brand lacks the on-air presence over the rest of the year when the majority of sales occur.

By planning for continuous reach, rather than mirroring competitors, you may lose slightly during the competitor burst, but you gain in the long term when that competitor has to go off air.

No more excuses!

As you can see, there really is no excuse *not* to plan for reach if you want to use the media budget wisely. In all categories and markets, achieving reach is important. Even in emerging markets, with large populations, fragmented media systems and large influxes of new category buyers, reaching out to the wider category-buying population is of paramount importance if you want to create an economically sustainable brand.

Advertise where you sell

Plan for reach where you have, or want, physical availability. A key purpose of advertising is to build up mental availability, which nudges the buyer towards brand. Once this is achieved, physical availability then enables the buyer to easily act on that nudge. If physical availability is poor, then even excellent, wide-reaching advertising will not generate sales.

If you only distribute on the east coast of the USA or in Harbin, China, then advertising outside of these regions is of little value. In such cases, regional media might be a smart choice to avoid advertising in areas where people can't buy the brand—but only if the cost of regionalising your media strategy does not outweigh the benefits. If you want to sell to buyers to a new region in the near future, advertising builds everyone's mental availability for the brand, including retailers and distributors. This can help secure distribution.

(More) valuable audience: Light and non-brand buyers

In Chapter 2 we discussed how light and non-brand buyers matter most for brand growth. We therefore need to reach these buyers, mindful that they buy and notice the advertising of the other brands as well. Exposure to our advertising gives our brand a better chance of being salient in buying situations, through freshening memory and neutralising the effects of competitors' advertising exposures.

This makes media that reach lighter and non-brand buyers extremely valuable. Typically, media that reach more category buyers also reach more of the buyers needed for your brand to grow. But there are three tactics that *reduce* the effectiveness of your media spend:

- *Trying to make buyers work for exposure.* High-engagement media that make buyers act in some way to qualify typically skew to heavy brand buyers who are the only ones motivated to go this extra step. Examples of this are given in Nelson-Field, Riebe and Sharp (2012) for Facebook fan pages, and Romaniuk, Beal and Uncles (2013) for social media and events.

- *Trying to make buyers work to identify your brand.* If you make the branding difficult and expect the audience to work hard to identify the brand, you will be very disappointed—most won't, and the few who do will be your past heavy brand buyers. You are left (only) preaching to the converted.

- *Unnecessary repetition.* A common mistake is to choose a large-reach media vehicle, but then schedule spots to create extensive short-term duplication within that medium. For example, advertising in *NCIS* but buying multiple spots in the same show: this is only of value if you have a very different audience in each ad break—are you confident of that?

Avoid making category buyers work to achieve your advertising goals; light and non-buyers simply won't make that effort, and you therefore miss your most valuable audience for growth.

Don't neglect light and new category buyers

Strategies aimed predominantly at the brand's customer base—even when wide-reaching—can still miss an important group: light and new category buyers. When categories grow, any influx of new category buyers presents an opportunity for the brand. And even in mature categories, new category buyers enter as circumstances change.

New category buyers know very little about the category, and the brands within it. This means lower competition for mental availability, and brands that make an impression at this nascent time have a 'blanker' slate to more easily establish a fresh brand in memory. Any media target should be broad enough to reach these buyers.

Choosing media platforms

Media scheduling should be buyer-centric, and this we know intuitively. The basic knowledge of *how many*, *how often*, *for how long* and *when* your category buyers consume different media is key to smart media planning. Unfortunately, we often lack robust buyer-centric media data to act on this intuition.

Luckily, media behaviour (across and within platforms) largely conforms to the law of double jeopardy. This means the *how often* and *for how long* directly correlate with *how many* (penetration) comprise the audience for the platform. Or put more simply, media that attract bigger audiences will be used more often and for longer by those audiences.

Figure 6.1 is from a sample of online users in Russia. We see the two most common media—going online with a personal computer and watching television—also have the most frequent users, with around 90% engaging in these activities on most days. In contrast, reading a magazine or going to the cinema have the double jeopardy double-whammy of the few people they do attract interacting less frequently.

Going online at an internet cafe is the obvious outlier in Figure 6.1, because it is something that only those without a computer do. A large proportion of the Russian internet-using population have computers, and so don't need to visit internet cafes. But those who do are active relatively frequently.

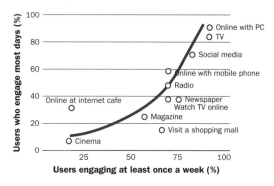

Figure 6.1: Media consumption habits of internet users in Russia 2014 (*n* = 800)

This application of the law of double jeopardy means that, in the absence of other evidence, you can assume that high-penetration media also attract their audience more often. But we do need to distinguish between a medium having large reach and a planner's ability to achieve extensive, unduplicated reach within that medium. For example, in China in 2012, people reportedly spent more time on the internet than watching television (Meeker & Wu, 2013), but the internet is infinitely more fragmented than even television's 350-odd channels. While category buyers might spend more time online, fragmentation might make it difficult to schedule for cumulative reach.

The double jeopardy law also generally holds within a platform (that is, for different television channels, radio stations and similar genres of websites). Decades of evidence show this holding for television viewing patterns around the world (Sharp, Beal & Collins, 2009), and we have seen this extend to radio, online site visitation and so on. In Table 6.1 we show double jeopardy in social media site usage of digitally literate samples in China and the USA.

Table 6.1: Penetration and frequency of social media usage by internet users only—in China (2014) and the USA (2015)

Chinese sites	Users (%)	Highly active* users (%)	US sites	Users (%)	Highly active* users (%)
Wechat	96	88	Facebook	84	82
Qzone	93	75	Twitter	49	65
Youku	87	60	Google+	47	51
Sina Weibo	86	70	Instagram	41	64

continued

Chinese sites	Users (%)	Highly active* users (%)	US sites	Users (%)	Highly active* users (%)
Tencent Weibo	80	56	Pinterest	41	51
Renren	62	41	LinkedIn	38	34
Douban	59	39	Tumblr	25	50
PenYou	58	45	Vine	23	45
Kaixin 001	50	41	Flickr	18	39
51com	43	40	Ask.fm	17	47
Diandian	34	32	Tagged	15	56
Jiepang	32	30	Meetup	14	48
Average	**62**	**49**	**Average**	**34**	**53**

*Highly active = use most days

It is easy to check double jeopardy for the media platforms you are selecting between. Simply order the channels', sites', stations' or publications' penetration and frequency or volume figures by market share. A quick scatterplot visually shows the relationship.

Fragmentation, both within and across channels, makes the few properties able to command large audiences particularly attractive. Once you advertise in a large-reach property, it is rarely a good investment to also advertise in a small-reach property in the same platform. Smaller media properties tend to attract heavy users of the platform/media—this means you have already reached them with the first, larger-reach, property. The addition of the smaller-reach property gives you lots of duplication, and very little additional reach.

For example, the audience for smaller social media sites such as Pinterest comprises people who are active on more other social media sites, including the big ones such as Facebook and YouTube (see Table 6.2 for examples from Mexico and Nigeria).

Occasionally smaller media vehicles have higher than expected frequency or time spent viewing but, as they attract such a small audience, the overall eyeballs or ears contribution of that vehicle remains small. These are often sold as attractive high-engagement media, but higher time spent or repeat exposures generate excess frequency unless the repeat views are carefully spaced. Remember each exposure costs the same, but close-together repeat exposures have lower returns.

The message is clear. First and foremost, choose media that attract a substantive audience. Then make sure you can cut through to reach category buyers in that medium.

Table 6.2: The repertoire size for social media and communications platforms by internet users in Mexico and Nigeria (2014)

Mexico	Penetration (%)	Number of other social media sites used by audience	Nigeria	Penetration (%)	Number of other social media sites used by audience
Facebook	91	2.1	Facebook	89	2.8
YouTube	84	2.3	WhatsApp	67	3.2
Twitter	45	3.2	YouTube	52	3.5
Instagram	21	4.2	Twitter	49	3.7
LinkedIn	14	4.3	LinkedIn	34	3.9
Badoo	10	5.1	Skype	22	4.1
Pinterest	8	5.6	Online Nigeria	20	3.8
Hi5	7	5.6	Instagram	15	4.8
Sonico	7	5.9	Pinterest	6	5.6
Metroflog	4	6.7	Tumblr	3	6.3
Average		**4.8**			**4.2**

Mixing a media cocktail

Sometimes you saturate a media channel to the extent that achieving any additional short-term reach will mean also paying for much more additional frequency. Then you have two options: add another medium to the mix or save the money for the next time period. Achieving unduplicated reach is the priority, and people consume multiple, different media. Given the paucity of buyer-centric data, how do we plan for unduplicated reach across multiple platforms?

We can draw on the duplication of purchase law from Chapter 3, which was actually first discovered in television viewing behaviour (Goodhardt & Ehrenberg, 1969). Applying this analysis across media, within media or both can help direct media choices (Redford, 2005). There are two points of particular of interest:

- excess audience sharing—which highlights media pairs to avoid, due to higher than expected duplication if both media options are chosen
- deficits in sharing—which highlights media pairs that together might help achieve more unduplicated reach.

Table 6.3 shows media audience sharing from China. It shows every other media channel shares around 80% of its audience with television, the biggest channel, and this pattern of diminishing sharing in line with media popularity is evident. However, there are deviations from this pattern for some media combinations. We now highlight how these findings can help inform media planning.

Table 6.3 shows that, in China, video ads via social media share more audience members with supermarket flyers/coupons, outdoor events, mobile and SMS advertising, and radio. This means that in a multi-platform campaign, a combination of a video ad on social media and an SMS campaign is likely to lead to higher audience duplication than, say a video ad on social media and an in-store promoter campaign. While the result of this type of analysis is only one input when designing a multi-platform campaign, because timing and costs also need to be factored in, this type of cross-media analysis can narrow the list down to more fruitful combinations, which is worth exploring further. The data can be collected by a well-designed survey.

Table 6.3: Sharing audiences across media in China (2012) (selected results)

Of those who were reached in the following media	Total reached (%)	Were also reached by (%)			
		Television ads	Social media video ads	In-store promoter advice	Peer word of mouth
Television ads	62	—	40	20	17
Social media video ads	31	80	—	7	5

Of those who were reached in the following media	Total reached (%)	Were also reached by (%)			
		Television ads	Social media video ads	In-store promoter advice	Peer word of mouth
Supermarket flyers/coupons	27	77	**63**	22	17
Free gifts/giveaways	22	83	18	**44**	**36**
Outdoor booths/events	17	84	**81**	16	12
In-store promoter advice	16	77	13	—	46
Ads via SMS or mobile	16	90	**82**	13	9
Ads for brands in-store	15	78	9	**58**	**46**
Peer word of mouth	13	85	12	**58**	—
Radio	10	89	**84**	15	9
Average	**16**	**83**	40	20	17

Figures in **bold** show excess sharing. Shaded figures show deficits in sharing.

The tactical routes to achieve maximum unduplicated reach are always going to vary. It's like making a good stir-fry: if you have the sound basics of a hot wok and oil with a high smoking point, you can mix any number of meat, vegetable and sauce combinations to get a great dish. These are some basic principles to remember for a good media mix:

- Because of the reach of its content (people like to watch television, as outlined in Barwise, Bellman & Beal, 2020) and the engaging potential of video, television is an invaluable part of any media mix, as many effectiveness examples show (Binet & Field, 2009; Rubinson, 2009). Don't abandon or avoid it lightly.

- Aim for the biggest reach medium first, and then only add to this if you achieve more unduplicated reach than duplicated reach in that week (Sharp et al., 2014)

- Look at media in different families, as this is more likely to lead to higher unduplicated reach (Romaniuk, Beal & Uncles, 2013). For example, mix social media and in-store, rather than two social media or in-store properties.

Conclusion

To build mental availability you need scale, and this is achieved by a sound reach-led media strategy, aimed at reaching as many category buyers, as continuously as possible. While today's fragmented media world and complex global markets can make achieving reach seem daunting, we provide some rules to simplify media choices:

- *First:* prioritise the audience for brand growth, which is light and non-brand buyers. These category buyers will usually be found in big-reach media. If in a growing category, look to reach light *category* buyers.

- *Second:* draw upon the law of double jeopardy to understand that small media properties tend to attract heavy media users, who are also found viewing larger media properties. Unless you can be assured of unduplicated reach, assume any investment in small media properties is likely to produce more frequency than reach.

- *Third:* when looking to engage in a multi-platform campaign, examine audience sharing across media options via duplication analysis to uncover more fruitful cross-platform avenues to explore.

7

Word-of-Mouth Facts Worth Talking About

Jenni Romaniuk and Robert East

Word of mouth (WOM) is treated as the superman of media—it's free, powerful and gives any brand the ability to leap bigger brands in a single campaign. Initially popular in the 1960s, WOM lost favour to other forms of influence, until last decade's surge in social media prompted a renaissance. More people with more opportunities to share about brands—now that's something to talk about! Ask buyers, and they will tell you that WOM is valuable to them. But does being (perceived as) valuable to buyers make it equally valuable to marketers?

WOM has particular resonance in emerging markets because it seems like a cure-all to two issues that plague marketers in these countries. First, many emerging markets score highly as collectivist cultures, where people express a greater desire to fit in with family and friends, leading to claims that WOM will be more influential than in other countries. The second issue is the challenge of media fragmentation making it more difficult to reach buyers with conventional media plans, combined with widespread adoption of social media, creating more opportunities for peer-to-peer communication about brands.

WOM's kryptonite is marketers' lack of control, which makes harnessing its power difficult. In this chapter we cover knowledge to help you to sensibly assess, focus and manage WOM activities as part of the larger media mix. We point out the strengths and limitations of WOM, and provide you with the knowledge to give all-important context to WOM metrics.

The lure of word of mouth

Once upon a time a brand became very big, purely through the power of word of mouth. Its buyers loved it so much they talked of it non-stop to their family, friends and anyone they happened to meet. As the word spread, more people bought the brand and they too told their family, friends, work colleagues and schoolmates, until gradually the brand was the number one in its category all over the country. The brand's manager got promoted and everyone lived happily ever after …

Sounds like a fairy tale? Well, that is because it largely is. WOM can be a useful addition to the marketing and media mix when harnessed correctly—but it is not the saviour that its (many) evangelists suggest. It's a small part of a big-picture brand-growth strategy. Myths about WOM's power often blind marketers to smart implementation and lead to inefficient allocation of resources through paying too much attention to trivialities. Indeed, the start-up world is littered with claims that brands were built with no advertising, totally on WOM. However, a quick review of the full stories behind these start-ups reveals that they succeeded *despite* the lack of advertising (due to no money being available) not because of it. One of the first thing founders do once they have the funds is start advertising to accelerate further brand building.

It is easy to see the attraction of WOM as a panacea to having small budgets in large, populous countries. For emerging markets, some commentators even go further to claim that WOM is even more powerful than in the developed world, as the reported collectivist nature of many emerging markets means buyers place more value on the advice of family, friends and colleagues.

Vague statistics are often used to support this claim, so look a bit more closely before trusting any findings. For example, McKinsey consultants claim that more people in emerging markets received recommendations about food and beverage categories before making purchases; and more Chinese consumers said they would consider recommendations from family and friends about moisturiser compared to US consumers (Atsmon & Magni, 2012). While these types of statements are easy to accept, as they support the prevailing view, this is hardly strong evidence. Receiving or considering WOM is not the same as acting upon the advice![1]

WOM routinely heads the list of sources that buyers self-report as important, and often-quoted statistics talk about the large volume of conversations that are about brands on a daily basis. But these statistics give a misleading picture of importance. First, we have a self-selection bias: we like to think we aren't fools swayed by advertising, and saying our purchase was based on advice from someone else is a more comfortable explanation. Second, while there are many conversations about brands, these conversations are by many people across many, many individual brands. The statistics for a single brand in a single category are much less exciting. We will also show how many of these conversations don't reach the necessary people to influence brand purchases.

That is not to say WOM is inconsequential. A large number of inexperienced buyers or buyers faced with major decisions might turn to WOM for guidance on choices. WOM has a long history as influential in new product adoption, particularly for disruptive innovations where more buyers need to directly hear about or see the product in action before buying.[2] But again, this is different from the effect of WOM on routine purchases or for existing products and categories.

---

1   The lack of strong evidence is probably why the collectivist stereotype is not universally accepted, with some arguing that the need for fitting in and approval from close family and friends is a personal, rather than country, characteristic.
2   For more background, see Bass and King (1968).

To use WOM effectively, you need to vaccinate yourself against myths. Currently many actions about WOM are built on the shaky foundations of many unsupported beliefs. In this chapter we dispel myths and provide evidence across a range of areas fundamental to good WOM practice, such as incidence, the impact of WOM and the interpretation of WOM metrics.

One characteristic of WOM is that it often has a valence, or direction, in that it is positive or negative for the brand. This leads to our first question: which is more important, positive or negative WOM?

Should I focus more on encouraging positive or combating negative WOM?

Allocating resources (attention, staff and money) to the most important areas is the first step to designing a smart strategy. WOM is often characterised as either positive, which is when someone says something good about the brand, or negative, which is when someone says something damaging about the brand. Some WOM is a neutral statement of fact (such as the store is open until 8 p.m.), but let's put these statements aside for now.

For the most part, positive WOM is good for the brand and negative WOM is bad for the brand,[3] so how much time or resources should you spend building up or encouraging positive WOM versus stopping or dealing with the fallout from negative WOM?

To answer this question, let's first dispel a common myth that negative WOM is more common than positive WOM: the evidence tells us otherwise. Positive WOM is much more common than negative WOM (East, Hammond & Wright, 2007). Figure 7.1 shows this for mobile phone handsets across ten countries, where positive WOM is two to five times more common than negative WOM.

---

3   A small amount of WOM has cross-effects—whereby positive WOM from someone from whom you have differing tastes could lead you to be less likely to buy the recommended brand or whose negative WOM could pique curiosity and lead to a higher probability of brand purchase—but this is usually confined to a small amount (around 3%) and to a few specific categories such as television programs, movies or fashion items.

Figure 7.1: Relative levels of positive to negative WOM for mobile phone handsets (2014)

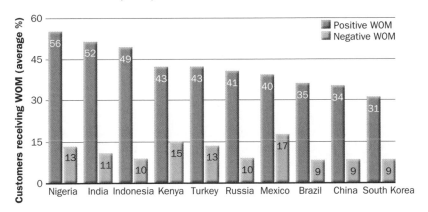

Even commonly talked-about categories such as restaurants and movies, or high-priced categories such as cars follow this pattern (see Figure 7.2). The volume of positive WOM is around three times higher than negative WOM, similar to the averages reported in East, Hammond and Wright (2007).

Figure 7.2: Comparison of volumes of positive and negative WOM across three categories in USA and China

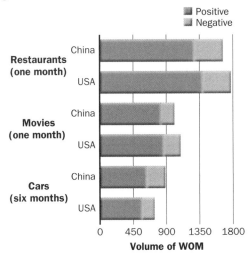

The greater volume for positive WOM is largely because many more people give, or receive, positive WOM than negative WOM (see Table 7.1 for three categories in the USA and China). Negative WOM spreads at much the same rate as positive WOM.

Table 7.1: Positive and negative WOM for three categories in China and the USA (2014)

Category and country	Respondents receiving at least one WOM incident (%)*		Frequency* (base = those receiving WOM)	
	Positive WOM	Negative WOM	Positive WOM	Negative WOM
Restaurants—China	62	28	3.5	2.2
Restaurants—USA	76	31	3.1	1.9
Movies—China	55	16	2.5	1.8
Movies—USA	57	18	2.6	2.0
Cars—China	47	21	2.2	2.0
Cars—USA	42	15	2.1	1.8
Average	**57**	**22**	**2.7**	**1.7**

*Time frame = one month for restaurants and movies, six months for cars

Why is positive WOM more common? Well, first to give negative WOM, you need a story. Most brands work as they should, so they don't provide any building blocks for (negative) conversation. This reduces the pool of people available to produce negative WOM, while there are still many more people are in the market to give positive WOM.

Another fear is that negative WOM is inherently more influential on recipients than positive WOM. This is also a myth. East, Hammond and Lomax (2008) provide comprehensive, multi-category evidence that positive and negative WOM have largely the same effect.

Overall, positive WOM is more influential on the brand's sales, reaching many more people with largely the same effect as negative WOM. Unless your brand is performing poorly (and in which case, fix the brand first!), don't dwell too much on negative WOM.

WOM equals conversation (about brands)

We call it *word of mouth*, which makes it easy to lose sight of the fact that for normal people, this is called *conversation*. The idea that everyone is seeking the advice of strangers is also largely a myth. Most WOM is shared between people who have a personal relationship. For example, in a 2014 survey we conducted in China, across three categories we found that 85% of WOM was from work colleagues, family members and friends. Only 15% of WOM was from people not very well known to the recipient.

For someone to receive WOM, someone else has to give it. That WOM occurs largely between people who are well known to each other means that the giver knows something of the interests and tastes of the people to whom they are talking, which shapes the direction of any conversation, including that about brands. When we converse with strangers, we test topics to discover mutual interests, but with family and friends we are pre-informed (and know, for example, they have no interest in sci-fi movies) and so talk about something of interest (and not the latest *Star Trek Discovery* episode).

Why do people talk about brands?

Jenni would like to share a story. The last time she was in Shanghai, she went to this great restaurant—Lost Heaven ... now from here, there are two ways to go:

- Jenni can tell you how great the food was, and how it was great value for money—now some of you have drifted off and stopped paying attention (please come back!), because you are not in Shanghai, have never been and have no plans to go. With this direction, her only interested audience are those currently in Shanghai, those who have been or those who are going in the near future.

- Jenni can tell you how it was fascinating to see the Burmese influence in the food because of how close Burma is to China, and talk about the recent political shifts in Burma, and China's influence in the region. Oh, and she might slip in the food was delicious and great value too. In which case she has kept the Shanghainese, and the past and future visitors interested, but also those interested in the region generally, political history and a wide range of interests. The reason is that the brand is part of the story, not the whole story. Some of those people interested in the region might end up in Shanghai, and now they have a restaurant recommendation for when they visit.

We often assume that a brand's actions are the primary triggers for WOM, but this is only part of the explanation. People also give WOM because they perceive it to be helpful to the recipient, or because it just came up in conversation (East et al., 2015; Mangold, Miller & Brockway, 1999). The brand can place itself in line for WOM by its actions; however, it is the situation of the giver that influences the actual delivery.

Understanding the full range of motives for giving WOM tells us the giver acts as a gatekeeper, picking the people with whom to share any specific piece of information. This constrains the reach of WOM as givers only give if *they perceive* the WOM will be of value to the recipient—either because they know that person is in the market to buy, or because the story is interesting or enjoyable (and so improves the conversation). Why give WOM if it doesn't have currency in the conversation?

This means conversation-worthy stories about the brand are particularly valuable, as they can be shared without an explicit need to know someone is in the market for a category or brand. Without a story to share, the giver is likely to wait for an external motivation to stimulate the WOM, such as someone indicating through their conversation that they are in the market or making a direct request for advice. Interesting stories allow the brand's WOM to circumvent those conversational conventions.

Marketers need to think about what brand stories are sufficiently compelling to be shareable in a conversation. It also means to consistently generate WOM, you need to provide fresh stories to pass on as people are unlikely to (deliberately) repeat the same story to the same people.

If your marketing plan is relying on WOM to drive purchase, consider how you can deal with these issues. The next point to consider is that people usually give WOM about brands they have experienced.

Experience with the brand matters

Experience gives us the stories to tell. People usually give WOM about brands when they have firsthand experience. Figure 7.3 shows examples, taken from East, Romaniuk and Lomax (2011), of givers of WOM from South Korea and Lebanon, as well as averages across fifteen categories in a range of developed and emerging markets. Positive WOM tends to be given by current users of the brand (East, Romaniuk & Lomax, 2011), as these buyers are more likely to have:

- formed an opinion about a brand they have confidence expressing to others;
- seen the brand's advertising, so have salient memories of the brand (Romaniuk & Wight, 2009; Vaughan, Beal & Romaniuk 2016); and
- had an unusual brand experience/story to share that is worth talking about.

Figure 7.3: (a) Positive and (b) negative WOM examples

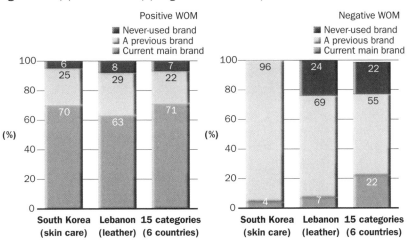

Source: East, Romaniuk & Lomax, 2011

In contrast, the brand's lapsed users or defectors give more negative WOM, as they:

- are most likely to have a negative experience to share; or
- have generated negative feelings to post-rationalise their defection from the brand (Winchester, Romaniuk & Bogomolova, 2008).

Current brand users thus dominate the pool of those who give positive WOM, while lapsed users and defectors dominate amongst those who give negative WOM. Very little WOM is generated from those who lack experience with the brand. This makes over-reliance on WOM a risky option for new brands, without many experienced customers, to rely on.

This correlation between defection and the giving of negative WOM highlights a key limitation of the *net promoter score* (Reichheld, 2003), which only captures willingness to give WOM from the brand's current customers. This can't capture negative WOM generated by brand defectors and so under-represents negative WOM (East, Romaniuk & Lomax, 2011).

Relax—your brand's level of WOM is probably normal

Like most brand-level metrics, WOM levels are highly correlated with market share (Uncles, East & Lomax, 2010). Brands with a larger share receive more positive WOM than smaller brands. Figure 7.4 illustrates this for major banks in Indonesia and Russia, where larger banks, such as Sberbank in Russia and Central Asia Bank in Indonesia, have more people receiving positive WOM than their smaller counterparts. Therefore a small brand will typically have less WOM than a big brand, simply because fewer people have sufficient experience to express an opinion.

Figure 7.4: Brands receiving positive WOM for banks in (a) Indonesia and (b) Russia (2014)

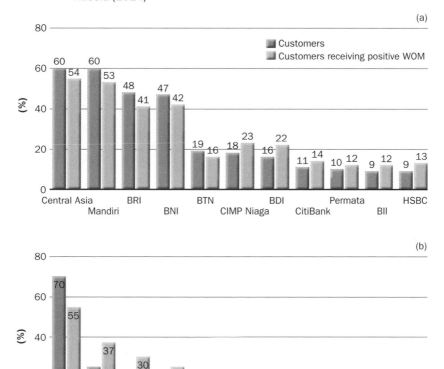

We see this relationship for the same brand across multiple countries, as illustrated with HSBC in Figure 7.5. In Brazil and China, where HSBC has more personal banking customers, positive WOM is higher than in Russia, where the brand has fewer customers.

A brand's share or usage level should set your expectations about WOM levels relative to other brands in the category. It is therefore possible to determine if the brand's levels of WOM are higher, lower or as expected for its size, rather than naively relying on the raw percentages. This is particularly useful for managers of global brands when comparing across countries where the brand differs in share.

Figure 7.5: Relationship between number of customers and incidence of positive WOM for HSBC across six countries (2014)

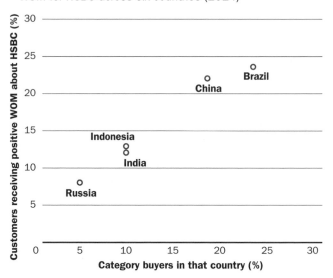

Positive WOM has the most influence when ...

The effect of a particular piece of advice depends on how likely the recipient was to buy the brand *prior to receiving the advice* (East, Hammond & Lomax, 2008). Without understanding the recipients' baseline probability of buying, it is easy to overestimate the effect of WOM on sales.

As Chapter 1 showed, the normal distribution of a brand's buying propensity looks like the reverse J in Figure 7.6, with lots of people with little or no propensity to buy the brand in the future.

What about those receiving WOM—how likely are they to buy the brand before hearing the WOM? Let's take positive WOM for cars in the USA as an example. Those who had received recent positive WOM about a car brand in the last six months were asked about their probability of buying that brand before and after receipt.[4] The difference between the

---

4   The survey was conducted in November 2014 amongst 600 respondents in the USA; this
      approach is the same as used in East, Hammond and Lomax (2008).

two is the impact, and in this case we see that positive WOM lifts the probability of buying a car brand by an average of +0.9 percentage points (no surprise here, but reassuring!).

Figure 7.6: Probability of considering Citibank for next banking product across India, China and Brazil (2014)

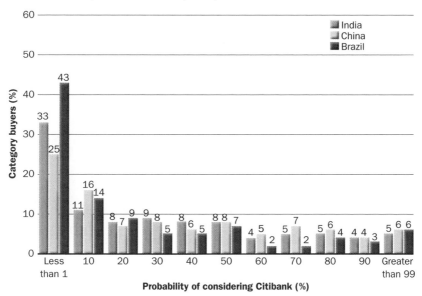

But is it the same lift across everyone? To test this, we plotted the impact for each probability of buying the car brand before receiving the WOM to see if it varied (see Figure 7.7). We also include the percentage of people at each probability level (from zero to 100), as this is crucial to contextualise the impact figures. High impact on only a few category buyers will still have only small overall return for the brand.[5]

---

5   Calculated as the difference between probabilities of purchasing a brand before and after receipt of WOM.

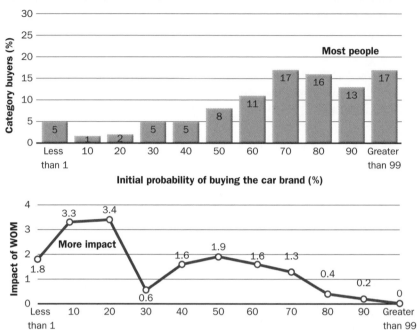

Figure 7.7: Incidence and impact of positive WOM for cars in the USA (2015)

From Figure 7.7, several key findings become apparent:

- Positive WOM has its greatest impact when it reaches those with a lower propensity (one or two chances out of ten) to buy the brand—this is more than double the average effect size.
- A mismatch exists between where the people are, and where impact peaks: 63% of people reached by positive WOM already had a 70% or more probability of buying the brand. At a probability of 70 or 80%, the impact halves to around 0.4.
- The very low probability group (close to zero or one) contains a few genuine brand rejectors who resist positive WOM.
- The audience for positive WOM skews to those with a high propensity to buy the brand, which needs to be taken into account when quantifying the effect of WOM.

This is not to dismiss the value of positive WOM reaching people with a higher prior probability of purchase, but rather to highlight that the return on investment (ROI) of WOM from these people is lower than it could be if the WOM reached people with a lower propensity.

WOM for cars in China follows similar patterns (see Figure 7.8). Impact is highest amongst low- but not zero-probability buyers of the brand; most recipients have a higher probability of buying, but WOM has more impact amongst low-propensity buyers. Cars are still quite a new category for many buyers in China, which is why the distribution is not as skewed to high propensity as it is in the USA.

Figure 7.8: Incidence and impact of positive WOM for cars in China (2014)

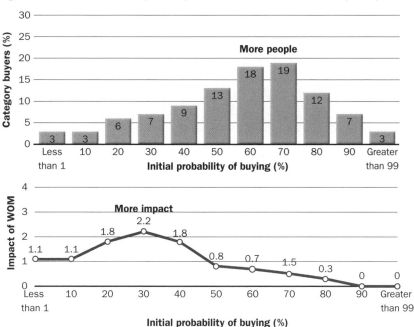

WOM's distribution is in the hands (mouths) of the givers, who look to talk to people whom they perceive have an interest in the category or brand. This skews the audience for WOM to those with an established interest. Calculations of the effect of WOM on sales need to account for this higher baseline, as does ROI modelling that compares WOM with other media without a skewed audience, such as television advertising. When the modelling includes the higher baseline of WOM, advertising can have as much, if not more, impact than WOM (Romaniuk & Hartnett, 2017).

What about the impact of negative WOM?

For negative WOM, the pattern reverses, with the biggest influence on those who have a high propensity to buy the brand (see Figure 7.9 for an example from restaurants in China where the average effect of negative WOM is a drop of 1.3 scale points). The effect is virtually zero for those who have low propensity to buy the brand and is greatest amongst those with a propensity of nine out of ten or more (90% or greater).

Figure 7.9: Incidence and impact[6] of negative WOM for restaurants in China (2014)

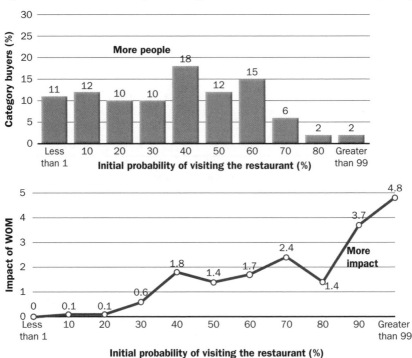

When negative WOM reaches someone with a high propensity to buy the brand, it can have a large effect: it just rarely reaches these people. This stifles the overall effect of negative WOM. We thus again see a mismatch between audience and impact, which curtails the possible impact of WOM. Both positive and negative WOM *can* have a big impact, but both tend to *fail to reach the right people* to do this. This highlights an issue with

---

6   Sign of impact is positive for convenience for the charts, but negative WOM stimulated a drop in propensity to buy the brand.

many market mix or ROI models that don't factor in the prior propensity of the audience reached, and that it might be positively skewed to heavy brand buyers. If this is not taken into account, it is easy to overstate the importance of small reach media with a skew to existing heavy brand buyers.

And the idea that WOM might have more influence in emerging markets than in the developed world? To test this we did an 'apples with apples' comparison between the USA and China, with similarly sourced internet panel samples across three categories, quantifying the effect of positive and negative WOM.

We compared the overall impact (see Figure 7.10), as well as the impact on only those who reported an initial probability of five out of ten (50%), to compare those who can equally move higher or lower in response to WOM (Figure 7.11).

The results show no evidence that WOM has more impact in China. We also don't see any evidence that negative WOM has more impact than positive WOM (consistent with East, Hammond & Lomax, 2008). For people with equal room to move, the impact of advice (positive or negative) is very similar: in the USA, average positive WOM impact = +2.3 and negative WOM impact = –2.1; in China, positive WOM impact = +1.2; negative WOM impact = –1.3.

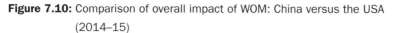

Figure 7.10: Comparison of overall impact of WOM: China versus the USA (2014–15)

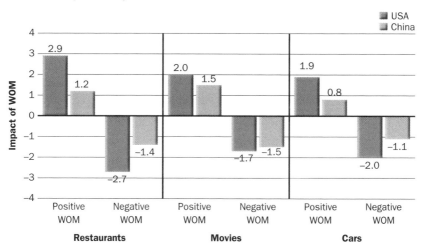

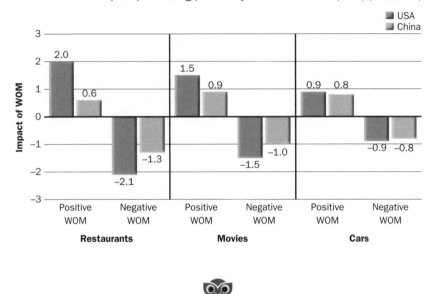

Figure 7.11: Comparison of impact of WOM: China versus the USA—only those with a prior purchasing probability of five out of ten (50%) (2014–15)

WOM as a reinforcer

While the skewed audience for positive WOM limits its influence as an acquisition force, WOM does the helpful job of reminding the giver of brands previously bought. While the receiver of a tweet might pay it scant attention, the composer of the tweet spent effort creating that message; and while the receiver of advice about a car might be daydreaming while the giver was talking, the giver was dredging their long-term memory and remembering past experiences to provide their advice. We should not neglect the power of WOM to remind the giver of how they feel about the brand. If this WOM is positive (which it largely will be), it can help the brand secure future sales from existing customers.

In repertoire categories, when advertising activity is low or when the brand is not obviously present in the environment, it is easy for the buyer to forget previously bought brands. The act of expressing WOM to others is an internal reminder, in effect acting as a self-generated 'advertising-like' exposure. For high involvement or visible purchases, giving positive WOM can help reassure the buyer of a decision made.

Don't neglect this impact of WOM; it's hard to measure but is useful to include in any reach calculations that, in giving WOM, the giver is also 'reached' by that same WOM.

Conclusion

WOM is an attractive source of promotion for brands, and our results show how to sensibly take advantage of the opportunities that WOM presents, without over-investing.

The strong correlations with market share give marketers a context for interpreting a brand's WOM levels: there's no need to panic if you have a small brand and low levels of WOM; and don't get excited if you are a large brand with higher positive WOM levels—these results are normal.

Negative WOM is rarely worthy of attention. It is uncommon and lacks influence. Don't be distracted by it unless a brand is new or undergoes a major change, such as a product reformulation.

Positive WOM has the most effect when it reaches those with a low or medium propensity to buy the brand. Stories or talking points that have a broad conversation value will help givers spread the word to a wider audience. Look for stories or gossip that people might want to share.

Taking into account the propensity to buy the brand prior to receiving the WOM is crucial to avoid overestimating the sales effects of WOM. But don't also neglect the value of WOM as a reinforcing form of self-generated advertising that reminds givers of their positive brand experiences.

Surprisingly, given the rhetoric on the power of WOM in emerging markets, our results for WOM in these markets mirror findings for the developed world, so we see no reason to adapt WOM strategy to these countries.

Finally, a reality check: advertising is often considered WOM's less attractive sibling—less memorable, less effective. But WOM has the same cut-through issues as advertising. Even WOM via social media suffers from this—just try it sometime: post something about a brand on whatever social network you use, and then find out how many people in your network actually saw it. And WOM reaches a biased audience. When audience biases are corrected, WOM and advertising have similar effect sizes, but advertising has much more effect overall because it reaches more brand buyers, particularly light and non-buyers (Romaniuk & Hartnett, 2017).

Peer-to-peer WOM is a capricious element to harness. Investing substantially in this at the expense of media where you can control content and distribution is a big risk to take with your media budget.

8

Building Physical Availability: Presence

*Magda Nenycz-Thiel, Jenni Romaniuk
and Byron Sharp*

This chapter is the first of two that cover physical availability, which is about making the brand easy to find and buy so that marketing activities can translate to (physical) behaviour towards the brand (buying, viewing, donating). The action can happen in a bricks-and-mortar store, online, on your way to work via your phone, even when you're sitting in front of your television while selecting which streaming service/channel to watch.

Building physical availability is about identifying and removing as many speed bumps to purchase as you can, no matter how small. The aim is to make the path between having the brand mentally available and actual purchase as smooth as possible, in order to realise the revenue promise of built mental availability. In this chapter we explain how physical availability is more than just gaining and keeping distribution, and cover the first pillar, *presence*. Chapter 9 delves into the remaining pillars of *portfolio* and *prominence*.

Why being 'easy to buy' can be quite difficult

Marketers make substantial investments to keep their brands mentally available. These are hard to justify without a link to a desirable behavioural outcome. As Chapter 4 explains, mental availability is about getting the brain ready to buy the brand, to increase the chance that it will be thought of as an option to buy. Physical availability is your brand's performance on the day (of buying). For changes in the brain to translate to behaviour, you want to remove any speed bumps between the brand being mentally available and actual purchase—in any sales environment.

A common misunderstanding is that building physical availability is just about distribution—getting into as many sales locations as possible. Getting widespread distribution is indeed part of the physical availability story, but it's only a starting point. What you do with those sales locations also matters.

Knowledge of the fundamental patterns of 'shopper' behaviour—that is, the pre-buying story—helps us to understand the challenges associated with building physical availability. First, shoppers have lives outside of the shopping task, which means their minds are often focused on things other than the task—on that project at work, a problem with the kids, whether the dog ate something they shouldn't, how exciting it will be to watch that new series on Netflix tonight … oh and that they need more laundry detergent/some pasta sauce/a new television. We just can't assume that, even when buying, all shoppers' mental attention is 'buying' attention.

Second, this mental clutter is accompanied by situational and competitive clutter—often dozens of brands are present alongside yours on the shelf in store, in an online supermarket, on a policy comparison website, out of a Google search, in the street. Alongside competitors are often other people and other marketing activities distracting the shopper away from noticing brands in the category. Being present doesn't guarantee being noticed in the moment. This means we can't assume that all 'buying' attention is 'buying our brand' attention.

Finally, shoppers come to *a* sales context with *a* need for today. *Which* sales context and *why* varies across shoppers and within each shopper across time. Understanding the *why* of the shopper is critical to making sure a brand offers suitable options to cover key contexts across people and time.

Another challenge for building physical availability is that while investments in mental availability linger in minds of reached consumers (for up to a few weeks), physical availability has no such long memory tail. When someone is looking to buy and *your brand is not easy to find, easy to pay for, easy to carry home and so on*, more often than not, another brand will be chosen.[1] Being *easy to find* in the most recently visited store doesn't help the brand when the buyer goes to buy in the next store.

With all those challenges, building physical availability means *minimising the chance* that when in a buying situation, shoppers walk away without your brand. This means addressing the three key speed bumps:

1 The brand is not where the shopper is.

2 The brand is not easily found in the sales environment.

3 The brand doesn't have something relevant to that buying context.

Our definition of physical availability highlights these key challenges:

Being easy: *highlights the need to fit into buyers' shopping behaviour*
... to find: *highlights the need to be prominent in any shopping environment*
... and buy: *highlights the need to cover the relevant (big and new) shopping occasions across time and people.*

This is captured in three pillars of presence, prominence and portfolio[2]—see Figure 8.1.

Figure 8.1: The three pillars of physical availability

Presence	**Prominence**	**Portfolio**
Is the brand present where buying happens (or could happen)?	Is the brand easy to find in sales environments?	Does the brand have a buyable option?

---

1   Sometimes people do not buy the category at that time.
2   This was previously referred to as relevance. We changed the name as we realised portfolio also began with 'P' (and is a better name)!

Why build presence?

Presence—being in a channel/retail outlet—is the backbone of physical availability. Regardless of whether the market is developed, emerging or somewhere in between, it is an obvious, but often neglected, fact that if a brand isn't available, it can't be bought. In packaged goods we see a clear relationship between distribution, measured by ACV% (all commodity value) and sales revenue (see Figure 8.2).

Figure 8.2: Distribution and market share relationship for pet food in Russia

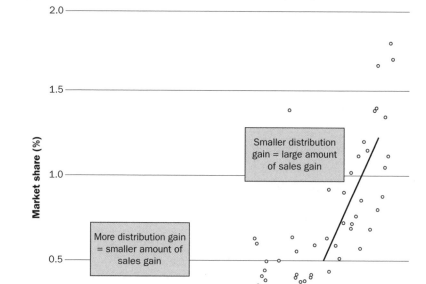

The relationship shows a double jeopardy–like pattern, whereby smaller brands typically suffer twice—they have lower distribution and sell less per point of distribution (Wilbur & Farris, 2013; Hirche, 2018). A higher ACV means the brand is reaching not just the big outlets, but also smaller retail outlets with successively smaller assortments. This gives the benefit of wider distribution *with* lower competition, where it is easier to win sales.

This double jeopardy pattern in market share and distribution highlights the value of large brands and large stock-keeping units (SKUs) in portfolios, as one brand is represented by many different SKUs of different sizes (see Chapter 9 for more on this). It also highlights there is an inflection point where the relationship flips from much more distribution = smaller sales gain to a little more distribution = much larger sales gains. The question is therefore: *Which of the SKUs that are below the ACV% inflection point can we move to the other side, so we get accelerated sales advantages from the increased presence?* The answer will involve careful analysis of the long tail. More on this in the discussion of portfolio in the next chapter.

Second, we notice that there are many small SKUs with varied levels of distribution (from single digits to 50–60%) before they reach the ACV% inflection point. Two SKUs can be on the same number of shelves but derive very different market share returns. This sub-pattern highlights that it is not just about distribution; other areas of physical availability—presence and prominence, as well as mental availability—also impact the market share achieved.

Presence = channel management

Being widely distributed sets up the conditions to help a brand achieve a higher market share. However, even for the largest brands, in today's fragmented, multi-channel environment, it is impossible to cover all possible buying locations, as each new distribution channel costs money and other resources. For example, developing a mobile app that has a sales function requires programming, encryption and financial services infrastructure, along with many skills that either need to be hired or bought from a consultant, often at great cost. Adding channels and retailers increases the coverage of category-buying occasions, but each addition needs to be weighed against the cost of establishing and managing a brand's presence in that new channel or outlet.

To make smart choices for presence, you need to two areas of shopper knowledge:

1 **Transaction view**—*where the transactions for your category are (or could be) happening*. Are transactions happening online versus offline; mobile versus desktop; rural versus urban; modern versus traditional

trade; retailer formats; or on-trade versus off-trade? What are the projected growth areas for transactions in the future?

2 **Category buyer view**—*how category buyers shop* across locations and time. What is the typical shopper repertoire? How many sales outlets do they shop from, and what factors shape their shopping choices? Do any outlets have a captive audience such as in movie theatres, in an emergency veterinarian clinic, or in the back of a taxi/Uber?

Together, these two views of buying help a brand achieve market coverage by revealing the options that *cover as many different buying occasions as possible for as few options as possible.* Put simply, you want to minimise the chance that someone buying the category can't find your brand.

Channelling choice

If we understand how people shop across channels, we can better prioritise outlets for the brand. For packaged goods in the developed world, distribution systems mean a well-trodden path with established supermarket retailers. While not immune to change, with the growth of online and mobile commerce providing opportunities to bypass supermarkets and sell directly to customers, the vast majority of grocery shopping is still conducted in modern brick-and-mortar retail channels.[3]

Emerging markets present a particular challenge for packaged goods' channel management for several reasons:

- the sheer size of the markets (both in population and geography), which makes central distribution locations inefficient, while multiple distribution locations add to costs and complexity
- the rapidly increasing presence of supermarkets and hypermarkets, which require training of both shoppers and distributors
- the residual strong traditional trade presence, particularly in rural areas
- the emergence of online shopping to further fragment channel options

---

3   Even during a pandemic. For example, Tesco reported that its online sales accounted for 16% of all sales, which is up from 9%, but says that 84% of its sales are still in-store (Lane, 2020). In the USA, online supermarket sales in total increased from 3.4% in 2019 to 10.2%, which is impressive growth but again still highlights that nine in ten grocery dollars come from the in-store shopper (Redman, 2020).

- the reliance on many small local stores (often referred to as extended pantries) to provide a source of spur-of-the-moment replacement purchases, as most homes have minimal storage.

For services and durables, the growing need for a combination of bricks-and-mortar outlets, online owned sites, online third party sites and mobile applications is shaking up distribution channel management. For example, Carvarna now distributes used cars via vending machines, so no more visiting strangers or car yards and hoping for the best! While in services, the use of brokers has also moved online with comparison sites such as comparethemarket.com or choosi.com offering a self-broker experience: people can compare brands and product offers themselves. This all adds up to a diverse and complex system of potential distribution paths to choose from and then manage. Knowing where to be, to reach potential buying occasions, is crucial for smart investment and growth.

Achieving market coverage

Brands within the same broad category sell to very similar types of buyers (see Chapter 3). Spending time and effort to identify and target a special sort of customer for your brand is therefore of little value— you should target all category buyers instead. Here we consider a similar proposition: Do different channels or retailers sell to different types of shoppers?

Given today's expanding retail options—the increasing role of online and mobile, and the complicated channel structures of today's emerging markets—are some channels overweighted to a particular, important demographic you can't reach elsewhere? The answer to this question is 'yes, sometimes', because the retailing environment largely dictates how people shop. Convenience matters: people generally shop in ways that are *easy to access*. When a channel is difficult to get to, fewer people use it. And while this shopping behaviour can change when the retail landscape changes, this change is more evolution than revolution.[4]

---

4   Often these changes are reported as large percentages, which occurs because the base is small. For example, there are many articles citing Walmart's online sales growing by 74% in 2020, but given that only 3–4% of US grocery sales are online, 74% means a rise to about 6–7%, which means Walmart's online sales are still a small part of the business (Kohan, 2020).

The accessibility of a retail option plays therefore a major role—much bigger than outlet type.

Coverage means reaching people in different locations, so it is useful to know what type of people live in a particular area, rather than be too concerned about trying to segment shoppers by retail type. Anyone will shop at a channel or retailer, if they are easy to access!

BEST BUY: HOW RETHINKING THE ROLE OF STORES HELPED STRENGTHEN THE COMPANY

Facing a decline of in-store shopping, most retailers have simply closed stores and relied on boosted online sales to take their place. Best Buy took a different approach with its 'renew blue' program, part of which is making the most of its store square footage (Team, 2020). It developed a 'ship from store' approach that harnessed the location and storage capabilities of its bricks-and-mortar stores to decrease shipping time by two days (Repko, 2020).

Best Buy's other innovations such as kerbside pick-up and deploying its 'geek squad' to do deliveries (Verdon, 2020) also decrease barriers to buy and improve its ability to operate safely in a pandemic. Excellence in e-commerce is not just about the website and ability to transact, as Best Buy shows—it is also about fulfilling orders. Best Buy has taken advantage of its internal resources to address this challenge. This has paid off in financial performance, with 2020 second-quarter domestic comparable store sales growing by 5% (Loeb, 2020).

Going beyond the cliché of the 'multi-channel world'

As more options become available, people expand their retail repertoire. It's not 'out with the old, in with the new' but rather 'let's add this new option to the collection'. As a consequence, channel proliferation for brands in a category also means channel proliferation for buyers. When the established mode of buying is challenged by an alternative, often the new channel buying behaviour is occasional; that is, it supplements the shopping outlet repertoire rather than dominates it. We see this in Table 8.1, which shows data from the skin-care category in China. Newer channels, such as social media or online variations, have a lower share of purchases (in this case around 10 percentage points) than more established channels.

Table 8.1: Channels for buying skin care in China over a 12-month period (2017)

Channel	Shoppers (%)	Share of skin-care purchases (%)
Department store counter	45	43
Retailer's online store	16	33
Skin-care brand's exclusive shop	44	43
Skin-care brand's online store	33	32
Social media	5	30

This means the investments in new channel presence have to be carefully paced. You need to consider the future (whereby you might slightly over-invest or under-invest in a channel compared to its sales revenue) but not waste too much money in the present.

To decide on new channels, we recommend asking the following questions:

1 How *large* is that channel today? This quantifies the short-term return on investment that can be achieved.

2 How *fast* is the channel growing in terms of absolute numbers of additional shoppers (as percentage growth can be deceptive)? This quantifies the potential future of the channel.

3 Does *the category buying behaviour* in the new channel differ in comparison to other channels where our brands are present? This checks if the skills and knowledge the company has gained in prior channels will transfer to this new one, or if new capabilities are needed.

4 What *growth levers* can we gain from this new channel that might make it more attractive for its (typically low) penetration (that is, unique shoppers, opportunity to charge higher prices)? This checks if there are other advantages that might not be obvious in the previous questions.

If the prior questions suggest this new channel has potential, ask:

5 What is the *best portfolio option* to start with at that channel? Do we currently sell that and/or what is our state of readiness to supply that (at scale if necessary)?

Using laws of (growth) shopping behaviour to prioritise channels and retailers

Channels help us to understand broader retail structures, but buyers actually shop in retail outlets. The good news is that shoppers 'shop' retailers similar to how they shop brands.[5] The following are some examples:

- Buyers have repertoires of retailers they visit within a category, and are rarely 100% loyal to one retailer, channel or store.
- The relationship between penetration and loyalty to retailers reflects a double jeopardy pattern.
- Competition across retailers for shoppers follows the duplication of purchase law, whereby retailers compete in line with the size of the competitor. Generally, retailers share more shoppers with the more popular retailers and fewer shoppers with the less popular retailers.

Retailers do have a number of structural differences between stores (format, pricing policy, location) that play a role in determining the relationship between penetration and loyalty. These differences help determine the relative importance of specific competitors as category structures get more complex. This means we can use the *main patterns* to set overall strategy but also harness the *deviations* to help in achieving some specific objectives.

Shopping around

Shoppers shop around—they shop around retailers, and they shop around channels. Covering multiple retailers and channels builds physical availability as shoppers rarely only shop at one outlet. We see this when we examine *retailer share loyalty* for grocery products. That is, how much does, say, a category buyer of laundry detergent or yogurt spend of their category money at any one retailer?

The figure for one retailer is typically under 50% of category spend, which means buyers spend more of their category money at other retailers.

---

5   For seminal work in the area of shopping behaviour patterns in developed and emerging markets, see Uncles and Ehrenberg (1990), Uncles and Hammond (1995) and Uncles and Kwok (2009).

In Figure 8.3 we see lack of high loyalty at retailer level for buying instant coffee, which ranges from 52% for Tesco to 31% for Lidl. Spend is fragmented across UK supermarket retailers. Another example comes from baby-product retailers in Australia, which is a category where we might expect greater retailer loyalty as category buyers learn to trust certain outlets. But we see a similar pattern of share loyalty between 25% and 34%. People shop at multiple outlets for their baby products.

Figure 8.3: (a) Retailer share loyalty for coffee purchases in UK supermarkets (2014) and (b) baby-product purchases from Australian retailers (2013)

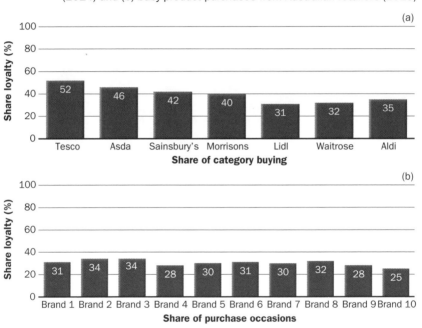

Sources: Kantar Worldwide Panel UK and Ehrenberg–Bass Institute survey

Loyalty to retailers follows a double jeopardy pattern

As with brands, loyalty to retailers can be measured in a variety of ways. These include: frequency of visiting, share of spend, repeat visitation, sole loyalty and length of time shopping at the retailer. Irrespective of the metric used, loyalty to channels and retailers follows a double jeopardy pattern. Channels/retailers with fewer shoppers also find those shoppers visit their retail chain a bit less frequently, as in Table 8.2, which gives the example of shampoo retailer choice in the USA, and in Table 8.3, which shows the pattern for alcohol buying both off premises and on premises in the UK.

Table 8.2: Double jeopardy in retailer choice for shampoo purchases in the USA

Store types	Penetration (%)	Average purchase frequency	Share of category requirements (%)
Walmart	44	3.2	65
Drug	16	2.2	43
Target	13	2.1	45
Dollar	10	1.9	33
Sam's Club	5	1.6	52
Costco	2	1.5	50
Beauty Supply	2	1.3	27
Online	2	1.4	24
Average	**11**	**1.9**	**44**

Source: Nielsen USA

Table 8.3: Double jeopardy in channel choice for alcohol purchases in the UK

Off premises	Market share (%)	Penetration (%)	Average purchase frequency	On premises	Market share (%)	Penetration (%)	Average purchase frequency
Super/ hypermarket	48	83	6.3	Standard pub	32	64	4.9
Convenience store	19	43	5.0	Standard restaurant	19	52	3.6
Discount retailer	17	37	5.2	Standard bar	18	40	4.4
Specialist store	4	14	3.1	Standard nightclub	10	26	3.8
Online	6	18	3.6	Premium restaurant	6	19	2.9
Duty/tax free	3	15	2.0	Premium bar	4	12	3.0

Source: Ehrenberg-Bass Institute survey

With double jeopardy in mind, we can easily see if retailer loyalty metrics are normal, or higher or lower than expected. With double jeopardy law providing context, we can better interpret shopping behaviour metrics and separate out normal royalty metrics, from where retailers gain higher or lower loyalty than they should, given the size of their customer base. This is useful information if you are a retailer or wanting to prioritise retailers to sell through.

Double jeopardy exists for shopper behaviour because of the underlying structure in retailer customer bases. Bigger retailers monopolise light shoppers, and smaller retailers attract a disproportionate amount of heavy category shoppers, while someone who shops at a smaller retailer typically also shops at the larger retailers. So bigger retailers get more of all types of customers, and smaller retailers get only those with split loyalties. Therefore, even if these heavy shoppers shop more frequently/spend more in total, they spend/shop less at the smaller retailer.

While typically low-penetration outlets have fewer shoppers, who shop there less often, there are some exceptions that can make a low-penetration retail channel more attractive:

- ability to reach shoppers who are tied into that outlet (for example, members of warehouse club stores like Costco; see Table 8.2)
- ability to reach shoppers not reached by other outlets (for example, due to geography)
- ability to capture different occasions (for example, in a vending machine next to a park or somewhere else *on the go*)
- ability to charge higher prices (for example, in restaurants or movie theatres, or in petrol or convenience outlets).

For example, take the warehouse club channel, which includes retailers such as Costco globally or Sam's Club in the USA. These are big-store formats that offer mainly large pack sizes or multi-packs, therefore largely mandating bulk buying of any category. While the penetration of those channels is low, they typically have an unusually high share of category requirements for any specific category buying (as shown in share of category requirements for Costco and Sam's Club in Table 8.2). Buyers who buy from club channels have already satisfied their category requirements for a long time and so are 'out of category' for a while. This means that if a brand is not in that channel, it effectively misses out on this group of shoppers for a long time.

There can also be a tactical advantage gained from using smaller retailers. They are in competition with larger retailers and looking for ways to add value to their shopper base. This means you might be able to negotiate to (cheaply) give your brand greater prominence in-store or to feature strongly in the outlet's above-the-line advertising activities. However, don't be taken in by claims of shopper exclusivity without independent shopper-centric data as back-up.

How retailers compete—applying the duplication of shopping law

When you rely on a retailer to get your product or service to category buyers, it is easy to feel they are all-powerful and you lack leverage to negotiate. Not too long ago Tesco in the UK and Walmart in the USA seemed all-powerful—like no one could topple them from their dominant retail perch. Now Tesco and Walmart face many challenges from nimble competitors such as Aldi and Lidl, as well as the giant that is Amazon. com. Retailers fear competition too—competition from other retailers. They are looking for any opportunities to protect the shoppers they have and gain new ones. This means understanding retailer competitive structure can be a superpower when negotiating with retailers. We return to the duplication of purchase law (see Chapter 3) as this provides the benchmarks needed to understand how channels/outlets share shoppers in any retail environment.

Retailer competition has not been as widely studied as other branded categories, but some published examples indicating evidence of a duplication of shopping law concern supermarket shopping in China (Uncles & Kwok, 2008, 2009) and wine retailers (Cohen, Lockshin & Sharp, 2012; Lockshin & Cohen, 2011). Here we can demonstrate that this law also holds for grocery buying across retailers (see Table 8.4 for shopping across UK retailers), but also for buying a specific category at different grocery outlets (see Table 8.5 for laundry detergents). Everyone shares more customers with the bigger retailers and fewer customers with smaller retailers.

Table 8.4: Shopping across UK retailers

Stores	Tesco	Asda	Sainsbury's	Morrisons	Marks & Spencer	Iceland	Aldi	Lidl	Waitrose
Tesco		48	48	38	26	26	23	25	15
Asda	67		45	44	23	28	30	26	10
Sainsbury's	70	46		39	33	23	23	25	22
Morrisons	65	54	46		29	27	29	28	14
M&S	70	45	63	46		25	24	25	29
Iceland	74	57	46	46	27		38	34	13
Aldi	68	63	48	49	26	38		39	11
Lidl	75	56	52	49	28	36	41		18
Waitrose	71	35	74	39	50	22	18	29	
Average	**70**	**51**	**53**	**44**	**30**	**28**	**28**	**29**	**17**

Source: Ehrenberg-Bass Institute survey

Table 8.5: Laundry detergent buying across UK retailers

	Penetration	Tesco	Asda	Sainsbury's	Morrisons	Aldi	Lidl	Waitrose	The Co-Op	Wilkinson
Tesco	37		22	19	17	14	10	5	4	5
Asda	25	33		16	21	16	11	3	4	6
Sainsbury's	21	36	21		20	12	10	8	5	6
Morrisons	20	31	25	18		16	12	4	5	6
Aldi	15	29	22	13	19		18	2	4	5
Lidl	12	30	23	15	20	26		3	4	5
Waitrose	7	39	16	34	16	9	8		6	4
The Co-Op	7	41	27	24	26	17	14	7		8
Wilkinson	7	39	33	24	27	20	13	4	7	
Average	**17**	**35**	**24**	**20**	**21**	**16**	**12**	**5**	**5**	**6**

Source: Kantar Worldwide Panel UK

The existence of the duplication of purchase pattern for retail outlets and channels means that covering the largest channels/retailers captures those who also shop at smaller channels/retailers. However, we can, on occasion, see a deficit in sharing of shoppers that can suggest good options for channel/outlet combinations. Excess sharing of shoppers, which can suggest less suitable retailer combinations, are also apparent on occasion.

E-commerce is a whole new ballgame?

Nothing gets publicity like a good growth story, and e-commerce is one such area. Examples range from the growth of Amazon.com, accelerated due to the COVID pandemic, to the continued rise of the Chinese juggernauts Taobao.com, TMall.com and JD.com. This is coupled with supermarkets' shares of sales from online increasing and the development of brands that bypass traditional routes to market and sell direct to the consumer online (Dollar Shave Club, Brooklinen, Away).

E-commerce has removed some of the channel barriers to entry that once existed for new brands, but many of these initially e-commerce retailers quickly move to become omni-channel (Sharp et al., 2017). For example, Dollar Shave Club, which was acquired by Unilever, is now available in Walmart, while Away luggage has opened its own retail outlets from Austin to London. Even Amazon.com has bought bricks-and-mortar stores through its Wholefoods acquisition, while Tesla has display stores in shopping malls such as White City in London and the Paragon in Bangkok.

When e-commerce was new, there was considerable speculation about both different shoppers and different shopping behaviour (for example, Nielsen, 2015). Differences in the profile of online shoppers versus the normal population was largely a by-product of the differences in the population online. Now that it is mainstream to be online, shopping online has become a mainstream activity, with more and more categories easily available to shop. For example, a supermarket's offline shoppers are more likely to become its online shoppers (66% overlap) (Dawes & Nenycz-Thiel, 2014). That is, Tesco offline shoppers are also likely to be Tesco's online shoppers.

Therefore, we need to be careful not to read too much into differences in e-commerce behaviour in a specific category, as these may simply be a function of it being a small channel.

Is e-commerce the loyalty builder?

There are several structural ways the online environment differs from offline. First is the searchable online brand list, whereby all brands are present. In-store, stock-outs can lead to some brands being temporarily unavailable, right at the time the buyer needs it, and the sale is lost to a competitor. A second difference is the function of saveable shopping lists and 'have you forgotten' systems to help remind people of the products or brands they last bought. Finally, delivery makes it easier to stockpile favourite brands (for example, when they're on special).

These differences make it easy to be more loyal to brands bought online. This higher loyalty will be at the expense of impulse, promotional or 'I'll just buy that brand because I can't find the one I want' brand purchases. Online buyers might still have a repertoire, but it will be smaller and more stable over time. Table 8.6 shows buying of a normal grocery category, toothpaste, online, compared to its purchases offline. We see that the law of double jeopardy holds for toothpaste purchasing in the online environment as well as offline—even the brand ranks are the same. In both the offline and online shopper worlds, the main difference between competing brands is how many people buy them, while loyalty varies much less and in line with brand penetration.

Table 8.6: Double jeopardy for toothpaste buying online and offline in the UK (2014)

Brand (rank order)	Offline sales (91% of total sales)		Online sales (9% of total sales)	
	Penetration over a year (%)	Average purchase frequency	Penetration over a year (%)	Average purchase frequency
Colgate	71	3.1	63	2.4
Aquafresh	23	2.1	27	2.3
Oral B	20	2.1	15	1.8
Sensodyne	15	2.4	12	2.1
Macleans	10	1.7	6	2.0
Arm+Hammer	9	1.9	4	1.8
Tesco Steps	1	1.6	3	1.8
Average	**21**	**2.1**	**18**	**2.0**

Source: Kantar Worldwide Panel UK

A direct comparison of online and offline buying data does suggest loyalty is higher in an online environment (see Table 8.7), but loyalty levels are still a long way from 100%, even though the online shopping conditions are conducive for them to be. However, the higher loyalty online makes it more challenging for small brands to enter buyer repertoires in this shopping environment. Even with a more levelled physical availability playing field, differences in mental availability mean big brands still have many advantages online.

Table 8.7: Average share of category requirements online and offline in the UK (2013–14)

Category	Share loyalty (2013)		Share loyalty (2014)	
	Offline (%)	Online (%)	Offline (%)	Online (%)
Dog food	21	33	20	34
Instant coffee	31	48	31	49
Nappies	28	42	33	41
Fabric softener	38	50	37	50
Toothpaste	35	43	37	41
Average	**31**	**43**	**32**	**43**

Source: Kantar Worldwide Panel UK

And for retailers?

Since the online space offers shoppers an additional channel and more retail brands to choose from, and all of this (almost) independent of location, multi-channel shopping also affects shopper loyalty to retailers. Shoppers do not substitute an offline store with an online option but rather expand their store repertoires and buy from more retailers in more channels. Over time, after the initial plunge into online grocery shopping, we see more competition between online channels. This shows that, once having entered the online world and bought at one online supermarket retailer (most likely the one which was their main chain offline), shoppers easily enter other supermarkets (that might be less geographically convenient) via their online stores. This means that online buying can negatively affect loyalty to *retailers* (Dawes & Nenycz-Thiel, 2014).

For durables, the majority of shoppers purchase a product in person, even if they found it, read reviews or compared prices online. We see this in a study we conducted into the pre-purchase shopping behaviour for 150 first-time buyers of mobile phones in India. There were two groups of first-time buyers: those buying a feature phone for the first time, and those upgrading to their first smartphone. We see no difference in the length of time from starting to think about the category to making a purchase—around one month for 70% of both types of new category buyers. Shopping outlets are also similar—around 95% researched the product online (the sample group were active internet active users and researching an electronic product), while around 70% visited bricks-and-mortar stores.

But, while both types of new category buyers visited the same number of online stores (around four), feature phone new buyers visited more bricks-and-mortar stores (around four) than smartphone new category buyers (only one or two stores). This means being easy to find in a physical presence is even more important to reach new smartphone buyers, who visit fewer stores during the purchase process.

Conclusion

Physical availability is more than just maintaining and expanding distribution; it is the mechanism to ensure buyers move from having the brand mentally available to buying it. Managing physical availability involves three components: presence—how well the brand covers places and times where buying happens; prominence—how easily buyers find the brand; and portfolio—how the brand covers the category buying situations. All three aspects are important because buyers have lives that exist outside of buying and limit the amount of time and energy they want to expend. What little attention buyers do give in the moment is easily diverted by situational and competitive clutter.

This chapter focused on presence. To build presence, cover as many buying occasions as possible and remember:

- shoppers shop across a variety of available channels. As more channels become available, people tend to add to their channel repertoire rather than switch completely from one to another. Therefore, all brands will need a multi-channel presence as categories evolve.

- The fundamental laws of double jeopardy and duplication of purchase (shopping) hold for channels and retailers, with some adjustment for format. Outlets with more shoppers will have those shoppers visiting more frequently and share customers more with other outlets. The shoppers who visit small outlets are rarely exclusive to that outlet. Use this knowledge to make smarter presence investments.

E-commerce is growing and is part of many brands' channel portfolios. Despite the possibilities the online environment creates, we are yet to see evidence that buying behaviour online is substantively different from that offline. There is slight evidence of higher loyalty online, although not close to 100%. This higher loyalty will, however, create an advantage for big brands while hampering smaller brands finding a customer base, particularly in packaged goods environments.

9

Building Physical Availability: Prominence and Portfolio

Magda Nenycz-Thiel and Jenni Romaniuk

This chapter unpacks the remaining two pillars of physical availability: prominence and portfolio (previously named relevance). Prominence is about being easily found in often-cluttered retail environments, which typically means standing out amongst competitors. This involves building 'shopping' distinctive assets, which are the specific assets buyers use to identify your brand when they shop.

Portfolio is about having something buyable for a particular category buyer on a particular buying occasion. Management of the portfolio means striking the right balance between the present (that gives you scale and revenue right now) and the future (portfolio investments that might take time to pay off but put the brand in good stead for the future).

Prominence: Is your brand easy to find in buyers' shopping environments?

A key aspect of being *easy to buy* is being *easy to find*. A brand's presence in any place where it can be bought can only be leveraged if the brand is easily found, particularly with competitor brands present. If your brand is not easily found, an alternative can fill the gap. Now you can buy prominence using end caps (Caruso et al., 2018; Tan et al., 2018), buying search terms or paying for higher listings on broker sites. However, in addition to the cost, all of these activities give more power to the intermediary. You can try to reduce the need for prominence by owning sales channels, but these are difficult to establish and costly to maintain. Therefore, in this section we focus on distinctive assets as something you can control.

In retail environments, clutter abounds. Brands are surrounded by *competitive clutter* from other brands; and shoppers experience *situational clutter*, such as other people in stores, advertising on websites, notifications and other apps on phones, or distractions in a mall or street making it difficult to find a retail outlet. These get added to the mental clutter of shoppers' internal monologue, which remind them of that unfinished project, that the kids didn't sleep well last night, or of their decision about whether it's time to get another dog.

It is easy to underestimate the level of clutter that shoppers experience. To get some sense of this, select a similar category you don't work on (to get a more typical buyer perspective) and look at the competing brands in different shopping environments. For example, a search on Amazon.com for a hairdryer revealed five pages of results, with over fifty options across twenty or so brands and prices ranging from $7.99 to $255, just on the first page. The different options had different attachments, some making claims such as they were the 'best for travel' or 'editor's pick', and some with price promotions signalled in green. Each of those twenty different brands was competing to capture the eye of the buyer, and this would have been more than enough for most buyers to make a selection. And if you go into electronics stores, how many different hairdryers do you see? This is a single, specific durable category. Imagine if we took a typical packaged goods category such as canned tomatoes, or home loan options, where you can shop for brands online, via a broker or at branches in a mall? A search on a credit card comparison site, where we clicked on 'rewards' as the most important quality for a card, revealed a long list of possible cards, each of which are the visual representation of the bank in this shopping environment. They were from eight different banks, and the first ten cards were all black or grey. The first card of any other colour was number 11, a *blue* Citibank card. In the first twenty cards the only ones that were not black or grey were two in blue and one in gold. Lots of clutter, with lots of brands, all looking the same.

Clutter varies from channel to channel and from outlet to outlet, so a brand needs to be prominent enough to be easily found irrespective of the environment. For example, a texture on a pack that works in a store where people can pick up a product might not stand out in a thumbnail two-dimensional image online. This means success in building and keeping prominence first comes from understanding the environments in which the brand needs to stand out.

Most outlets offer (sometimes costly) ways to make a brand more prominent, but you can build prominence by creating a strong subset of visual distinctive assets (see Chapter 5) that we call 'shopping' distinctive assets. Shopping distinctive assets are assets present in sales channels that have also been built in the memory of category buyers. This subset of assets can help build physical availability by making a brand more noticeable in its shopping environment (Romaniuk & Caruso, 2018). Examples of common shopping distinctive assets are logos (such as the yellow M on poles to signal a McDonald's restaurant), images (such as the white glass and a half of milk image on Cadbury Dairy Milk chocolate pack) and shapes (such as the HSBC diamond present on ATMs and branches).

Mental availability helps your brand be one the buyer is looking for; shopping distinctive assets can help the buyer find your brand. Strong visual distinctive assets that have been built up via out-of-shopping activities catch the category buyer's eye in competitive shopping contexts. Strong shopping distinctive assets can help act as a bridge for the brand in many different sales environments. An example of this is Heineken's use of the red star. It features on the core bottles and cans, but also on outer packs, beer taps in bars, take-home kegs, glasses and even in the brand's zero-alcohol range.

Just because an asset has been on a pack for a long time doesn't mean it is a strong asset. As explained in Romaniuk and Caruso (2018), results from 1001 packaging assets show that some of the more commonly tested assets, such as colours, fonts or words on packs, performed poorly (on average less than 25% fame). These results are reproduced in Figure 9.1.

Figure 9.1: Performance of packaging assets as distinctive assets

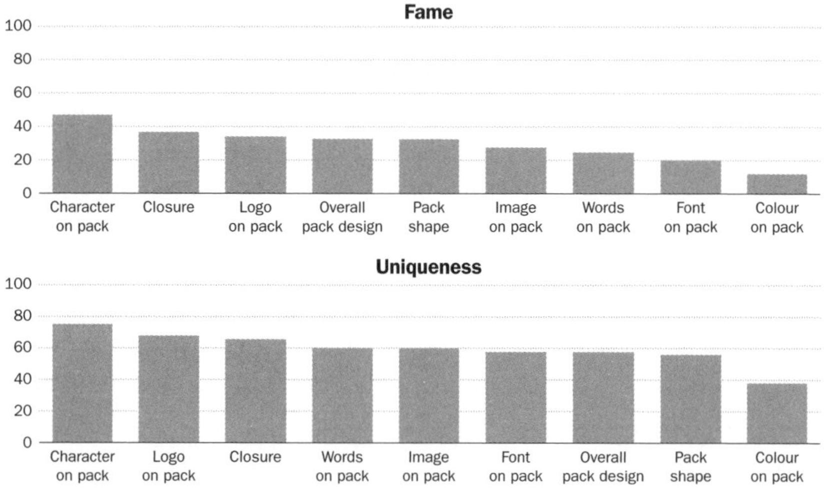

Source: Romaniuk, 2018a, p. 54

In *Building Distinctive Brand Assets* (Romaniuk, 2018a), the role of distinctive assets specifically in building physical availability is covered in more detail. We encourage readers who want to explore this topic in more depth to go to that resource.

Finally, we must mention a dangerous yet common idea. The idea is that in order to stand out and attract attention, brands should be constantly striving to look different, to employ whacky eye-catching colours, shapes and gimmicks. Some people think this is what it means to be distinctive. This idea leads to dangerous behaviours of regularly changing packaging, and inadvertently not looking like you. These practices slow down buyers' recognition of the brand; they make the brand harder, not easier, for people to find. Once you have identified and built the brand's shopping distinctive assets, these should not be changed, even temporarily. You want to be distinctive from other brands, not from what looks like your brand.

Portfolio: Is your brand buyable?

Building physical availability means offering formats that buyers *can* or *want* to buy, so the product is relevant to the buyers' context at that time. Portfolio management is different from segmentation. It about designing for a buying context, rather than a person, as it acknowledges that, over time, the same person can experience many different buying contexts when they encounter a category. Therefore, what makes *a good buyable option at the time* varies over buyers and over time. While we might want to offer more colours than just black, we can't offer everything to everyone because of production and logistics costs. This means narrowing down a possible portfolio to a viable portfolio. Even in services, without factory production costs, there are still additional internal costs in human capital when adding to a portfolio, as well as the external search costs for the buyer who then has more options to consider.

The questions critical to portfolio management are:

1 Does the brand have the right portfolio (composition and size)?

2 How important is the core part of the brand's portfolio?

3 How are decisions on what to take out from the 'tail' made?

4 How do we decide on new introductions/expansions to the portfolio?

We provide five portfolio management principles to address these key questions. Figure 9.2 provides a summary of these.

Figure 9.2: Five portfolio management principles

1 Be buyable (over buyers and over time)

2 Benchmark your portfolio for your market share

3 Identify and prioritise the brand's core

4 Manage your long tail; get rid of freeloaders

5 Make only disciplined additions to the brand's portfolio

Principle #1: Be buyable over buyers and over time

Being buyable effectively means covering the market for the highest penetration opportunities across locations, people and time. Buyers shop across different channels and stores for needs that vary across time. We also know buyers have repertoires of brands—if your brand does not have an important variant (for example, jumbo pack size, orange flavour, gluten-free, 30 days interest free, freezer at the bottom, OLED screen, 90 cm width oven), another brand with that option could get the sale. However, similar to presence, additional portfolio options bring with them additional resource needs.

We need to prioritise portfolio options to avoid fragmentation and cannibalisation as well as to keep costs under control. To do this, a product or service portfolio should aim to have these characteristics:

- *Capture current sales*—have an option to buy in all the variants that capture substantial volume. Scale is important to gain cost efficiencies and also get any intermediaries on board to build presence. Therefore having variants that sell to a lot of people is a key starting point for any portfolio.
- *Look to future sales*—have options to compete in areas that are growing in popularity (for example, gluten-free in bread, plant-based options in ready-made meals and dairy).
- *Compete in major partitioned sub-markets*—have an option in any major sub-market where a subset of brands might compete more closely with each other than with other brands, thereby locking out some sales from options that do not offer the partition-defining quality. This includes different pack sizes that might be linked to specific channels (for example, Aldi or Costco).
- *Minimise duplication*—avoid overweighting in any one area and over-cannibalising, particularly at the premium end where the buyer base is smaller (for example, offering three types of whitening toothpaste or five 'titanium' credit card options).

Ensuring your portfolio has these characteristics will mean your brand will cover as many buying situations as possible and take advantage of future category growth areas, but you will avoid over-investing in small areas.

Product-type competition analysis, which combines duplication analysis (for example, across pack sizes, flavours and/or price points if price tiering exists), brand performance and the segment's growth rate, can be useful inputs into a brand's portfolio decisions. This will allow you to assess category and sub-category size and trajectory, and therefore future attractiveness.

Principle #2: Benchmark your portfolio size for your market share

Portfolios can have many options or only a select few, so how do you know if your portfolio is the right size?

Larger share brands do tend to have larger portfolios (Tanusondjaja et al., 2018a). However, while being bigger means you'll usually have more stock-keeping units (SKUs), just adding more SKUs does not mean the brand will capture more market share, as some will not get bought and others might cannibalise your existing portfolio sales and so you won't add incremental sales (Tanusondjaja et al., 2018b).

Why do big brands have bigger portfolios? It's a combination of resources, diversity of channels and retailers and greater ability to launch products. As brands grow and get more resources, so too does the portfolio. For example, let's look at Tesla's portfolio over time (see Figure 9.3). It started in 2008 with a single two-door Roadster, with a top speed of 125 miles per hour. It could travel up to 200 miles per charge and cost around US$100,000 (Muoio, 2016). At the end of 2021, Tesla proposes having five models, ranging in price from under US$40,000 to more than US$150,000. They will have top speeds from 135 to 200 miles per hour, and will be able to travel from 244 to 520 miles on a single charge (www. tesla.com). Tesla's vehicles now include sedans, SUVs and trucks. The Roadster is also reported to be making a comeback in 2022, but with four doors rather than the original two. Yes, technology has helped evolve the products, but now Tesla has a much wider portfolio to cover different category entry points for the automobile market, which will help fuel future growth.

2008	2010	2012	2015	2016	2020	2021	2022
							Roadster* US$200K Now four-seater Removable glass roof
							Cybertruck* US$40K First pick-up truck design Armoured Optional solar panel to generate energy
						Semi* US$150K First semi truck design Autopilot for driving on highways	**Semi** US$150K First semi truck design Autopilot for driving on highways
					Model Y US$52K More compact SUV	**Model Y** More compact SUV	**Model Y** More compact SUV
				Model 3 US$35K Four-door sedan Dual-motor all-wheel-drive	**Model 3** Four-door sedan Dual-motor all-wheel-drive	**Model 3** Four-door sedan Dual-motor all-wheel-drive	**Model 3** Four-door sedan Dual-motor all-wheel-drive
			Model X US$74K SUV design 'Ludicrous' mode Autopilot (can also summon car)	**Model X** SUV design 'Ludicrous' mode Autopilot (can also summon car)	**Model X** SUV design 'Ludicrous' mode Autopilot (can also summon car)	**Model X** SUV design 'Ludicrous' mode Autopilot (can also summon car)	**Model X** SUV design 'Ludicrous' mode Autopilot (can also summon car)
		Model S US$105K Luxury sedan	**Model S** Luxury sedan Add dual motor all-wheel-drive option	**Model S** Luxury sedan Add dual-motor all-wheel-drive option	**Model S** Luxury sedan Add dual-motor all-wheel-drive option	**Model S** Luxury sedan Add dual-motor all-wheel-drive option	**Model S** Luxury sedan Add dual-motor all-wheel-drive option
	Roadster 2 US$109K Better engine, better interior, touting eco-friendly credentials	**Roadster 2** Better engine, better interior, touting eco-friendly credentials					
Roadster US$98K First production electric vehicle to use lithium-ion battery cells Two-door	**Roadster** First production electric vehicle to use lithium-ion battery cells	**Roadster** First production electric vehicle to use lithium-ion battery cells					

*proposed

Principle #3: Identify and prioritise your core

The 'core' of your portfolio is the top-selling part of the portfolio. These are the biggest selling flavours, pack sizes and/or formats. For example, for ice-cream, vanilla will be a core flavour for all brands. This part of the portfolio has the highest penetration as even the lightest category buyer knows vanilla as a flavour and can probably easily find it on shelf. Even something as simple as Netflix has three subscription options (basic, standard and premium), but of those three options, there will be one option that is the most common choice for subscribers. That is the core offering. Prioritise it. Protect it.

What is your brand's core worth?

It's easy to take for granted the sales workhorses we have within the portfolio and forget these sales are not automatic but need to be earned through investments in the core's mental and physical availability. Memories fade without reinforcement, and customer bases decline without acquisition. Unless the core is supported, its sales will decline (Hartnett et al., 2021). If that happens, you need the sales from the new innovations to at least replace lost core sales.

A simple exercise is to calculate, for the last few years, the proportion of your sales revenue that have come from the core. Tanusondjaja and colleagues (2018a, b) show that in packaged goods, the top SKU accounts for 50% of penetration—an impressive number given how long the rest of the portfolio could be. Nine of the fourteen categories covered had an average penetration between 46% and 53%.

Now look at your brand portfolio's marketing spend. What proportion went to the core only (really just the core—not a new launch that you hope will spill over to the core)? Do the figures align? If they do, then you have a good start; however, if marketing spend is much lower than sales revenue, you are most likely bleeding your core. If by some chance your spending on your core is greater than its sales revenue, then you may be under-investing in innovation. This puts the brand at risk of not evolving with market trends, as in the case of Maxwell House and Folgers, which took a long time to innovate into coffee pods, the growing part of the category (see Gasparro, 2018).

The main aim here is to get the evidence to make sure you keep prioritising the core over other parts of the portfolio for mental and physical availability investments. The reason it is important is the core tends to be bought by light category buyers, who need to be reminded of its existence both in brand and type. Without keeping up mental availability investments, these people can forget to buy (your brand). The core is often an area of major competition from other players and so we need to (at minimum) neutralise the effects of competitor advertising on category buyers. Finally, the small but sustained decline in brand revenue that accompanies declining support can send the brand on a downward trajectory that is difficult to climb out of.

The top 50% SKUs brings on average 75% of sales, which leaves just 25% for the rest. This brings us to the last portfolio management principle, which is about the 'tail' of the portfolio—the group of SKUs that do not sell a lot (Tanusondjajaet al., 2018b).

Principle #4: Manage your long tail

Often, the unintended consequence of being a big brand with a larger portfolio is having many SKUs that contribute little to sales. This leads to low sales per point of distribution. However, this does not mean that you should remove all SKUs in the (long) tail—some small-sales SKUs can make an important contribution. But there are some small-sales SKUs that just languish in the tail, and there will be little loss (and perhaps a gain) if you delete them. Your brand's portfolio tail can include 'working' SKUs in the following three categories (see Figure 9.4):

- *specialist buyer SKUs*—variants that attract unique buyers (for example, gluten-free, hypoallergenic)
- *specialist retailer SKUs*—variants needed to sell at certain retailers (for example, unique pack size/style for Costco or Aldi)
- *newbies*—very new variants that are yet to establish themselves.

These types of small sales SKUs are all useful additions to the profile as they gain sales the core can't. However, intermingled with these three useful tail SKUs are:

- *freeloader SKUs*—low-selling variants that have been in the tail for a while, and get sales just because they are on 'shelf', but cost money to produce and distribute.

This group of SKUs should be reviewed, and actively targeted for replacement with one of the working SKUs. This step is critical as delisting and losing shelf space will be detrimental to manufacturer sales. While getting additional facing for our core could be one of the options, space for new SKUs is another. Which leads to the question: what makes a good addition to a portfolio?

Figure 9.4: Types of variants in the long tail

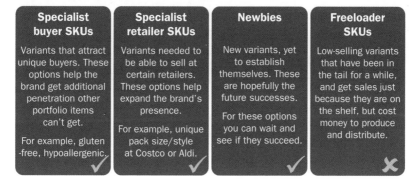

Principle #5: Make only disciplined additions to the brand's portfolio

There is much excitement about launching a new SKU (see Chapter 10 for more on this), but before a launch is the decision to green-light the development. Making the case for a new SKU and justifying the investment means answering the following questions:

- *How big is the opportunity? What does it offer?* Have a clear size of the opportunity and the objective as well as a standard set of KPIs to assess the introduction against.

- *Where will the sales most likely come from?* Introducing something new is rarely going to generate 100% incremental sales. This typically only happens if you are breaking down barriers to enter into a new channel, retailer or geographic location. We know that SKUs compete with each other in line with market share (the duplication of purchase law). Therefore, we can predict, using the duplication of purchase analysis, where the buyers are most likely to come from and how much duplication with the core and any of the brand's other SKUs in the category is normal. It can also be used to scenario-test the financial consequences of additional cannibalisation (see Chapter 10), which allows you to confirm what level of cannibalisation will still allow the introduction to be financially viable.

- *Where will the budget for marketing activity come from?* A new introduction needs out-of-store support to generate early excitement (get retailers on board) and to sustain sales after the end of any extra in-retailer presence (for example, a gondola end in a supermarket for a packaged good, or a gift card with a new television purchase). Be careful about just moving the money from the rest of the portfolio. Even 'successful' additions can cause damage if they draw resources away from the core offering.

Portfolio addition can also be viewed through the lens of barrier removal. Can the new introduction remove a barrier and make the brand easier to buy? Barriers that a portfolio addition can address includes can include:

- *Size*—specific buying or shopping contexts can make some pack sizes more or less attractive. In emerging markets, for instance, single-use sachets, while more expensive per unit, can make something an occasional treat and widen the potential market (buyers and buying occasions). Small formats also are easier to transport for someone who lacks a car and is travelling by public transport or on a bicycle. At the other end of the spectrum, bulk packs can be essential to be a viable option for households with a large number of people.

- *Price-point variety*—buyers are not 100% loyal to price points but have a repertoire based on availability and share of offering (Romaniuk & Dawes, 2005; Scriven & Ehrenberg, 2003). Having an option for when a buyer wants to splash out in a category, as well as for when someone is feeling frugal, helps maximise coverage. Different occasions also demand different price levels—such as a bottle of wine for a dinner with my work colleagues to celebrate success as opposed to at home for an everyday dinner.
- *Payment options*—wanting to buy is different from being able to buy, and flexibility in payment options is one way to remove this barrier. This can include instalment plans, credit services or mobile transfer of funds so the buyer can transact easily.

Think creatively about what the brand can bring to market to smooth the path to purchase.

Conclusion

After presence, prominence and portfolio are the two other pillars of physical availability. Prominence, along with portfolio, help realise sales revenue from channel investments.

Prominence is about standing out in shopping environments. The aim is to help the brand be noticed despite clutter from competitors and the (often chaotic) environment. Building prominence you control means creating 'shopping' distinctive assets, which are visually present on the brand in sales environments—mobile apps, online brokers, websites, third-party retailers, bricks-and-mortar stores, car yards, travel agents— any environment where people can buy the brand.

Portfolio management is about providing options that shore up current revenue and set the brand up for the future. To improve the quality of a brand's portfolio, design for the buying occasion, not the buyer. Buyers typically experience many different types of occasions for a category, and so ideal formats and price points will vary accordingly. This is a brand portfolio strategy rather than a segmentation strategy—having options that are buyable but being less concerned about who makes the purchase. The following four questions provide a checklist for future-proofing a brand's portfolio:

1 Does the brand currently have the right portfolio (composition and size)?
2 How important is the core part of the brand's portfolio and are we protecting this revenue?
3 Have we removed 'freeloaders' from the 'tail'?
4 Do we have a disciplined approach to new introductions/expansions to the portfolio that does not unnecessarily compromise the core?

Answering these four questions can help shape your current portfolio so that it is better placed to serve current and future category buyers, and therefore the company.

10

New Brands and New Buyers of Brands

Jenni Romaniuk and Byron Sharp

New brand launches are exciting but risky endeavours. In this chapter we highlight some assumptions that adversely affect new launch marketing strategy, unwittingly lessening the chances of success. We reveal how the mental structures of new brand buyers look like light brand buyers, rather than someone who recently underwent a radical conversion to buy the brand. And we discuss what this means for activities that aim to grow penetration.

We also examine new buyers of (existing) brands. To build penetration we need to recruit new 'brains' to brands—you can think of this as the zombie strategy. To survive and grow, the brand needs to go out and reach (gobble up) as many new brains as possible. We explain how to use mental and physical availability to recruit these very important buyers, and the implications for media planning.

We show how recruiting heavy category buyers is a necessary but not sufficient condition for success and reveal how to benchmark the *normal* cannibalisation a new brand will generate if you launch an additional brand or variant into your category, to easily identify if cannibalisation should be of concern.

A special occasion: The birth of a new brand

The launch of a new brand is an activity full of promise and opportunity. Nothing else can galvanise the marketing department to the same extent, as careers have blossomed (and crashed) based on the performance of a new launch. The *promise* of what the launch might be makes it easier to ask for money and other resources. Secret new teams are formed, with code names worthy of a James Bond movie. But with this investment come great, but sadly often unfulfilled, expectations.

Figure 10.1: The birth of a new brand is an exciting event

> **Birth notice: Bingo! Plc**
>
> **After a long labour of feasibility studies and fighting over budgets, the marketing department of Bingo! Plc are delighted to announce the birth of new brand 'Bango' into the Upper Volta toothpick market on December 3 2015, weighing between 50 and 200 in pack size.**
>
> **The proud parents hope that Bango will attract a substantial, loyal buyer base and find its own profitable place in a cluttered, competitive category.**

New launches can add to the portfolio within a category or be a company's first entry into a new category. Additions can be totally new brands or variants/extensions that are released under an existing name. Variants/extensions can gain from a head start in building both physical and mental availability but risk excess cannibalisation, and often fail to win incremental sales or profits. Only 40% of new variants launched are still on sale two years after launch (Victory et al., 2021).

The 'arduous' path to first purchase

The cold reality is that, when a new brand enters a category, most category buyers just continue buying the brands they always have. Why is this? The traditional (exaggerated) explanation is that a buyer needs to be convinced of some benefit to change from their existing repertoire: that they need a reason or an intense emotional desire to change past behaviour. The textbook recommendation is for a new launch to have a value proposition that exceeds existing brands, that it must be very differentiated, and that the advertising must be very persuasive. If people don't buy a new brand, it's thought to be because it failed to be worthy or convincing enough—or both.

But let's come down to earth and look at markets full of busy buyers, who are naturally loyal and who have managed to make satisfactory category purchases without the new launch. Low brand knowledge, even for the buyers of an existing brand, is the norm.

Let's go back to 2015 and take a brand when it was relatively new then, Coke Zero, and compare the level of knowledge across three buyer groups: very light and non-buyers; recent new buyers who bought the brand for the first time in the last three months; and longer-term buyers who have been buying the brand for more than three months.

We see in Figure 10.2 that in terms of brand knowledge, recent new buyers sit somewhere in between very light and non-buyers and longer-term buyers. These recent buyers know something about the brand, but six in ten of new buyers don't know very much, with fewer than three brand associations (out of a possible 18). This is not unusual: of longer-term Coke Zero buyers, *four in ten buyers also know very little about the brand.* It is quite normal for a brand to have the majority of its buyers with only a few accessible mental structures; recent new buyers skew even more to having little accessible brand knowledge.

Figure 10.2: Recent new buyer brand associations for Coke Zero

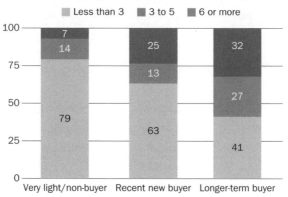

Brands are therefore fairly 'new' (unknown) to most category buyers, whether they are long established or new launches. For many buyers, brands that were launched years ago are still unknown to them. This tells us that perhaps the process for a new brand attracting a new buyer is not that different from an existing brand attracting a new buyer. In both cases, it is a question of what mental availability needs to be built for someone to buy a brand for the first time.

To answer this question, we first look at buying behaviour: the metrics of new launches, and the buying patterns of buyers of a newly launched brand. Then we move onto the underlying mental structures of new brand buyers and how you can build that army of new brains for the brand.

New brands grow in the same way as existing brands

Research examining new launches shows that the metrics of new brands settle down remarkably quickly to be very similar to existing brands of similar share (Ehrenberg & Goodhardt, 2001; Wright & Sharp, 2001). New brands, even in emerging markets, grow more via penetration than improvement in loyalty metrics. As an example, Table 10.1 shows a toothpaste brand launched in China—year-on-year penetration grew considerably more than either loyalty metric.

Table 10.1: The growth of a new toothpaste brand in China

Year	Value share (%) and change (%)	Penetration (%) and change (%)	Purchase frequency (%) and change (%)	Share loyalty and change (%)
1	0.002	0.02	0.9	10
2	0.25 (+1200)	0.4 (+1900)	1.1 (+22)	10 (+0)
3	1 (+292)	1 (+150)	1.4 (+27)	13 (+30)

New launches in any market are initially (very) small brands with few customers. Unsurprisingly then, they need to recruit new customers to grow, yet it's not uncommon for new launch marketing plans to focus on winning the loyalty of a few rather than reaching out to acquire the masses.

A common but fanciful idea is that it's best to win over a few opinion leaders in the hope they become advocates for the brand. The enormous risks associated with this sort of strategy are too often glossed over. Marketing consultants sell secret techniques to identify a special group of consumers whom the new brand is supposed to be targeting. The names change, but the idea is old: golden households, innovators, super consumers, brand influencers, micro influencers. It's all very entertaining, and good business for the consultants, but you needn't part with your money as it's actually very easy to predict which buyers are the most likely to buy your new brand first, and who you need to recruit to grow the new launch.

Who buys first?

Heavy category buyers look like tempting targets for new launch activities. These buyers do tend to be a sizeable portion of a new brand's initial buyers—they notice and buy the brand sooner than other category buyers. However, these buyers are simply in the market more often and their timing of their buying is more likely to overlap with when the new launch is making a splash. Their disproportionate buying of a new brand is often because of their dipropionate opportunity to buy any brand in the category, by virtue of being a heavy/frequent category buyer.

Statistically, a heavy category buyer is more likely to buy a new brand than a light category buyer (Taylor, 1977)—but what happens after that? Such heavy category buyers, who buy the category a lot, could also easily become super loyal to the brand; they certainly make enough category purchases to be able to do so. Unfortunately, the vast majority of heavy category buyers become *light buyers of the new launch*, maintaining a large number of other brands in their repertoire (Trinh, Romaniuk & Tanusondjaja, 2015). The new launch becomes part of the repertoire's entourage, rather than the dominant star.

Remember, a natural characteristic of heavy category buyers is that they buy more brands. This is illustrated in Figure 10.3 for soft drinks in Turkey, Nigeria and Mexico. Those buying soft drinks less than once a month only bought two or three brands, while those buying more frequently, at least once a day, bought between six and seven brands.

As the new launch slips into their repertoires usually quite a long way down, the heavy category buyers do not typically end up being of substantial value *per customer* to the new launch. This means one should be cautious about paying a great deal to acquire heavy category buyers.

Figure 10.3: The relationship between frequency of buying and number of brands bought for soft drinks in Turkey, Nigeria and Mexico (2014)

New (and small) brands have a customer base skewed to heavier category buyers; to grow, they have to correct this skew by recruiting lighter category buyers—as this is what the customer base of large, established brands looks like (Tanusondjaja, Trinh & Romaniuk, 2016). Put simply, recruiting heavy category buyers is not enough—it's impossible to grow without extending the brand's footprint out so that it recruits an awful lot of light category buyers.

New launches need to hang around long enough to reach medium and light category buyers

Existing brands, particularly the medium and big ones the new launch is aspiring to be, have many light brand buyers who buy them once or so over a longer time frame. Many of these light brand buyers are also light category buyers. To grow, new launches have to (eventually) attract these infrequent category buyers. This can only happen if the brand continues to advertise beyond the initial launch period, so it is active when these category buyers make that infrequent purchase.

What about loyalty?

What of the role of loyalty in the ongoing success of a new brand? New launches have systematically lower loyalty when compared to existing brands of similar market share (Trinh, Romaniuk & Tanusondjaja, 2015). This lower loyalty is not a sign of impending failure and is seldom due to people trialling and then rejecting the brand (all brands are rejected a little but not much). Rejection by first-time buyers is seldom a reason for failure today, because most marketers conduct decent tests beforehand to prevent such disasters. The main reason for this slightly lower loyalty is that new brands temporarily buy physical and mental availability, and even give price discounts, all of which results in some purchases that fail to be repeated when this support for the brand disappears (that is, when it gets a bit harder to buy for some people).

Singh and colleagues (2012) examined fairly successful brand extensions—that is, those that secured more than 0.5% market share and stayed in the market for at least a couple of years. They found a group of these brands that within a year started to decline. In other words, they did rather well at winning share for two or three quarters but then faltered. Interestingly, while the penetration and purchase-frequency metrics for these particular brands always looked about normal, their quarter-to-quarter repeat rates were low. This fits with a brand attracting sales through temporary in-store displays and discounts, and bursts of advertising.

Perhaps the lesson here is *start as you mean to go forward*. Planning a special launch, with a burst of enticements, sounds like the right sort of thing to build mental and physical availability for something new. But if the schedule is heavy on temporary inducements and then followed by a trough, this is unlikely to build the mental and physical availability necessary to sustain the brand's share.

BASES, Nielsen's sales forecasting consultancy, once pointed out that Apple's launch of the iPod featured a steady and increasing media spend, each quarter more than the previous one. Yes, we saw it at launch, but we also saw it over the longer term as well. It didn't just make an entrance and fade away. More recently, throughout 2019 and 2020, the social network TikTok grew in the USA, and part of that growth was fuelled by advertising on TV including mainstream channels such as ABC and NBC (Spangler, 2020).

So why do many new launches fail? Typically they fail to gain *both* penetration and loyalty. This is because they fail to do the hard work to build the necessary mental and physical availability. One of the reasons for this is, in the thrill of the new launch, marketers overestimate the excitement their new brand might generate. A few excited new buyers won't replace the investment that builds widespread mental and physical availability.[1] They bank on any excitement and word of mouth doing too much of the work. It would take astonishing amount of excitement to make up for shortfalls in mental and physical availability.

The common launch strategy of an intense burst of activity, followed by silence until more budget is available, delivers low cumulative reach. It also means that many future category purchases will not have been preceded by recent ad exposure for the new launch, and past mental availability has decayed away.

---

[1] Even if these excited buyers are super-influencers, they only will account for a small amount of word of mouth. See Watts and Dodds (2007) for more on word-of-mouth diffusion.

A two-stage launch strategy

Think about a new launch in two stages.

Stage 1: Attract enough initial sales to secure and build the brand's physical distribution. Remember, you don't need to target heavy category buyers specifically—their natural buying patterns mean that they will find you! Choose wide-reaching activities and realise that heavier category buyers are more likely to initially respond. Minimise frequency to keep funds for Stage 2, but make sure every exposure counts with strong branding and advertised messages that resonate with many category buyers, but in particular with heavy category buyers.

Stage 2: Be continually 'on air' to reach medium and light category buyers as they enter their buying cycles. Make sure your messages are relevant to these buyers, which might mean broadening the messages from initial launch. Ensure the branding is strong enough to be noticed by viewers with partial, transient attention, who might be only mildly interested in the category.

CANNIBALISATION: HOW MUCH IS TOO MUCH?

One of the major concerns on second brand or variant launches is cannibalisation—where the new launch 'steals' sales from an existing brand from the same company. Some level of cannibalisation is normal but how much is too much?

The duplication of purchase law (see Chapter 3) gives a benchmark for how much cannibalisation to expect. It shows how much the overlap between your two brands' customer bases should be. Avoid any more overlap than this benchmark. Only accept a higher rate when the new brand is simply to block a competitive launch, and this is a strategic choice to steal your own sales rather than have competitor steal them from you.

How to avoid excessive cannibalisation? The traditional strategy is to target the brand towards a different type of buyer, but this may hamper the chance of a new brand being successful. Brands (which survive their launch) end up selling to much the same sort of customers as their rivals. Dreaming of positioning the new brand so that it does not sell to the same sort of people who buy your existing brand is largely, well, wishful thinking—and may backfire by limiting the brand's sales.

Excess sharing can be avoided or rectified in these ways:

- *building physical availability*—widening distribution of the smaller brand so that it is not just overlapping with the existing brand.
- *building mental availability*—avoiding poorly branded advertising as this will only work on buyers of the parent brand. You need non-buyers of the parent brand to also notice the new launch.

These strategies are likely to enhance overall sales, as well as prevent excess stealing from the parent brand.

Priority mental structures for a new brand (buyer)

What might you need to know before you buy a brand for the first time? It's a useful exercise to consider what are essential memories for potential buyers. Essential memories are those that, if absent, make it unlikely that they will buy your brand. Contrary to marketing textbook logic, these are not beliefs concerning the brand's superiority or its difference from other brands.

The first, most essential memories to build are simply what this brand is and what it looks like (so that it can be found). Often this is a case of saying 'we are an(other) accounting service' or 'we are an(other) soft drink'—and this is our name, this is what we look like, and this is where and how you can buy us. That Avocado is a mattress company is not a natural leap most people will make without advertising. If you don't get these facts into category buyer memory, then your new launch has very little chance of being bought.

It should be obvious, yet a surprising amount of new brand marketing communication does a very poor job of communicating these fundamentals. All too often the marketing plan is instead focused on teaching (part of) the market what is different or better about the brand. People aren't looking for difference: they are looking to understand the brand, and for signals as to where it would be useful to store the brand in their memory.

TIP: BORROW MEMORIES

A brand that is new to a market, even if it is famous overseas, suffers from a lack of mental availability. Its lack of physical availability and sales mean that few consumers see other consumers using the brand or hear them mention it—so no groundswell supports your own marketing activities. A lack of distinctive assets means branding relies on the name, which makes quickly building mental availability difficult. This all sounds daunting, and it is, but it's not impossible to overcome.

One tip is to start by working with existing cultural memory structures. Know how potential buyers already see the category and brands within it. Advertising must also work with the collective knowledge, symbolism and mores of the particular market (the local culture). And look out for archetypes, colours and symbols that have immediate communication power to associate your brand with the category. These can visually support the category entry points (CEPs) you are developing to build mental availability. This strategy needs to be coupled with a distinctive asset palette (see Chapter 5). The aim is to attach new brand memories to established category memories.

Snack-food marketer Mars had a problem in India that chocolate is an after-meal treat, but not something that could be taken to work as a snack. Its Snickers chocolate bar suffered from a lack of mental linkage to these very important consumption situations. By linking Snickers to *tiffin*, which in India refers to light, between-meal snacks and to the silver tins used to transport them, Mars was able to borrow these between-meal memory structures and visual images of Snickers in the silver tins and attach the brand to this common potential consumption occasion (for an advertising example, see <www.youtube.com/watch?v=ouwr2HeTjGI>).

Buying a brand for the first time doesn't require a major conversion, just a little mental availability. Think of new brand buyers as lighter users, rather than converted disciples (Trinh, Romaniuk & Tanusondjaja, 2015). This makes sense: remember, most of your buyers are like this. New recruits do not suddenly leap to the top of the attitude or image charts—they just have enough useful mental structures and sufficient physical availability to get them over the line to buy when an occasion presents itself.

After establishing links to the category, the next important step is to broaden mental availability amongst category buyers, and have the brand compete as a viable option in different buying situations. To build to this, the new brand, like any other, needs to form links to category entry points (CEPs). Like any other brand, in the long run the more links to more CEPs, the better placed the brand will be. But a new brand is usually in a race to generate initial sales, which are necessary to hold and win more physical availability. This makes some memories more important to lay down first.

Prioritise common CEPs—this is how you capture volume

CEPs vary in how often they 'come up' for buyers in a category. Some CEPs occur often for many people, while others are rarely used by anyone. Commonly encountered CEPs are more valuable for a brand, as they create more opportunities where the brand *could* be salient. For example, comparing the relevance of CEPs for whisky, *something to help me relax* is more common than *a special gift*. Signalling the brand is useful in a gifting or a treat context is useful but, as it rarely comes up, it might not be the best starting point for the brand that needs initial sales to keep distribution and justify further investments. Strong links to this CEP will only help in these (rare) occasions.

A commonly used CEP has more brands competing for retrieval (Romaniuk & Gaillard, 2007). This means excellent branding is needed to avoid confusion or helping competitor brands already embedded in buyers' memories.

Prioritise branding quality across all touch-points

The brand anchors the advertised message in the right place in buyer memory. Advertising exposure can't build mental availability if the viewer can't correctly identify the advertised brand. Broadly speaking, two types of branding tactics exist:

- directly by showing or saying the brand name
- indirectly via distinctive assets (covered in Chapter 5).

Being new to the category, a new launch won't have distinctive assets to use, as these take time and repeat exposure to build. New launches can set the goal of building distinctive assets and incorporate these future assets into marketing activity across mental and physical availability activities. But launch campaigns need to have crystal-clear execution of the brand name, both for effective advertising and to lay the groundwork for building distinctive assets for the future.

Remember that the first buyers of a new launch are likely to be heavy category buyers who use many brands and so notice the advertising of these brands. These buyers could easily think of and buy many other brands if the advertisement reminds them only of the category (and not also the new brand). Strong branding requires using smart execution tactics to make the brand a prominent and noticeable part of the advertisement (or indeed any other marketing activity).

The general rule is that your brand should be obvious to everyone, including those who have little or no knowledge about the brand or who are paying very little attention when they are viewing or listening to the advertisement—or both.

In practice this means branding in advertising that:

- is placed where the eyes or ears first experience the ad
- is spaced out across many parts of the ad (including over time where relevant)
- has both visual and audio components where possible.

(See Romaniuk, 2009 for more evidence and background to effective television or brand placement execution tactics.)

But what about more unusual CEPs—won't they be easier to win?

The illusory Holy Grail is where the new launch finds one CEP it can own. This search for a unique CEP is risky for two reasons:

- A CEP that is rarely used by rivals is usually also less commonly used by category buyers. The fewer occurrences where the brand might be retrieved makes it harder to achieve the volume of sales needed in a short period of time.

- These less common CEPs are usually less relevant to light category buyers, who have more general category needs. Uncommon CEPs are more likely to be used, on the rare occasion they are relevant, by heavy category buyers. Therefore while an uncommon CEP might help initially gaining interest from heavy category buyers, unless framed very carefully, ongoing promotion of that same message will hamper the recruitment of lighter category buyers. This is why new launch messages should be tested on both heavy and light category buyers.

Selecting an uncommon or unique CEP might be a route into a market, but this is not a recipe for large sales volumes. Remember from Chapter 4 that a brand that is big will be considered applicable to all of the major CEPs in the category. Again, why not start as you mean to go on!

Rejection check—is anything holding the brand back?

For a new launch it is useful to monitor the level and reasons for brand rejection to highlight any immediate issues. This early-warning system gives you the opportunity to fix any issues you can, to give the brand the best chance to succeed. Nenycz-Thiel and Romaniuk (2011) outlined some common reasons for rejection:

- *low perceived quality*—often judged by extrinsic qualities such as packaging; having cues that cause possible new buyers to question the brand's performance
- *bad past experience*—product not performing as expected
- *spillover*—particularly for private labels, where negative perceptions of the type of brand in one category carry over to another category, which may affect variants if they are not distinct from the parent brand
- *too expensive*—the price puts off potential buyers and is a disincentive to try the brand, unless the purpose of the new launch is to penetrate a premium section of the category, in which case this might be acceptable as long as the buyers of other like brands do not find the price unreasonable.

But don't assume that any lack of repeat buying in a short period of time means that the category buyer has rejected the brand. Carefully word any survey questions about brand rejection. A common flaw in brand rejection measurement is to lead the buyer to construct (make up) reasons to rationalise non-buying. Leave room in the possible responses for the fault not being the new launch but rather the marketing, with examples like these:

- a media plan that failed to gain enough reach to build mental availability; or
- a physical availability plan has not made the brand easy to (re)buy.

This stops you from jumping at shadows and fixing exaggerated attitude problems that distract you from more proactive marketing activities.

Conclusion

New launches are risky. We have concentrated on trying to reduce that risk by highlighting some areas where it is easy to go astray in thinking and action. Penetration rules (again); to succeed, you need to recruit many category-buyer brains.

While new launches grow by acquiring new customers, who will repeat buy as time progresses, the initial customer base of a new launch will skew to heavy category buyers with larger-than-average repertoires, most of whom become light buyers of the new brand. The reasons for this are largely statistical, which is why you should not spend a great deal of money on targeting and recruiting heavy category buyers. These buyers are the easy fish to catch.

For longer-term growth, new launches need to recruit medium and light category buyers. It is therefore dangerous to burst marketing spend at launch, and then have silence for a long period of time. While an initial burst might be needed to help gain physical availability, advertising spend should be spread out as much as possible to avoid wasting money on excess frequency.

Potential buyers of a new launch know very little about it, and potential new buyers of existing brands are in the same boat. Therefore the mental availability challenge is largely the same. A brand doesn't have to be new to be 'new to you'.

To build mental availability, attach the brand to CEPs that are relevant for the wider spectrum of buyers in the category. New launch advertising also needs these characteristics:

- clear category cues to give it context in buyer memory
- excellent branding to build mental availability and to lay the groundwork for building distinctive assets.

Finally, physical availability continues to be vital; advertising (and sales effort) helps to keep as well as build distribution.

11

Getting Down to Business-to-Business Markets

Jenni Romaniuk

This chapter examines the laws of growth in a B2B context, and the implications of these laws for building mental and physical availability. The aim is to highlight the similarities between B2B and B2C contexts, as well as any notable differences for B2B marketers looking to grow their brand.

This will allow B2B marketers to learn from knowledge gained in B2C categories, and not reinvent the wheel. As well as highlighting relevant evidence of how B2B brands grow, the chapter also provides a framework of key questions to help a B2B marketer adapt the laws of growth approach to their specific circumstances to grow their brand/company.

One B2B description to rule them all?

The term 'B2B marketing' is often used as if it describes a single, homogenous category. However, there is no single B2B market. The only common link is that the B2B market involves selling to another business. The businesses on both sides of the B2B coin come in many shapes and sizes, from small businesses with one or two employees to large multi-nationals. B2B businesses can sell consumables, durables or services. B2B categories can vary in price from discounted to luxury, and in whether the relationship with the buyer is subscription or repertoire in nature (as described by Sharp, Wright & Goodhardt, 2002). This makes it risky to claim any discovery to improve marketing effectiveness can generalise to all B2B contexts.

Therefore, this chapter starts by showing evidence of two relevant, important laws of growth in different B2B contexts. While this will not cover all of the possible B2B conditions, it will hopefully be sufficient to highlight what B2B marketers can learn from knowledge established in a B2C context. If you feel the examples here do not adequately cover the B2B context you encounter, these examples can illustrate how to conduct your own tests.

The rest of the chapter then discusses mental and physical availability through a B2B lens.

Why might laws of growth hold in B2B contexts?

It is easy (and common) to focus on the differences between B2B buying and B2C buying, such as the contracts, switching costs and more structured purchase cycle rather than the similarities, such as customers having a wide range of competing options and little time to process all the information available. However, remember it is the same B2B customer, with the same brain, who is also buying toothpaste, cars, weekends away, chocolate, whisky, a luxury watch and home insurance. This perspective makes similarities between personal and business buying less surprising and the empirical question of whether laws of growth hold in B2B contexts worth addressing.

The answer to whether the fundamental laws of growth hold in a B2B context is 'yes'. The laws of double jeopardy and duplication of purchase both hold. Next are some examples, and at the end of the chapter is a list of published research in the area for those wanting more evidence beyond that provided here.

Double jeopardy in B2B categories

Chapter 1 contained an extensive background to the law of double jeopardy, but as a reminder, the double jeopardy law is that smaller brands suffer twice: they have fewer buyers, and those few that do buy have lower loyalty to the smaller brand. The law is evidence that the path to growth is by increasing the size of the customer base, which means getting more buyers in any time period. Double jeopardy also provides a warning that brands can't grow predominantly by loyalty, as if they could, the law would not exist. The evidence is demonstrated in Tables 11.1 and 11.2, which contain examples of the double jeopardy law from service, durable and consumable product B2B categories. The examples cover a range of different loyalty metrics including number of products, brand attitude and average purchases per buyer. Smaller B2B brands/companies have many fewer customers, who are also slightly less loyal. This is normal.

As is the case in B2C categories, there can be exceptions to double jeopardy at B2B brand level. For example, in Table 11.2, Firm F for concrete contracts has slightly higher loyalty than might be expected for its size (around 50% more than Firm G with a similar penetration). These deviations should not distract from the overall fit of double jeopardy law to this B2B category. Remember it is because of the law that the exception is easier to spot—*you know what the loyalty for Firm F should be, given its penetration, so you can quickly see that it is odd.*

Table 11.1: Example of double jeopardy from B2B banking in the UK (2019)

Bank	B2B customers (%)	Number of business banking products	Customers saying it is favourite (%)
Barclays	41	5.7	31
HSBC	30	5.4	45
Natwest	25	4.9	32
Lloyds	25	5.0	39
Nationwide	21	3.9	31
Santander	19	3.4	34
Halifax	16	3.3	31
RBS	13	3.3	15
Metro	11	3.2	15
TSB	10	3.7	23
Average	**21**	**4.2**	**30**

Source: Data collected by the Ehrenberg-Bass Institute

Table 11.2: Examples of double jeopardy from concrete and aeroplanes

Concrete contracts	B2B customers (%)	Average number of contracts	Aeroplane buying	Business customers (%)	Number of purchases per buyer
Firm A	50	7.1	Boeing	86	101
Firm B	41	4.3	Airbus	82	95
Firm C	40	3.5	Canadair	18	47
Firm D	35	3.4	Embraer	16	37
Firm E	33	3.5	Other	16	31
Firm F	29	4.2			
Firm G	28	2.9			
Other	10	1.8			
Average	**33**	**3.8**		**44**	**62**

Sources: Pickford & Goodhardt, 2000; Bennett, Anesbury & Graham, 2018

In service categories, probability of defection on next renewal occasion is a common loyalty metric. The same double jeopardy pattern holds, but in reverse because defection is negatively correlated with brand penetration.

Bigger brands have more customers and proportionally fewer of those defect, while smaller brands have fewer customers and proportionally more of those defect (see also Sharp et al., 2002).

Figure 11.1: Defection rates in the B2B commercial property insurance category in the USA

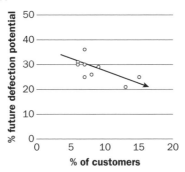

Double jeopardy is not a license to ignore or underservice current customers

Growth comes from expanding your brand's customer base, but this does not mean you can ignore or underservice existing customers. The key is to understand the defection that is normal for a brand of your size and invest sufficient resources to maintain that level—without over-investing. There is currently little evidence that B2B growth can come from resources being successfully directed to lower the B2B defection level beyond the normal level. The key reason for this is because often reasons for defection are beyond your brand's control, and so any intervention you do, no matter how successful, will not address the majority of the reasons for defection (for an example from financial services, see Bogomolova & Romaniuk, 2009). Double jeopardy is not about ignoring current customers; it is about being realistic about your capacity to control their behaviour. Therefore, to mitigate risk, you need to make sure there is always a pipeline of new customers ready to replace those that do defect, and hopefully grow.

Duplication of purchase law

Double jeopardy shows us that gaining more customers is an essential ingredient for growth. The next key law, the duplication of purchase law, shows us the source of these new customers. Duplication of purchase provides understanding and quantitative benchmarks for a brand's sharing of customers with competitors. The law states that brands share customers with other brands in line with competitor size. That is, all brands share more customers with bigger competitors and fewer customers with smaller competitors. This means if your company/brand grows, more of your new customers will come from the bigger brands in the category, and fewer from the smaller brands in the category. This law also holds for B2B categories.

Before we go into the actual numbers, it is important to remember that duplication of purchase is about multi-brand buying, so it needs purchase data where people have had the opportunity to buy from different brands. This can take different forms, depending on the category buying patterns:

B2B multi-purchase markets—if you are in a category that has multiple purchase opportunities in a time period, and for each of those purchases there is the opportunity to select the same brand or a different brand, then you can look at cross-brand buying, or the percentage of Brand A's customers who are also a customer of Brand B. For example, see Table 11.3, which shows the duplication of purchase law from the US business insurance category, covering 16 different business insurance products including commercial auto insurance, crime coverage, business income interruption insurance, travel insurance and professional liability insurance. It shows that 26% of State Farm's B2B customers are also B2B customers of Allstate, while only 12% of State Farm's B2B customers are also B2B customers of Humana. This can also be used for broader category definitions, such as all business insurance products, which allow for more than one brand to be bought. For example, B2B customers could use a different brand for the company's disability insurance than for its business travel insurance.

Table 11.3: Duplication of purchase table for US business insurance (across 16 insurance products)

Business customers of	Penetration (%)	Businesses who are also a customer (%)										
		State Farm	All State	Geico	Progressive	Hartford	Nationwide	Liberty Mutual	Farmers	Travelers	AIG	Humana
State Farm	25		26	18	16	14	14	10	10	13	6	12
Allstate	23	27		25	15	14	19	13	16	14	14	13
Geico	17	26	34		22	15	23	13	20	12	13	14
Progressive	16	26	23	24		19	17	15	11	9	14	11
Hartford	15	22	21	17	19		16	12	13	19	13	15
Nationwide	13	26	33	29	20	18		15	22	13	7	12
Liberty Mutual	13	19	24	18	18	14	15		6	14	13	18
Farmers	12	20	31	28	15	16	24	7		15	19	12
Travelers	11	30	30	19	13	27	16	16	16		10	21
AIG	11	14	30	21	20	18	9	15	21	11		14
Humana	10	30	32	25	18	23	17	23	15	23	15	
Average	12	24	28	22	18	18	17	14	15	14	12	14

Source: Data collected by Ehrenberg-Bass Institute, 2019

B2B subscription markets over time or long inter-purchase interval durables—if you are in a category here, only one brand is bought at one time, but the duplication of purchase law holds when you look at data over time and examine patterns in defection from brands and acquisition to other brands. To easily gather this data, you can capture brands bought at the current point in time, then ask buyers to time travel back to 12 months ago and ask them what brand they bought at that time. For example, see Table 11.4, which shows that of those B2B customers who defected from a bigger UK bank such as Barclays or HSBC, 62% went to another bigger bank, 20% went to a medium bank and 18% went to a smaller bank.

Table 11.4: Business banking defection and acquisition patterns in the UK (2019)

	Who defected to			
Customers of	**Bigger banks**	**Medium banks**	**Smaller banks**	**Total**
Bigger banks	62	20	18	100
Medium banks	56	25	19	100
Smaller banks	70	12	18	100
Average	**63**	**19**	**18**	**100**
	Acquired customers from			
Customers of	**Bigger banks**	**Medium banks**	**Smaller banks**	**Total**
Bigger banks	54	20	26	100
Medium banks	58	25	17	100
Smaller banks	54	15	31	100
Average	**55**	**20**	**25**	**100**

These are both expressions of the same law, just drawing on different data types to capture the (potential for) multi-brand category buying needed for analysis.

In the same vein, when dealing with large multinational companies with many different departments and financial reporting lines, it might be useful to adapt your definition of 'customer' to cover multiple people or departments within a company, defined as holders of different budgets with independent decision-making capabilities, rather than a single entity of the company as a whole. A key factor in deciding whether someone can be defined as a different B2B customer within a company is whether the person has the capability to make a choice that will bring revenue from a new budget source to your business.[1] This allows you to be more granular in your definition of 'B2B customer', to allow for the fact that one department in a company might defect from a brand, but another department within that company might remain with a brand.

To return to Table 11.3, the average sharing figures reveal how sharing declines in line with brand penetration. Every brand's business customer base is more likely to also have another policy with State Farm, Allstate or Geico, than with Travelers, AIG or Humana.

Brand defection and acquisition patterns over time

B2B brands grow by getting more customers. More of these customers will come from bigger share brands, and fewer customers will come from smaller share brands. This shows up over time in the defection and acquisition patterns. Let us revisit the UK business banking category, as shown in Table 11.4. In this analysis, banks were divided into bigger (such as Barclays and HSBC), medium (such as Halifax and Nationwide) and smaller (such as Standard Chartered and Handelsbanken) business banks to more clearly display the duplication of purchase pattern.[2]

Table 11.4 shows how every sized bank had more of its main financial institution customers defect to bigger banks and fewer to smaller banks. Also, every sized bank acquired more if its new main financial institution customers from bigger banks and fewer from smaller banks. This is the duplication of purchase law: that growth comes from acquiring new

---

1   If you are struggling to determine how to test duplication of purchase or double jeopardy in your category, do get in contact and we might be able to help.

2   This is due to sample size issues at brand level, as with even over 500 businesses, defection/acquisition is a relatively rare event so the small sample sizes can easily obscure the patterns. If you have a larger sample size or a category with higher churn then you can do this same analysis at brand level.

customers from all other competitors, largely in line with competitor size. It also means that if a brand declines, it also loses its customers to other competitors, again largely in line with competitor size. This means your biggest competitors (to stimulate growth or stave off decline) are the biggest brands in the category.

This is a sample of the evidence that B2B businesses grow by expanding the company's customer base and we hope other examples emerge as more data becomes available. The apparently logical idea of growing via loyalty/ retention is actually the difficult, if not impossible, path to growth.

So how do we grow a B2B brand? For this we turn to mental and physical availability. While companies have policies and procedures, they are made up of people who create and implement these policies and processes. Those people have the same brains, memory processes and challenges to attention that any other category buyer experiences. In the next section we will explore mental availability through a B2B lens.

Mental availability in a B2B context

Even knowing what I know about mental availability I am still surprised when one of our corporate sponsors says something like, 'Oh I didn't know you offered distinctive asset measurement'. From my perspective, distinctive asset measurement is a core Institute product, an area of research I pioneered, and one that I even wrote a book about! How could anyone, particularly a current Institute sponsor, not know/remember we offered this?

However, taking a buyer perspective, it's much easier to see how this can happen. The Institute is only a small part of our buyers' day-to-day activities. Commissioning research is only one item on a long list, and distinctive assets measurement only a small part of that portfolio. Our customers have their own staff to manage, administrative tasks to complete and other parts of their own organisation to engage with. Also, they deal with other suppliers. So yes, they know the Ehrenberg–Bass Institute exists and that we offer research services, but we have to fight to be mentally available.

All businesses that sell to other businesses face the familiar mental challenges of transient, partial, divided buyer attention, fading memories and competitive interference. It's an ongoing struggle to be a contestant in the race to be bought. This is the battle of mental availability. And the battle takes place in B2B just as much as B2C.[3] We now examine the three components of mental availability—reach, branding and messaging—through a B2B lens.

Achieving reach

As discussed in Chapter 6, the key principles of reach are (as laid out by Sharp et al., 2014, Sharp et al., 2017):

- Try to reach all category buyers, as often as feasible given budget constraints, over time.
- Space out your contacts so you don't have too many close together but also don't have large gaps in contact.
- Adjust a bit for any seasonality, but not too much.

This strategic approach for media planning in B2C categories also holds in B2B categories. However, the tools and tactics can vary in B2B settings where options range from more mass media television to more targeted but expensive and smaller-reach trade events/expos. The sales force is also often a potential resource to deploy. This more complex 'reach-getting' mix means it is easy to make sub-optimal decisions. Here are a few of the more common mistakes:

- *Prioritising avoiding wastage over achieving reach*—this leads B2B marketers to avoid larger, more mass activities in favour of smaller, more exclusive audiences. It doesn't matter how many irrelevant people you reach, what matters is the cost of how many relevant buyers you reach. Sometimes a bigger reach activity with more 'wastage' actually delivers greater and more cost-effective reach amongst your category buyers.

---

3   Much of the precursor work into mental availability drew on data from services (banking, insurance and telecommunications) in both B2C and B2B categories (Romaniuk, 2000).

- *Prioritising a big splash campaign over continuity over time*—smaller budgets and more defined audiences can lead B2B marketers to spend money on expensive events and sponsorships that happen at only one point in time and neglect the other 300-odd days of the year when buying happens. A big splash campaign can create memories—it just can't sustain them. Without refreshment, B2B buyer memories are lost. Putting all your eggs in one basket around one big activity ignores the role of memory decay over time and that even your best activity can be nullified by a well-timed competitor campaign.

- *Prioritising talking to buyers you know over buyers who don't know you*—focusing on existing customers over new customers, or prioritising existing contacts within a company over new contacts, risks spending all your marketing dollars on preaching to the converted. It's always difficult to start up a conversation with a relative stranger, but it is necessary if you want to grow. Any 'reach-getting' part of the mix should include reaching non-customers as a key performance metric.

While as in other categories, the planning aim is 1+ cumulative reach, the media channels, platforms or timing can differ depending on the audience you need to reach. The key thing is to test and evaluate to improve your ability to deliver that goal with the budget you have. Measuring reach is a big challenge for most B2B categories. But at minimum, your customer relationship management (CRM) systems should be able to cover exposure of category buyers to your company's activities, which will allow you to evaluate your 1+ reach in any time period. With this approach you can improve the efficiency of your media plan by identifying reach activities with high duplications with other activities that can be reduced or removed.

A final reach factor for the B2B context is the presence of multiple buyer 'brains' within the same organisation. Therefore, reach should be based not only on a count of businesses, but also of 'business buyer brains with budget'.

Branding

Branding is about making sure every marketing activity is easily identifiable as being from your company, whether it's an advertisement, an email, a direct mail piece, a proposal PowerPoint deck, a stand at an expo, a corporate box at a stadium, or a LinkedIn post. As with B2C, branding can be in the form of the brand name (direct) or distinctive assets (indirect).

The distinctive assets worth building will vary with the media and buying environments for each category. If you cover both business and consumer categories, consistency in brand identity is important as buyers don't change brains when the context changes from personal to business. If you want to separate the brand's identity in a B2B context from how it is represented in a B2C context, adapt the guidelines for building distinctive assets for sub-brands outlined in *Building Distinctive Brand Assets* (Romaniuk, 2018a). The adapted steps are:

1 Identify your core brand assets, which represent the brand's identity in any context, B2C or B2B, but also with shareholders, board members, key government officials—basically any relevant audience for the brand.

2 Separate out fixed qualities, which are mandatory inclusions (for example, colour assets) from optional qualities, where you can decide whether to include the asset type or not (for example, a tagline or specific image).

   a Fixed core brand assets need to remain the same with the B2B brand, so if your core brand colour is red the B2B brand needs to have red as its dominant colour as well.

   b Optional core brand assets can be included or excluded depending on the need, so if your core brand asset has a tagline that won't work in a B2B context, then don't use it. But if it could work, then you can use it if the B2B environments are conducive to a tagline being a useful priority asset.

   The combination of these fixed and optional core brand assets can form the basis of the bridge between the core brand to the B2B-specific brand identity.

3 Map your B2B branding environments (media and sales) to identify asset types that will be more useful options for investment.

4 If you want an asset to create a visual difference between your B2B brand and the core brand in other contexts, draw on any useful non-core asset type that is specific to the B2B brand, and can be used in the B2B branding environments. This ensures the new asset separates the B2B brand from the core, without clashing with the identity of the core brand.

Finally, remember the key role of distinctive assets is to brand, and the strongest meaning the asset should have is your company/brand name. Don't select a specific asset based on any perceived meaning (particularly colours), as this makes it more likely you will look the same as everyone else (hello corporate blue!). Select an asset type based on what is useful in the environments you need to brand, and select a specific asset form based on what is ownable and helps the brand stand out from competitors.

Messaging

And yes, you also need to build useful mental structures in the brain of the B2B customer. While B2B category entry points (CEPs) differ from B2C CEPs in the same category, across three different service categories (a financial service, a personal service and a professional service), the influence of the B2B's customer on what makes a good supplier was notable. We found 50–70% overlap in the CEPs for business customers and consumers within the same category.

While the same Ws framework discussed in Chapter 4 can be used across categories, and the specific CEPs will depend on the category, the B2B context does entail an additional layer to consider. Just as when dealing with a category such as children's beverages, a buyer might take into account how they think the child will react, it is useful to take into account the three constituents that a business buyer can have on their mind.

Themselves—even though the person will have the company interests in mind, there is also a personal agenda to recognise. So, do consider what the B2B buyer, as a person, might be thinking, feeling and wanting to achieve/receive/avoid. Examples include getting recognition or promoted; making an impact; and avoiding disappointing others or getting fired.

Their work colleagues—a B2B buyer is likely to also the thoughts or anticipated reactions of other people within the company. This can be 'higher ups' such as senior management and board directors, but also peers and subordinates.

Their customers—your business customer most likely has their own customers, and can be thinking of their *perceived* needs, wants and objectives. For example, if your B2B customers are beauticians, they can be thinking about their clientele's reactions to the product, particularly if it is one the clientele will notice or choose as part of the service.

It can be useful to create sub-groups from each of the three areas, under each W, to make sure you have coverage. For example, under 'hoW feeling', a personal consideration might be the B2B buyer *feeling proud of the job being done*, an internal company consideration might be *wanting an option the boss will feel reassured by*, while an external customer consideration for a beautician might be that *their customers will walk out feeling confident and sexy*. Not all sub-groups will be relevant to all categories or all Ws, just as not all Ws are relevant to all categories. However, going through the process of checking these three groups helps minimise the chance of neglecting important areas.

Did you bring your brain to work?

In a B2B world, the context changes, the brands change and the buying processes change, but the responses to questions about brand memories follow the same patterns as in the B2C world. B2B buyers bring to the workplace the same brains they used to select the wine to drink with mates, what to cook for dinner, the present to give their mum and what channel or streaming service to watch. They use this same brain to choose the next business indemnity insurance supplier. We see this manifested in the fundamental patterns of buyer memories that hold for brands in B2B categories amongst business customers.

For example, a brand's B2B customers are more likely to respond to any business attribute than non-customers, and lapsed B2B customers are more likely to respond positively about a brand than those who have never been a customer. This is illustrated in Table 11.5 for B2B insurance, across six attributes that cover a range of areas including expertise, relationship building, efficiency, claims process and quality (also Romaniuk, Bogomolova & Dall'Olmo Riley, 2012). This also highlights the value of keeping in touch with lapsed customers, as they tend to have more positive memories about the brand than those who have never been a customer (as articulated in Bogomolova & Romaniuk, 2009).

Table 11.5: Attribute response patterns for B2B insurance (average across 10 insurers, 2019)

Attribute	Current customers (%)	Lapsed Customers (%)	Never been a customer (%)
Advice and expertise to help people with their business	51	35	23
Build a strong long-term relationship	51	37	21
Efficient processes	50	34	25
Trust to provide security in times of uncertainty	51	33	23
Reasonable when making a claim	50	37	22
Good-quality products and services	56	46	27
Average	**52**	**37**	**24**

But what about building up a positive attitude/combating rejection?

There are two ideas that hold all marketers back. The first is assuming that non-buying has a cause, a barrier/objection that needs to be overcome. The second is that external opportunities are limited and expensive, thus there is a need to prioritise retention over acquisition (the 'bird in the hand' mentality). Both of these limiting ideas are discussed in prior chapters in a B2C context, and they permeate the B2B world as well.

First, let's look at brand rejection. Does being more informed make B2B customers more prone to reject brands? To answer this, we can compare the levels of rejection for B2B and B2C brands from the same category (see Table 11.6 from UK business banking). B2B rejection is typically lower than B2C rejection. This is further supported in Table 11.7, which shows most business customers do not actively reject B2B brands. Nor do most people hold negative perceptions about any brand, but particularly not about B2B brands they have never used (see Table 11.8).

Table 11.6: Comparison of UK banking B2B and B2C rejection levels

Brand	B2B rejection (%)	B2C rejection (%)
Barclays	10	24
Halifax	8	12
HSBC	10	12
Lloyds Bank	11	14
NatWest	8	15
RBS	19	21
Santander	11	18
Average	**11**	**17**

Source: Romaniuk, 2021, p. 4

Table 11.7: Comparisons of B2B and B2C average rejection levels across five categories (2017–2020)

Across categories	B2B (%)	B2C (%)
Finance product	13	10
General banking	11	17
Insurance	7	5
Retail service	7	4
Website use	5	5
Average	**9**	**8**

Table 11.8: Attribute response patterns for business banking (average across eight banks, collected 2019)

Attribute	Lapsed customers (%)	Current customers (%)	Never been a customer (%)
Wouldn't care about businesses customers	24	13	8
A risk to use	14	11	7
Likely to be expensive for what it provides	28	19	14
Not interested in the well-being of communities where it operates	25	15	12
Doesn't care about the environment	18	16	10
Average	**22**	**15**	**10**

Lapsed users have the highest propensity to give negative perceptions, but this is a surprisingly low average of 20%, given the behavioural rejection from this group (this is also evident in B2C categories: see Winchester & Romaniuk, 2008). Therefore, stop creating imagined barriers to acquisition to overcome, and instead focus on the real barrier to acquisition: lack of mental availability.

Physical availability

Physical availability is about being easy to find and buy. The goal of physical availability is to make sure that any mental availability built can be easily acted upon. Chapters 8 and 9 discussed the three pillars of physical availability: presence, prominence and portfolio. While mental availability has the advantage of drawing on the same brain, physical availability is more dependent on the category's sales environments. R&D into physical availability in B2B categories is nascent, and so focus on asking the right questions, drawing on the knowledge from B2C categories, and testing in your own context wherever possible. The first thing to remember is that building physical availability is about reducing the odds that the brand will not be bought because:

1 Our business is not present where the buyer 'shops'.

2 Our business does not stand out in sales environments.

3 Our business lacks something relevant to key buying contexts.

Now we will go through each of the pillars and how they can be applied in a B2B context.

Presence

Presence is about being where buying is happening (or could happen), and having as much coverage as feasible (given resources) across different sales channels. Two areas of 'B2B shopper' knowledge are:

1 *How do channels deliver sales?* Are transactions happening local versus national versus international; preferred supplier lists or open tender; inbound versus outbound; personal contact versus electronic contact?

2 *How do channels deliver customers?* How do B2B buyers buy across locations and time—what is the typical B2B buyer repertoire for

channels to source suppliers over a year? What proportion is ad hoc arrangements versus longer-term contracts?

The aim is for your channel choices to deliver market coverage across B2B customers and time, particularly within the channels you are currently operating.

Prominence

In the B2B sector this means mapping the sales environments where B2B buyers 'shop' and identifying the level and nature of competitor or situational clutter that is likely to hamper the brand being found. B2B contexts have visual tools to utilise such as presentation deck formats, email signatures, word templates, website layouts—any channels where you might present your company's offering. Some of these environments will require your brand to visually stand out in a competitive environment (for example, as a stand at an expo), and some of these options will involve making sure the brand is processed by category buyer brains when they see/review the offer and that it is memorable afterwards (for example, in a proposal deck that is one of five or six reviewed one after another).

Use distinctive assets to brand each visual tool individually, but also to build a mental bridge between the disparate set of marketing activities to which the customer is exposed. This is a particular challenge for B2B marketers when customers are likely to be exposed to the brand in a wide range of infrequent activities.

Start small with the number of 'shopping' distinctive assets you want to build in the B2B space, as one or two strong assets are better than five weaker ones.

Portfolio

Portfolio management means developing a portfolio that is buyable across different contexts. This means addressing the following areas (adapted from Chapter 9):

1 *Portfolio (composition and size)*—does your company's portfolio cover the main areas in the category (for scale), the growing areas (for the future) and the major partitioned areas (for coverage), while minimising duplication?

2 *The core*—which products or services make you the most money? Are you adequately resourcing the marketing and R&D of these products? And not under-investing in the present for a risky future bet?

3 *The 'tail'*—have you cleaned out the clutter from the tail, the product options that sell little and are unlikely to increase?

4 *Budget for new introductions/expansions*—where will the customer's budget for any new introduction come from? Is it a budget we are already accessing (and thereby risking cannibalisation) or is it a new budget line? How do we fund the marketing of a new product? Will it mean requisitioning resources from the core (and potentially weakening a key income stream)?

More R&D is needed to build up our empirical laws in this area. Hopefully by the next edition of this book, we will have more findings to help answer these questions.

Building mental availability, physical availability or both?

There are some B2B marketing activities that could build mental *and* physical availability. These activities can build/freshen buyer mental structures and provide them with a means to transact and buy the brand. For example, at trade events potential customers can interact with and learn about the brand, as well as place orders. In a similar vein, sales teams that can interact with existing customers, or reach out to new ones. Direct mail can build mental structures around CEPs, and also contain an offer to buy within a time frame, and mobile apps can act as a reminder due to their presence on customers' phones but can also be used to place an order.

It is important to separate out the key activities and performance evaluation for each, as the best way to evaluate activities will differ depending on whether you are examining mental availability or physical availability (see Table 11.9). Note these are not mutually exclusive. Both types of metrics can be used for the same activity, and the activity can be good at one and poor at the other—that doesn't mean the activity in total is a bad decision, just that it has one dominant role rather than two. However, when an activity is poor at both, money could be better spent somewhere else.

Table 11.9: Mental and physical availability evaluation questions for B2B marketing activities

	Mental availability	Physical availability
Scale	How many people are reached via this channel/outlet?	What proportion of total sales come from this channel/outlet?
Branding	Is the brand easily recognised and does it cut through creative and situational clutter?	Can the brand stand out from competitive and situational clutter?
Relevance	Do the people exposed to the activity take away a relevant message (ideally based on a CEP)?	How quickly can category buyers find the different products in the brands product portfolio? Are we missing any major payment forms?

Conclusion

We find two fundamental laws of growth to hold in a B2B context: the law of double jeopardy, which tells us that brands grow by expanding their customer base, and the duplication of purchase law, which says B2B brands compete largely on size, and that if you grow, more of your new customers will come from bigger competitors and fewer from smaller competitors. This does not mean that you ignore or skimp on the quality or service you offer existing customers, just that you can't look to your existing customers as the primary source of sales to grow your brand/company.

All businesses that sell to other businesses face the familiar mental challenges of transient, partial, divided buyer attention, fading memories and competitive interference. This why building mental availability is important. This means:

- *Reaching* out to all potential B2B buyers, continuously over time, spaced out so the contracts are not too close together, but not so far apart that large gaps emerge where your brand can be forgotten.

- *Branding* to ensure every marketing activity is easily identifiable as being from your company, via the brand name or distinctive assets. If you operate in both B2B and B2C categories, remember your B2B buyers bring the same brain to work, so the brand identities of both need to work together.
- *Messaging* to build relevant memory structures, such as CEPs. In a B2B context remember the buyer is not just thinking about the company in an overall sense, but themselves, their work colleagues and their customers. The anticipated thoughts of these constituents can influence the CEPs B2B buyers use.

The evidence also shows that B2B buyers are not more likely to reject brands, or more likely to hold negative thoughts about brands than B2C customers. Remember, it's the same brain. Don't imagine barriers to acquisition that do not exist.

The three pillars of physical availability can also be adapted to a B2B context. This means understanding the 'shopper' behaviour of B2B customers to reduce the odds that your company will not be bought. The pillars are:

- *Presence*—this means understanding how channels deliver sales and customers and having a substantial presence in both of those. Channel choices should deliver market coverage across B2B customers and time.
- *Prominence*—in the B2B sector this means mapping the nature of competitor or situational clutter in sales environments that is likely to prevent the brand being found, and drawing on 'shopping' distinctive assets to help the brand stand out.
- *Portfolio*—this means balancing protecting current sources of revenue and innovating to make sure the company is not left behind as buyers and categories evolve.

Finally, there are some marketing activities that could build mental or physical availability. The key is to evaluate the activity according to the objective, so you can determine if it does both, is dominant in one or the other, or is weak in both and should be either fixed or removed.

FURTHER READING ON LAWS OF GROWTH IN THE B2B SECTOR

Bennett, D, Anesbury, Z & Graham, C 2018, 'Buying in a heavy industrial context', Report 88 for corporate sponsors, Ehrenberg–Bass Institute for Marketing Science, Adelaide.

Bowman, D & Lele-Pingle, S 1997, 'Buyer behavior in business-to-business services: the case of foreign exchange', *International Journal of Research in Marketing*, vol. 14, no. 5, pp. 499–508.

Ehrenberg, A 1975, 'The structure of an industrial market: aviation fuel contracts', *Industrial Marketing Management*, vol. 4, pp. 273–85.

McCabe, J, Stern, P & Dacko, S 2013, 'Purposeful empiricism: How stochastic modeling informs industrial marketing research', *Industrial Marketing Management*, vol. 42, no. 3, pp. 421–32.

Michael, J & Smith, P 1999, 'The theory of double jeopardy: an example from a forest products industry', *Forest Products Journal*, vol. 49, no. 3, pp. 21–6.

Pickford, C & Goodhardt, G 2000, 'An empirical study of buying behaviour in an industrial market', Academy of Marketing Annual conference, University of Derby, Derby, England.

Stern, P 1994, 'Prescriptions for branded and generic pharmaceuticals', *Journal of Brand Management*, vol. 2, no. 3, pp. 177–83.

Uncles, M & Ehrenberg, A 1990, 'Industrial buying behavior: aviation fuel contracts', *International Journal of Research in Marketing*, vol. 7, no. 1, pp. 56–68.

Wright, M & Riebe, E 2010, 'Double jeopardy in brand defection', *European Journal of Marketing*, vol. 44, no. 6, pp. 860–73.

12

And Finally, a Bit of Luxury

Byron Sharp and Jenni Romaniuk

An implication is that symbolic brands and even super expensive luxury brands often need to advertise widely. Advertising for luxury watches is not just directed towards billionaires, partly because most people aren't billionaires and because most of the people who buy luxury watches aren't billionaires.

How Brands Grow (2010)

In this chapter we tackle a sacred cow of marketing: the luxury brand. Do luxury brands obey special marketing laws? This chapter illustrates how the laws of growth hold for luxury categories and brands, and we dismantle some assumptions that hold back luxury brand growth.

Who buys luxury brands?

Luxury brands don't just sell to rich people. The super-rich buy more luxury brands per capita than the rest of us, but it's the middle classes who do most of the buying, because they outnumber the billionaires thousands of times over.[1] This means that while luxury brands don't sell to everyone, they still compete in mass markets. This statement comes as a surprise, even a rude shock, to many marketers (and marketing theorists) who are openly hostile to the idea. It conflicts with their belief that exclusivity and scarcity is the secret to success for any luxury brand.

The idea is that scarcity sells (or at least maintains high prices) and that being seen as popular is supposed to be a kiss of death. In this chapter we explore these notions, because if they are true then luxury brands need different marketing from that advocated in *How Brands Grow*.

Does familiarity breed contempt?

Back in 1995 a French marketing professor and an American marketing consultant attempted to directly study this question. Dubois and Paternault (1995) surveyed 3000 Americans about a list of thirty-four luxury brands.[2] They asked respondents which of the brands they were aware of, which they had actually purchased in the past two years, and, finally, they asked respondents to imagine that if they had won a contest and could choose a beautiful present, which five brands they would like best. From this survey, for each of the thirty-four brands, they calculated three metrics:

- awareness
- ownership
- desirability.

---

1   Actually, globally there are around 1.3 million members of the middle class for every single billionaire!

2   The brands were from various product categories: mainly cosmetics, clothing, a few luxury watch brands, one audio equipment brand (Bang & Olufsen), one crystal-ware (Waterford) and one chinaware (Lenox).

Their key thesis was that ownership would reduce desirability, so brands that were owned by many people (high penetration) wouldn't be as desirable.

This is indeed what Dubois and Paternault claimed to find, but the research was flawed. Mixing categories and brands of vastly different price levels meant that ownership was high for the cosmetic brands like Lancôme and Revlon but desirability less so, while desirability was high for expensive brands like Rolex and Gucci but not ownership. Unsurprisingly, people would prefer an expensive luxury watch as a prize than some comparatively cheap lipstick (particularly the men!). Mixing brands of vastly different product categories and different prices guaranteed the authors found what they expected. It was an unfortunately flawed study.

Interestingly, the Pierre Cardin brand did rather well on desirability, and not just because of its level of awareness—it scored higher on desirability than some other brands with similar levels of awareness. This result for Pierre Cardin is very interesting and odd—because this brand was the poster child for failing to practise 'exclusivity marketing'. Back in 1995 there would have been many business schools teaching that Pierre Cardin had lost its cachet because it became widely available, and because the brand was no longer just used on haute couture clothing but also perfume, cosmetics and wine. There is a 2005 *Harvard Business Review* article that says Pierre Cardin overextended itself in the 1990s (Reddy & Terblanche, 2005). Yet oddly the data showed the brand was still desirable to US consumers. Also interestingly, many other haute couture brands have followed Pierre Cardin's lead; for example, today it's very normal for an haute couture house to also sell multiple perfumes and cosmetics under its name.

As often happens, real-world data doesn't nicely fit with (armchair) marketing assumptions. We decided to replicate the original study, and collected awareness, ownership and desirability of luxury brands across several countries. To avoid the mistakes of the past research we endeavoured to carefully compare brands within the same category and of similar price and quality levels (see Tables 12.1, 12.2 and 12.3). Now would ownership reduce desirability? Would being owned by few (low penetration) make a luxury brand be perceived as more desirable, more exclusive or more cool?

First of all, we found a very tight relationship between awareness and ownership (a very high correlation of around 90%: see Table 12.1). This is unsurprising. People are far less likely to buy any brands that they haven't heard of (Hoyer & Brown, 1990; Macdonald & Sharp, 2000)—possibly this is especially true for expensive luxury items. But of course, if you remember you own a brand then you are also likely to recognise it in a survey. Secondly, in each category, awareness is much higher than ownership (see Tables 12.1, 12.2 and 12.3), which is not unexpected: it shows that awareness is not only due to ownership and that advertising, publicity, word of mouth and seeing other people with the brand also create awareness.

The relationship between awareness and desirability is also strong (with an average correlation of 85%: see Table 12.1). Many luxury brands are not well known, and people don't desire brands they don't know.

Prada and Rolex are the only slight deviations with extra-high desirability (see Tables 12.2 and Table 12.4, respectively). Both also have the highest awareness in their categories (Prada was also presumably helped by the book and movie *The Devil Wears Prada*). But perhaps they are not really deviations at all, but rather this is simply a strong double jeopardy effect, where the awareness leaders will also dominate in desirability.

Finally, and directly related to the theory we are testing, the relationship between ownership and desirability is not quite so strong for clothes and watches (correlations of 57% and 52%) where the Prada and Rolex outliers and low variation amongst small brands reduce the fit, but the relationship is a very strong for champagne (correlation of 91%).

The very expensive Patek Philippe[3] and Vacheron Constantin also deviate—unsurprisingly, their desirability is slightly higher considering their level of ownership and awareness. But neither reach the desirability of the high-awareness brands. These results don't support the familiarity-breeds-contempt theory. They strongly suggest that having more owners (greater penetration) does nothing to depress demand.

---

3   We attempted to include brands that were of similar price and quality to avoid the mistake of the original research by Dubois and Pernault, but didn't quite get it right—these deviations show up the huge flaw in the original research.

Table 12.1: Average Pearson's correlation co-efficients between awareness, ownership and desirability for luxury brands

	Fashion	Champagne	Watches	Average
Awareness and ownership	83%	96%	92%	90%
Awareness and desirability	85%	91%	79%	85%
Ownership and desirability	57%	91%	52%	67%

All correlation co-efficients are p<0.05.

Table 12.2: Brand awareness, ownership and desirability for fashion brands in the USA, Russia and China (2015)

	Awareness (%)	Ownership (%)	Desirability (%)
Prada	68	21	27
Hugo Boss	59	29	11
Burberry	56	27	16
Givenchy	54	18	10
Fendi	44	13	5
Mark Jacobs	42	16	7
Kenzi	38	18	5
Moschino	31	12	3
Balenciaga	30	7	7
Bottega Veneta	26	6	4

Table 12.3: Brand awareness, ownership and desirability for champagne brands in the USA, Russia and China (2015)

	Awareness (%)	Ownership (%)	Desirability (%)
Moët & Chandon	36	18	22
Joseph Perrier	23	8	15
Perrier Jouët	23	8	8
Verve Cliquot	22	9	11
Mumm	18	8	7
Lanson	16	5	5
Tattinger	16	2	4
Piper Heidseick	15	5	9
Philipponnat	12	2	4
Nicolas Feuillatte	12	3	6

Table 12.4: Brand awareness, ownership and desirability for luxury watch brands in the USA, Russia and China (2015)

	Awareness (%)	Ownership %	Desirability %
Rolex	85	17	47
Omega	72	22	11
Longines	50	15	6
Rado	41	10	4
Patek Philippe	37	6	12
Zenith	34	6	2
Piaget	32	4	8
Vacheron Constantin	31	4	2
Breitling	25	4	3
Girad Perregaux	15	2	3

If I own it, does it lose its sparkle?

Finally, to test the proposition that familiarity can breed contempt even further, we looked at individuals', rather than brand-level, scores. We looked at people who were aware of a brand and compared the desirability scores of those who owned the brand against those who didn't. Would ownership reduce desirability? Would owners want to collect another, different, luxury brand? If so, how large might this effect be?

But, in spite of some variety seeking that must exist in every market and that leads people to want what they don't have, owning a luxury brand actually results in higher desirability for the brand, even once we have controlled for awareness. Table 12.5 shows the data for luxury clothing brands. We compared two groups of consumers who were aware of the brand: people who owned the brand with people who did not. Desirability was highest amongst owners. Remember that desirability was measured by asking respondents to imagine they had won a competition and could choose a lovely present; they had to select which three brands they would like from each product category. Table 12.5 reports the percentage of owners and non-owners aware of the brand and how many selected the brand as their first choice. We also analysed the results for any choice out of three and the pattern was the same.

Table 12.5 is further evidence that ownership does not decrease desirability. While it is possible that these owners desired the brand even more *before* they bought it, the practical ramifications, if this were true, would be minor; this group still desire the brand more than people who are aware but haven't bought yet.

Table 12.5: Relationship between ownership and desirability for luxury clothing in China, Russia and the USA (2015)

Clothing brand	First-choice desirability (%) amongst owners	First-choice desirability (%) amongst aware non-owners
Prada	43	29
Burberry	23	18
Bottega Veneta	21	8
Hugo Boss	18	11
Givenchy	16	10
Marc Jacobs	14	9
Kenzo	9	7
Balenciaga	9	14
Moschino	8	6
Fendi	8	5
Average	**17**	**12**

Honestly, we expected that there would be a degree of variety seeking large enough to mean that owners would show slightly less desirability than aware non-owners, but the data suggest variety seeking is pretty minor. Instead it seems that loyalty is the natural and dominant behaviour; having bought a brand means you are more likely to buy it again than other consumers who know the brand but haven't (yet) bought it.

This effect was weaker for luxury watches, and this fits the idea of variety seeking. Having bought a Rolex, it makes sense that some owners would then prefer another brand as the next to add to their collection. Desirability for Rolex was 51% amongst owners and 51% amongst aware non-owners. Overall the average desirability score across brands was 13.4% for owners and 13.3% for aware non-owners—a much smaller difference than observed for luxury clothes (17% compared with 12%)

and champagne (22% compared with 14%). So, there is evidence of more variety seeking for luxury watches, but it is still very hard to argue that ownership does much to decrease an individual's desire for that brand.

Does being 'easily available' cheapen a luxury brand?

In another set of data collected in a different survey, this time for a corporate sponsor of the Ehrenberg–Bass Institute, we directly measured perceptions of luxury and exclusivity and we also measured perceptions of physical availability. Would brands with (perceived) restricted distribution be seen as more exclusive, more luxurious?

No. Indeed, we found the opposite—brands that were perceived as luxurious and exclusive by more people scored lowest on *not available everywhere* (see Table 12.6). This means perceptions of exclusive distribution do not correlate with perceptions of exclusivity or luxury. We need to look to other aspects of the marketing mix for the sources of exclusivity (like high price); there is no need to restrict physical availability to make a brand be seen as exclusive or luxurious. Indeed, investigations into luxury buyers' perceptions of luxury brands show that they follow patterns observed in non-luxury brands (Romaniuk & Huang, 2019). Associations for Gucci have similar structure as associations for Gatorade.

Table 12.6: Perceptions of luxury and relationship with awareness, exclusivity and restricted distribution for alcoholic spirits in the USA (2013)

Luxury brand	Bought in year (%)	Aware (%)	Brand associated with luxury (%)	Brand has a sense of exclusivity (%)	Brand is not available everywhere (%)
Russian vodka	65	91	32	22	8
Mexican tequila	52	80	28	24	13
Scotch whisky 1	46	77	22	19	13
Scotch whisky 2	37	56	19	17	21
European vodka	26	50	15	14	19
US bourbon	21	38	18	15	17
Average	**41**	**65**	**22**	**19**	**15**

Does small mean niched?

These tests of the familiarity-breeds-contempt theory strongly suggest the speculation is wrong: that luxury brands compete like normal brands, within their luxury market. That luxury buying behaviour data matches the laws set out in *How Brands Grow* supports this contention.

Further support for normal growth patterns for luxury brands appears when we look at how luxury brands compete. We see the familiar duplication of purchase law, where brands share customers with all other brands in the category, and more with the larger brands and less with the smaller brands. In Table 12.7 we see that every luxury fashion brand shares about half of its customers with Prada, while they all share far less (about a fifth of their customers) with Bottega Veneta. For those with a deeper interest in the category, a few deviations also worthy of attention appear in the tables: the customer bases of Balenciaga and Bottega Veneta overlap more than expected, perhaps because they are both owned by the same French luxury goods house, and Kenzo and Marc Jacobs under-share customer bases, as do Balenciaga and Hugo Boss. The duplication of purchase law clearly highlights these deviations.

The duplication of purchase law also describes well the customer overlap between skin-care brands (see Table 12.8). Once we know the expected pattern, it is easy to see unusually high sharing between Burberry and Givenchy in this category. Normally this sort of oversharing occurs between brands with the same owner (and therefore sold through the same distribution network and by the same sales team). That isn't the case here. It may be partly because these two are the smallest brands (note that the two smallest brands of luxury fashion also have high sharing). Buyers of small brands tend to, on average, be heavier category buyers (natural monopoly law), and this may partly explain the high sharing between the two smallest brands in the analysis.

This natural monopoly law is shown in Table 12.9, which contains repertoire-size data for luxury watch buyers of each brand. The pattern is clear: owners of smaller brands of luxury watch have larger repertoires. In other words, they are heavier buyers of the category. Remember (from Chapter 2), it's called the natural monopoly law because larger brands tend to *monopolise* the category's light buyers.

Table 12.7: Duplication of purchase table for luxury fashion in top 25% income holders in China, Russia and the USA (2015)

Customers of	Penetration (%)	Customers also buying (%)									
		Hugo Boss	Burberry	Prada	Givenchy	Kenzo	Marc Jacobs	Fendi	Moschino	Balenciaga	Bottega Veneta
Hugo Boss	31		49	46	42	44	31	27	27	12	15
Burberry	30	52		48	38	31	34	32	28	19	16
Prada	24	59	58		43	42	32	40	29	19	14
Givenchy	21	62	54	50		48	33	37	38	22	20
Kenzo	21	66	44	49	49		25	27	37	16	16
Marc Jacobs	17	57	60	47	42	31		34	29	26	25
Fendi	15	55	61	63	51	37	37		35	25	24
Moschino	13	65	63	55	61	60	38	41		22	23
Balenciaga	10	39	59	49	48	34	46	39	30		39
Bottega Veneta	8	57	57	41	53	41	51	45	37	47	
Average	19	57	56	50	47	41	36	36	32	23	21

Table 12.8: Duplication of purchase table for skin care—top 25% income holders in China, Hong Kong, and Singapore (2015)

Customers of	Penetration (%)	Customers also buying (%)									
		Estée Lauder	Chanel	Dior	Shu Uemura	Shiseido Pres.	Laneige	Gucci	YSL	Burberry	Givenchy
Estée Lauder	21		43	37	23	25	21	21	20	18	15
Chanel	19	46		48	21	23	18	25	25	20	17
Dior	16	47	57		26	28	20	28	29	22	17
Shu Uemura	10	47	40	41		33	36	25	33	22	24
Shiseido Pres.	10	53	46	47	36		26	24	25	23	21
Laneige	10	44	36	34	39	26		24	25	19	21
Gucci	9	47	53	49	28	25	25		29	31	23
YSL	9	46	53	51	37	26	27	30		23	24
Burberry	7	54	55	52	33	33	27	42	31		32
Givenchy	6	51	52	44	39	32	33	34	34	34	
Average	**12**	**48**	**48**	**45**	**31**	**28**	**26**	**28**	**28**	**24**	**22**

Table 12.9: Penetration and repertoire size for luxury watches in China, Russia and the USA (2015)

Brand	Owned (%)	Average number of brands ever owned
Omega	67	2.2
Rolex	52	2.1
Longines	45	2.4
Rado	31	2.5
Patek Philippe	19	2.6
Zenith	18	2.8
Breitling	13	2.8
Vacheron Constantin	12	2.7
Piaget	11	2.8
Girard-Perregaux	5	2.9
Average	**27**	**2.6**

If you've only ever bought one luxury watch, then this watch is much and more likely to be an Omega or Rolex. But if you own a Girard-Perregaux, then you are probably a bit of a luxury watch collector.

We don't want to overstate the effect; the natural monopoly law is seldom dramatic, but it does show up in market after market, for prosaic items like butter and margarine, toothpaste or fast food, and, it seems, for luxury items too.

Buyer profiles of luxury brands seldom differ

Much of the profiling in the luxury sector is on the difference between buyers and non-buyers of luxury. Patrick, along with other Institute researchers, decided to test whether luxury brands that compete in the same luxury category/price point differ substantively from each other in terms of who buys them, thus suggesting that efforts to differentiate the brand and/or target a specific type of luxury buyer have worked. The answer is no. Luxury brands in the same category (that is, around the same price point) each sell to very similar sorts of buyers. A study quantified the variation in customer bases of luxury brands in five categories for luxury brands (over 200 brands in total). The data was collected from over 1900 luxury buyers who are in the top 25% of income earners within the USA, China, Singapore, Taiwan, Indonesia and Hong Kong.

The categories and a sample of the brands are:

- *Alcohol* (30 brands)—Balvenie, Hennessy, Penfolds, The Macallan, Dalmore, Louis XIII
- *Fashion/accessories* (45 brands)—Louis Vuitton, Hermès, Christian Louboutin, Prada, Shang Xia, Chloé, Alexander McQueen
- *Make-up/skin care* (48 brands)—Chanel, Guerlain, SKII, YSL, Dior, Giorgio Armani, La Mer, La Prairie
- *Watches/jewellery* (42 brands)—Rolex, Jaeger-LeCoultre, Cartier, Van Cleef & Arpels, Patek Philippe, Audemars Piguet
- *Cars* (24 brands)—Aston Martin, Bentley, Ferrari, Spyker, Lamborghini, Jaguar, Ferarri, Maserati, Porsche
- *Hotels* (23 brands)—Four Seasons, Ritz Carton, St Regis, Oberoi, Shangri-la.

Analysis covered a wide range of variables including demographics, motives for buying luxury brands and luxury buying habits. The results showed mean absolute deviations between luxury brands within a category to vary between 2 and 5 percentage points. A sample of the results from Patrick and colleagues (2018) is shown in Table 12.10. The mean absolute deviations in the table quantify the variation in that characteristic across all brands within the category. For example, alcohol brands tended to vary in age profile by +/-2 percentage points, which means if the average brand has 35% aged 30–39 years, then the majority of brands had the proportion of 30–39-year-olds between 33% and 37%.

Table 12.10: Brand user profiles hardly differ—examples of results from luxury brands in Patrick et al. (2018)

Mean absolute deviations	Alcohol (30 brands)	Fashion/ accessories (45 brands)	Make-up/ skin care (48 brands)	Watches/ jewellery (42 brands)	Cars (24 brands)	Hotels (23 brands)
Age	2	2	2	2	2	2
Gender	4	4	5	4	3	3
I mainly buy luxury when travelling	4	3	3	4	4	4

Mean absolute deviations	Alcohol (30 brands)	Fashion/ accessories (45 brands)	Make-up/ skin care (48 brands)	Watches/ jewellery (42 brands)	Cars (24 brands)	Hotels (23 brands)
Buy luxury because people recognise the brand	3	3	3	4	4	3
Buy luxury because of the quality	2	3	3	3	3	3
Buy luxury because of the exclusivity	4	3	3	3	3	3

Buyer profiles seldom differentiate luxury brands from one another, and nor do those buyers' attitudes to luxury differ greatly. Luxury brands are different from non-luxury brands in that they are higher quality and have a much higher price. But luxury brands compete with other luxury brands. Versace's buyers are similar to Gucci's, just as Nike's buyers are similar to those who buy Adidas. Their buyers' motivations and perceptions are similar, and classic luxury characteristics like glamour, style, craftsmanship, uniqueness and quality matter equally across competing brands.

Managers of luxury brands should always assume that their brand competes head on with other luxury brands selling (potentially) to all category buyers. Embracing this knowledge opens up significant opportunities for brand growth: anyone who buys luxury goods is a potential buyer of your brand.

Conclusion

In this chapter we tested the widely held beliefs that luxury brands are fundamentally different because high penetration would result in a loss of desirability and hamper future sales as a luxury brand, and that effective marketing in this area needs to follow different rules to compete—for example, avoiding mass advertising. These turned out to be myths.

The really obvious difference about luxury brands is that they are more expensive, very high quality and often beautifully designed. Their high quality cannot always be instantly assessed: it may take years of use of a leather bag or a watch to truly appreciate the craftsmanship. Though the quality might be inferred from a high price, there is some danger in using this heuristic and buyers know it. Consequently, it can take a brand many years to build a reputation for extreme quality.[4] The higher price creates a natural 'exclusivity' barrier to the luxury brand being a regular, everyday purchase. Therefore there is not only no need to put additional barriers to purchase in place by restricting distribution, but putting up these barriers just means it's most likely your more accessible luxury competitor will be bought instead.

Many buyers, particularly those new to a category, don't trust their ability to choose something that is high quality (for example, wine) or fashionable. They look to cues such as price, advertising (how much is it?, how expensive does it look?), and how many other people respect or buy the brand—the fact that they have heard of the brand, or not, consequently has a powerful effect on the purchasing decision. It's very hard for small, largely unknown brands to sell to these buyers.

All this suggests that luxury brands need a good deal of advertising to build and maintain mental availability. It also suggests that it will take a good deal of time to build the reputation they desire. Ideally, a luxury brand has consistently made beautiful products of exemplary quality for many years. It certainly helps to signal to the market that you have been around for many years: 'Dunhill since 1907', 'Gucci 1921 collection' or 'Berry Bros. & Rudd established 1698'. Heritage helps.

---

4   And it takes decades for a fine wine to prove that it can age and turn into something special. Most wines don't. Similarly it takes decades for a luxury brand (of watch, car, furniture or jewellery) to prove that it retains its value on the secondary (for example, auction) market.

Finally, it's important to remember that despite what can seem like outrageous prices, luxury brands get most of their sales from the middle class, not a small cadre of billionaires. More bottles of Château Lafite Rothschild and Penfold's Grange are sold to doctors and lawyers than billionaires.[5] Indeed, many bottles of fine wine are bought by currently impoverished medical and law students, saving or pooling their money to try something special now and then (for example, on a special occasion, such as graduation). The European Commission states that there were 1.8 billion people in the global middle class in 2009, that this number rose to 3.5 billion in 2017 and that it will reach 4 billion by the end of 2021 (European Commission, 2020). In comparison, there are only 3000 or so billionaires on the planet, far too small a market to sustain most luxury brands.

---

5   The few billionaires on the planet can only drink so much wine. Indeed some drink none: for example, Warren Buffet does not consume any type of alcoholic drink—though this has not deterred him from investing in alcohol distribution companies.

A Final Note

Thank you for reading this updated version of *How Brands Grow, Part 2*. We hope it will help you make evidence-based marketing decisions and grow brands with greater success.

These laws are now more commonplace in brand strategy discussions—more marketers, for example, now query how a tactic might help move the brand up the double jeopardy line, draw on the duplication of purchase law to identify opportunities in a category, and quantify the strength of their distinctive assets. With this rigour, marketing is evolving into a serious science, something that can start to be taken seriously in the boardroom, although there is still much more work to be done.

We also hope that the ubiquity of these laws makes you think twice when a new technology or media claims to revolutionise marketing practice. Tactics might change, but the fundamental need to build mental and physical availability doesn't. In this update, we have provided revised chapters on these two concepts, drawing on our ongoing research streams to provide additional insight into how to grow brands.

Further, while people may say their market is different, and it might be (a bit), rarely does any difference rewrite the laws of growth. Here, we've expanded the boundaries of many laws and provided new material on B2B (which now has its own chapter), as well as new examples from services, durables and luxury brands. We encourage you to use this knowledge to test these laws in your own categories.

Despite the developments you have read about here, there is still much more work to be done. Teams of Ehrenberg–Bass Institute researchers continue to build knowledge in areas such as category growth, new launches, how small brands grow, and the efficacy of different media in achieving mental availability. It is an exciting time as we continue to build marketing's age of enlightenment.

Our work continues.

Jenni and Byron

www.marketingscience.info

Reference List

Allsopp, J, Sharp, B & Dawes, J 2004, 'The double jeopardy line—empirical results', Australia and New Zealand Marketing Academy (ANZMAC) conference, 29 November, Victoria University, Wellington, New Zealand.

Anderson, J & Bower, G 1979, *Human Associative Memory*, Lawrence Erlbaum, Hillsdale, NJ.

Anesbury, Z, Winchester, M & Kennedy, R 2017, 'Brand user profiles seldom change and seldom differ', *Marketing Letters*, vol. 28, no. 4, pp. 523–35.

Anschuetz, N 2002, 'Why a brand's most valuable consumer is the next one it adds', *Journal Of Advertising Research*, vol. 42, no. 1, pp. 15–21.

Atsmon, Y & Magni, M 2012, 'Meet the Chinese consumer of 2020', *Treasury Management International*, vol. 205, p. 28.

Baldinger, A, Blair, E & Echambadi, R 2002, 'Why brands grow', *Journal of Advertising Research*, vol. 1, pp. 7–14.

Barker, A 2021, 'Using double jeopardy to forecast small brand growth', Masters thesis, Ehrenberg–Bass Institute, University of South Australia, Adelaide.

Barnard, N & Ehrenberg, A 1990, 'Robust measures of consumer brand beliefs', *Journal of Marketing Research*, vol. 27, no. 4, pp. 477–84.

Barwise, P, Bellman, S & Beal, V 2020, 'Why do people watch so much television and video?: implications for the future of viewing and advertising', *Journal of Advertising Research*, vol. 60, no. 2, pp. 121–34.

Bass, F & King, C 1968, 'The theory of first purchase of new products', Purdue University, Institute for Research in the Behavioral, Economic, and Management Sciences.

Bennett, D 2008, 'Brand loyalty dynamics—China's television brands come of age', *Australasian Marketing Journal*, vol. 16, no. 2, pp. 39–50.

Bennett, D, Anesbury, Z & Graham, C 2018, 'Buying in a heavy industrial context', Report 88 for corporate sponsors, Ehrenberg–Bass Institute for Marketing Science, Adelaide.

Binet, L & Field, P 2009, 'Empirical generalisations about advertising campaign success', *Journal of Advertising Research*, vol. 49, no. 2, pp. 130–3.

Bird, M & Channon, C 1969, 'Brand usage, brand image, and advertising policy—part I', *Admap*, vol. 6, pp. 27–46.

Bird, M, Channon, C & Ehrenberg, A 1970, 'Brand image and brand usage', *Journal of Marketing Research*, vol. 7, no. 3, pp. 307–14.

Bogomolova, S & Romaniuk, J 2009, 'Brand defection in a business-to-business financial service', *Journal of Business Research*, vol. 62, no. 3, pp. 291–6.

Caruso, W, Corsi, A, Bogomolova, S, Cohen, J, Sharp, A, Lockshin, L & Tan, P 2018, 'The real estate value of supermarket endcaps: why location in-store matters', *Journal of Advertising Research*, vol. 58, no. 2, pp. 177–88.

Ceber, M 2009, 'The importance of light TV viewers and how to reach them', Masters thesis, Ehrenberg–Bass Institute, University of South Australia, Adelaide.

Cohen, J, Lockshin, L & Sharp, B 2012, 'A better understanding of the structure of a wine market using the attribute of variety', *International Journal of Business and Globalisation*, vol. 8, no. 1, pp. 66–80.

Danenberg, N, Kennedy, R, Beal, V & Sharp, B 2016, 'Advertising budgeting: a re-investigation of the evidence on brand size and spend', *Journal of Advertising*, vol. 45, no. 1, pp. 139–46.

Dawes, J 2020, 'The natural monopoly effect in brand purchasing: do big brands really appeal to lighter category buyers?', *Australasian Marketing Journal*, vol. 28, no. 2, pp. 90–9.

Dawes, J & Nenycz-Thiel, M 2014, 'Comparing retailer purchase patterns and brand metrics for in-store and online grocery purchasing', *Journal of Marketing Management*, vol. 30, no. 3–4, pp. 364–82.

Dubois, B & Paternault, C 1995, 'Understanding the world of international luxury brands: the "dream formula"', *Journal of Advertising Research*, July/August, pp. 69–76.

East, R, Hammond, K & Lomax, W 2008, 'Measuring the impact of positive and negative word of mouth on brand purchase probability', *International Journal of Research in Marketing*, vol. 25, no. 3, pp. 215–24.

East, R, Hammond, K & Wright, M 2007, 'The relative incidence of positive and negative word of mouth: a multi-category study', *International Journal of Research in Marketing*, vol. 24, no. 2, pp. 175–84.

East, R, Romaniuk, J & Lomax, W 2011, 'The NPS and the ACSI: a critique and an alternative metric', *International Journal of Market Research*, vol. 53, no. 3, p. 15.

East, R, Uncles, M, Romaniuk, J & Dall'Olmo Riley, F 2015, 'Factors associated with the production of word of mouth', *International Journal of Market Research*, vol. 57, no. 3, pp. 439–58.

Ehrenberg, A 1959, 'The pattern of consumer purchases', *Applied Statistics*, vol. 8, no. 1, pp. 26–41.

Ehrenberg, A 1972, *Repeat Buying: Theory and Applications*, American Elsevier, New York.

Ehrenberg, A 2000, 'Repeat-buying: facts, theory and applications', *Journal of Empirical Generalisations in Marketing Science*, vol. 5, pp. 392–770.

Ehrenberg, A & Goodhardt, G 2001, 'New brands: near-instant loyalty' *Journal of Targeting, Measurement and Analysis for Marketing*, vol. 10, no. 1, pp. 9–17.

Ehrenberg, A, Goodhardt, G & Barwise, T 1990, 'Double jeopardy revisited', *Journal of Marketing*, vol. 54, no. 3, pp. 82–91.

Epstein, E, 2014, 'The Johnnie Walker brand: a rich blend of design and progress', *Mashable*, 3 May, <http://mashable.com/2014/05/02/johnnie-walker-marketing-strategy>.

European Commission 2020, 'Developments and forecasts of growing consumerism', <https://knowledge4policy.ec.europa.eu/foresight/topic/growing-consumerism/more-developments-relevant-growing-consumerism>.

Fader, P & Schmittlein, D 1993, 'Excess behavioral loyalty for high-share brands: deviations from the Dirichlet model for repeat purchasing', *Journal of Marketing Research*, vol. 30, no. 4, pp. 478–93.

Gasparro, A 2018, 'Folgers wakes up with a new premium cup of coffee', *The Wall Street Journal*, 21 February, <www.wsj.com/articles/waking-up-a-brand-with-a-new-folgers-in-your-cup-1519209001>.

Graham, C, Bennett, Franke, K, Henfrey, C & Nagy-Hamada, M 2017, 'Double jeopardy—50 years on. Reviving a forgotten tool that still predicts brand loyalty', *Australasian Marketing Journal*, vol. 25, no. 4, pp. 278–87.

Goodhardt, G & Ehrenberg, A 1969, 'Duplication of television viewing between and within channels', *Journal of Marketing Research*, vol. 6, May, pp. 169–78.

Greenfield, S 2000, *The Private Life of the Brain*, Allen Lane, London.

Hammett, E 2019, 'P&G puts focus on reach: It's a more important measure than spend, *Marketing Week*, 17 June, <www.marketingweek.com/pg-reach-ad-spend>.

Hammond, K, Ehrenberg, A & Goodhardt, G 1996, 'Market segmentation for competitive brands', *European Journal of Marketing*, vol. 30, no. 12, pp. 39–49.

Harrison, F 2013, 'Digging deeper down into the empirical generalization of brand recall', *Journal of Advertising Research*, vol. 53, no. 1, pp. 181–5.

Hartnett, N, Beal, V, Kennedy, R, Sharp, B & Gelzinis, A 2021, 'When brands go dark: examining sales trends when brands stop broad reach advertising for long periods', *Journal of Advertising Research*, pp. 1–30.

Hartnett, N, Romaniuk, J & Kennedy, R 2016. 'Comparing direct and indirect branding in advertising'., *Australasian Marketing Journal*, vol. 24, no. 1, pp. 20–8.

Hirche, M 2018, 'An empirical analysis of stock-keeping units deviating from the Reibstein-Farris distribution and market share model: the role of product- and distribution-related characteristics', PhD dissertation, Ehrenberg–Bass Institute, University of South Australia, Adelaide.

Holden, S & Lutz, R 1992, 'Ask not what the brand can evoke; ask what can evoke the brand?', *Advances in Consumer Research*, vol. 19, no. 1, pp. 101–7.

Howard, J & Sheth, J 1969, *The Theory of Buyer Behavior*, John & Wiley Sons, New York.

Hoyer, W & Brown, S 1990, 'Effects of brand awareness on choice for a common, repeat-purchase product', *Journal of Consumer Research*, vol. 17, no. 2, pp. 141–8.

Jones, J 1990, 'Ad spending: maintaining market share', *Harvard Business Review*, vol. 68, no. 1, pp. 38–43.

Kearns, Z, Millar, S & Lewis, T 2000, 'Dirichlet deviations and brand growth', Australia and New Zealand Marketing Academy (ANZMAC) conference, 28 November – 1 December, Griffith University, Gold Coast, Queensland.

Keller, K 1993, 'Conceptualizing, measuring, and managing customer-based brand equity', *Journal of Marketing*, vol. 57, no. 1, pp. 1–22.

Kennedy, R & Ehrenberg, A 2001, 'Competing retailers generally have the same sorts of shoppers', *Journal of Marketing Communications*, vol. 7, no. 1, pp. 19–26.

Kennedy, R, Ehrenberg, A & Long, S 2000, 'Competitive brands' user-profiles hardly differ', Market Research Society Conference (UK), 15–17 March, Brighton, UK.

Kohan, S 2020, 'Walmart's online sales have surged 74% during the pandemic', *Forbes*, 19 May, <www.forbes.com/sites/shelleykohan/2020/05/19/walmart-revenue-up-86-e-commerce-up-74/?sh=53f76bdb66cc>.

Kooyman, C & Wright, M 2017, 'Double jeopardy benchmarks for political polls', *Australasian Marketing Journal*, vol. 25, pp. 180–4.

Lane, I 2020 'Big retail winners: supermarkets benefit from coronavirus online shopping boom', *The New Daily*, 25 August, <https://thenewdaily.com.au/finance/consumer/2020/08/25/tescos-pandemic-coles-woolworths>.

Lavin, F 2018, 'How to win and retail loyal customers in China', *Forbes*, 21 May, <www.forbes.com/sites/franklavin/2018/05/21/how-to-win-and-retain-loyal-customers-in-china/?sh=6096ba312806>.

Livaditis, M, Sharp, A & Sharp, B 2012, 'Evidence of naturally bias behaviour—seating habits at a lecture', Australia and New Zealand Marketing Academy (ANZMAC) conference, 3–5 December, Ehrenberg–Bass Institute for Marketing Science, Adelaide.

Lockshin, L & Cohen, E 2011, 'Using product and retail choice attributes for cross-national segmentation', *European Journal of Marketing*, vol. 45, no. 7/8, pp. 1236–52.

Loeb, W 2020, 'Best Buy successfully changed its strategy to lead in the pandemic', *Forbes*, 26 August, <www.forbes.com/sites/walterloeb/2020/08/26/best-buy-successfully-changed-its-strategy-to-lead-in-the-pandemic/?sh=3cbfed843dab>.

Macdonald, E & Sharp, B 2000, 'Brand awareness effects on consumer decision making for a common, repeat purchase product: a replication', *Journal of Business Research*, vol. 48, no. 1, pp. 5–15.

McDonald, C & Ehrenberg, A 2003, 'What happens when brands gain or lose share?: customer acquisition or increased loyalty?', Report 31 for corporate sponsors, Ehrenberg–Bass Institute for Marketing Science, Adelaide.

McPhee, WN 1963, *Formal Theories of Mass Behaviour*, The Free Press of Glencoe, New York.

Major, J, Tanaka, A & Romaniuk, J 2014, 'The competitive battleground of colours, logos and taglines in brand identity', in G Muratovski (ed.), *Design For Business*, pp. 42–59, Intellect Ltd, Bristol, UK.

Mangold, W, Miller, F & Brockway, G 1999, 'Word-of-mouth communication in the service marketplace', *Journal of Services Marketing*, vol. 13, no. 1, pp. 73–89.

Martin, C, Jr 1973, 'The theory of double jeopardy', *Journal of the Academy of Marketing Science*, vol. 1, no. 2, pp. 148–56.

Meeker, M, & Wu, L 2013, 'Internet trends, D11 conference', *KPCB*, <www.slideshare.net/kleinerperkins/kpcb-internet-trends-2013>, accessed 25 June 2015.

Muoio, D 2016, 'Here's how Tesla's cars have changed over the years', *Business Insider*, 12 September, <www.businessinsider.com/how-tesla-cars-have-changed-over-time-photos-2016-9?r=AU&IR=T#tesla-garnered-a-lot-of-attention-in-2008-when-it-released-its-very-first-electric-car--the-wildly-sexy-tesla-roadster-1>.

Mundt, K, Dawes, J & Sharp, B 2006, 'Can a brand outperform competitors on cross-category loyalty? An examination of cross-selling metrics in two financial services markets', *Journal of Consumer Marketing*, vol. 23, no. 7, pp. 465–9.

NCES 2019, 'Adult literacy in the United States', <https://nces.ed.gov/datapoints/2019179.asp>.

Nelson-Field, K, Riebe, E & Sharp, B 2012, 'What's not to "like"?: can a Facebook fan base give a brand the advertising reach it needs?' *Journal of Advertising Research*, vol. 52, no. 2, pp. 262–9.

Nenycz-Thiel, M, Dawes, J & Romaniuk, J 2018, 'Modeling brand market share change in emerging markets', *International Marketing Review*, vol. 35, no. 5, pp. 785–805.

Nenycz-Thiel, M & Romaniuk, J 2011, 'The nature and incidence of private label rejection', *Australasian Marketing Journal*, vol. 19, pp. 93–9.

Nielsen 2015, 'The future of grocery: e-commerce, digital technology and changing shopping preferences around the world', *Nielsen*, <www.nielsen.com/content/dam/nielsenglobal/vn/docs/Reports/2015/Nielsen%20Global%20ECommerce%20and%20The%20New%20Retail%20Report%20APRIL%202015%20%28Digital%29.pdf>.

Pare, V & Dawes, J 2011, 'The persistence of excess brand loyalty over multiple years', *Marketing Letters*, vol. 21, no. 2, pp. 163–75.

Patrick, S, Romaniuk, J, Beal, V & Sharp, B 2018, 'Comparing the customer profiles of rival luxury brands', Report 81 for corporate sponsors, Ehrenberg–Bass Institute for Marketing Science, Adelaide.

Pickford, C & Goodhardt, G 2000, 'An empirical study of buying behaviour in an industrial market', Academy of Marketing Annual Conference (AM2000), 5–7 July, University of Derby, Derby, UK.

Press Trust of India 2013, 'Samsung beats Nokia to top spot in India, Apple posts strong gains: survey', *NDTV Gadgets*, 21 August, <http://gadgets.ndtv.com/mobiles/news/samsung-beats-nokia-to-top-spot-in-india-apple-posts-strong-gains-survey-408478>.

Reddy, M & Terblanche, N 2005, 'How not to extend your luxury brand', *Harvard Business Review*, December, <https://hbr.org/2005/12/how-not-to-extend-your-luxury-brand>.

Redford, N 2005, 'Regularities in media consumption', Masters thesis, Ehrenberg–Bass Institute, University of South Australia, Adelaide.

Redman, R 2020, 'Online grocery to more than double market share by 2025', *Supermarket News*, 18 September, <www.supermarketnews.com/online-retail/online-grocery-more-double-market-share-2025>.

Reichheld, F 2003, 'The one number you need to grow', *Harvard Business Review*, December, pp. 46–54.

Repko, M 2020, 'Best Buy tops estimates on strong online sales, but shares fall on lack of holiday forecast', *CNBC*, 24 November, <www.cnbc.com/2020/11/23/best-buy-bby-q3-2021-earnings.html>.

Riebe, E, Wright, M, Stern, P & Sharp, B 2014, 'How to grow a brand: retain or acquire customers?', *Journal of Business Research*, vol. 67, no. 5, pp. 990–7.

Roberts, K 2004, *Lovemarks: The Future Beyond Brands*, Murdoch Books, Sydney.

Rogers, A, Daunt, K, Morgan, P & Beynon, M 2017, 'Examining the existence of double jeopardy and negative double jeopardy within Twitter', *European Journal of Marketing*, vol. 51, no. 7/8, pp. 1–35.

Romaniuk, J 2000, 'Brand image and loyalty', PhD dissertation, University of South Australia, Adelaide.

Romaniuk, J 2003, 'Brand attributes—"distribution outlets" in the mind', *Journal of Marketing Communications*, vol. 9, June, pp. 73–92.

Romaniuk, J 2006, 'Comparing prompted and unprompted methods for measuring consumer brand associations', *Journal of Targeting, Measurement and Analysis for Marketing*, vol. 15, no. 1, pp. 3–11.

Romaniuk, J 2008, 'Comparing methods of measuring brand personality traits', *Journal of Marketing Theory and Practice*, vol. 16, no. 2, pp. 153–61.

Romaniuk, J 2009, 'The efficacy of brand-execution tactics in TV advertising, brand placements and internet advertising', *Journal of Advertising Research*, vol. 49, no. 2, pp. 143–50.

Romaniuk, J 2013, 'Modeling mental market share', *Journal of Business Research*, vol. 66, no. 2, pp. 188–95.

Romaniuk, J 2018a, *Building Distinctive Brand Assets*, Oxford University Press, Melbourne.

Romaniuk, J 2018b, 'Developing a "sound" strategy', in J Romaniuk, *Building Distinctive Brand Assets*, pp. 153–62, Oxford University Press, Melbourne.

Romaniuk, J 2021, 'Brand rejection in B2B: incidence, reasons and implications', Report for LinkedIn B2B Institute, Ehrenberg–Bass Institute for Marketing Science, Adelaide.

Romaniuk, J, Beal, V & Uncles, M 2013, 'Achieving reach in a multi-media environment: how a marketer's first step provides the direction for the second', *Journal of Advertising Research*, vol. 53, no. 2, pp. 221–30.

Romaniuk, J, Bogomolova, S & Dall'Olmo Riley, F 2012, 'Brand image and brand usage: is a forty-year-old empirical generalization still useful?', *Journal of Advertising Research*, vol. 52, no. 2, pp. 243–51.

Romaniuk, J & Caruso, W 2018, 'Building physical availability with distinctive assets', in J Romaniuk, *Building Distinctive Brand Assets*, pp. 43–55, Oxford University Press, Melbourne.

Romaniuk, J & Dawes, J 2005, 'Loyalty to price tiers in purchases of bottled wine', *Journal of Product and Brand Management*, vol. 14, no. 1, pp. 57–64.

Romaniuk, J, Dawes, J & Nenycz-Thiel, M 2014, 'Generalizations regarding the growth and decline of manufacturer and store brands', *Journal of Retailing and Consumer Services*, vol. 21, no. 5, pp. 725–34.

Romaniuk, J & Gaillard, E 2007, 'The relationship between unique brand associations, brand usage and brand performance: analysis across eight categories', *Journal of Marketing Management*, vol. 23, no. 3, pp. 267–84.

Romaniuk, J & Hartnett, N 2017, 'The relative influence of advertising and word-of-mouth on viewing new season television programs', *European Journal of Marketing*, vol. 51, no. 1, pp. 65–81.

Romaniuk, J & Huang, A 2019, 'Understanding consumer perceptions of luxury brands', *International Journal of Market Research*, vol. 62, no. 5, pp. 546–60.

Romaniuk J, & Nenycz-Thiel, M 2014, 'Measuring the strength of color–brand name links', *Journal of Advertising Research*, vol. 54, no. 3, pp. 313–19.

Romaniuk, J, Nenycz-Thiel, M & Truong, O 2011, 'Do consumers reject brands? Which, where and how often', Report 61, Ehrenberg–Bass Institute for Marketing Science, Adelaide.

Romaniuk, J & Nicholls, E 2006, 'Evaluating advertising effects on brand perceptions: incorporating prior knowledge', *International Journal of Market Research*, vol. 48, no. 2, pp. 179–92.

Romaniuk, J & Sharp, B 2000, 'Using known patterns in image data to determine brand positioning', *International Journal of Market Research*, vol. 42, no. 2, pp. 219–30.

Romaniuk, J & Sharp, B 2004, 'Conceptualizing and measuring brand salience', *Marketing Theory*, vol. 4, no. 4, pp. 327–42.

Romaniuk, J & Wight, S 2009, 'The influence of brand usage on responses to advertising awareness measures', *International Journal of Market Research*, vol. 51, no. 2, pp. 203–18.

Romaniuk, J & Wight, S 2014, 'The stability and sales contribution of heavy buying households', *Journal of Consumer Behaviour*, vol. 14, no. 1, pp. 13–20.

Romaniuk, J, Wight, S & Faulkner, M 2017, 'Brand awareness: revisiting an old metric for a new world', *Journal of Product & Brand Management*, vol. 26, no. 5, pp. 469–76.

Rubinson, J 2009, 'Empirical evidence of TV advertising effectiveness', *Journal of Advertising Research*, vol. 49, no. 2, pp. 220–6.

Safi 2015, 'About us', *Safi*, <http://safi.com.my/web-en/about-us/safi-philosophy.php>.

Sawyer, A, Noel, H & Janiszewski, C 2009, 'The spacing effects of multiple exposures on memory: implications for advertising scheduling', *Journal of Advertising Research*, vol. 49, no. 2, pp. 193–7.

Scriven, J & Ehrenberg, A 2003, 'How consumers choose prices over time', Report 32 for corporate sponsors, Ehrenberg–Bass Institute for Marketing Science, Adelaide.

Sharp, B 2009, 'Detroit's real problem: it's customer acquisition, not loyalty', *Marketing Research*, Spring, pp. 26–7.

Sharp, B 2017, *Marketing: Theory, Evidence, Practice*, second edition, Oxford University Press, Melbourne.

Sharp, B, Beal, V & Collins, M 2009, 'Television: back to the future', *Journal of Advertising Research*, vol. 49, no. 2, pp. 211–29.

Sharp, B, Nenycz-Thiel, M, Martin, J, Anesbury, Z & McColl, B 2017, 'Are big brands dying?', Report 74 for corporate sponsors, Ehrenberg–Bass Institute for Marketing Science, Adelaide.

Sharp, B, Newstead, K, Beal, V, Tanusondjaja, A & Kennedy, R 2014, 'Key media principles', Report 66, Ehrenberg–Bass Institute for Marketing Science, Adelaide.

Sharp, B, Newstead, K & Danenberg, N . 2011, 'A guide to continuous-reach advertising', Report 57 for corporate sponsors, Ehrenberg–Bass Institute for Marketing Science, Adelaide.

Sharp, B, Riebe, E, Dawes, J & Danenberg, N 2002, 'A marketing economy of scale— big brands lose less of their customer base than small brands', *Marketing Bulletin*, vol. 13(May), pp. 1–8.

Sharp, B & Romaniuk, J 2007, 'There is a Pareto law—but not as you know it', Report 42 for corporate sponsors, Ehrenberg–Bass Institute for Marketing Science, Adelaide.

Sharp, B, Romaniuk, J & Graham, C 2019, 'Marketing's 60/20 Pareto Law', available at SSRN 3498097, Ehrenberg–Bass Institute for Marketing Science, Adelaide.

Sharp, B, Trinh, G & Dawes, J 2014, 'What makes heavy buyers so heavy? Do they favour you or just eat a lot?' Report 65, Ehrenberg–Bass Institute for Marketing Science, Adelaide.

Sharp, B, Wright, M & Goodhardt, G 2002, 'Purchase loyalty is polarised into either repertoire or subscription patterns,' *Australasian Marketing Journal*, vol. 10, no. 3, pp. 7–20.

Singh, J, Scriven, J, Clemente, M, Lomax, W & Wright, M 2012, 'New brand extensions: patterns of success and failure', *Journal of Advertising Research*, vol. 52, no. 2, pp. 234–42.

Spangler, T 2020, 'TikTok launches biggest-ever ad campaign as its fate remains cloudy', *Variety*, 18 August, <https://variety.com/2020/digital/news/tiktok-advertising-brand-campaign-sale-bytedance-1234738607>.

Sylvester, AK, McQueen, J & Moore, SD 1994, 'Brand growth and "phase 4" marketing', *Admap*, September, available from *Warc*, <www.warc.com>.

Tan, PJ, Corsi, A, Cohen, J, Sharp, A, Lockshin, L, Caruso, W & Bogomolova, S 2018, 'Assessing the sales effectiveness of differently located endcaps in a supermarket', *Journal of Retailing and Consumer Services*, vol. 43, pp. 200–8.

Tanusondjaja, A, Nenycz-Thiel, M, Dawes, J & Kennedy, R 2018a, 'Does size matter? How product portfolio size is related to brand penetration and revenue', Report 80 for corporate sponsors, Ehrenberg–Bass Institute for Marketing Science, Adelaide.

Tanusondjaja, A, Nenycz-Thiel, M, Dawes, J & Kennedy, R 2018b, "Portfolios: patterns in brand penetration, market share, and hero product variants', *Journal of Retailing and Consumer Services*, vol. 41, pp. 211–17.

Tanusondjaja, A., Trinh, G & Romaniuk, J 2016, 'Exploring the past behaviour of new brand buyers', *International Journal of Market Research*, vol. 58, no. 5, pp. 733–48.

Taylor, J 1977, 'A Striking Characteristic of Innovators', *Journal of Marketing Research*, vol. 14, February, pp. 104–7.

Taylor, J, Kennedy, R & Sharp, B 2009, 'Making generalizations about advertising's convex sales response function: is once really enough?', *Journal of Advertising Research*, vol. 49, no. 2, pp. 198–200.

Team, T 2020, 'Best Buys stock still attractive at 118?', *Forbes*, 15 October, <www.forbes.com/sites/greatspeculations/2020/10/15/best-buys-stock-still-attractive-at-118/?sh=cd962fe15548>.

Trinh, G, Romaniuk, J & Tanusondjaja, A 2015, 'Benchmarking buyer behavior towards new brands', *Marketing Letters*, vol. 27, pp. 743–52.

Truong, O 2014, 'Do consumer behaviour empirical generalisations hold in emerging markets?', Masters thesis, Ehrenberg–Bass Institute, University of South Australia.

Truong, O, Faulkner, M & Mueller Loose, S 2012, 'An examination of consumer profiles across brands in emerging markets', Australia and New Zealand Marketing Academy (ANZMAC) conference, 3–5 December, Ehrenberg–Bass Institute for Marketing Science, Adelaide.

Tulving, E & Craik, F 2000, *The Oxford Handbook of Memory*, Oxford University Press, Oxford.

Uncles, M 2010, 'Retail change in China: retrospect and prospect', *International Review of Retail, Distribution and Consumer Research*, vol. 20, no. 1, pp. 69–84.

Uncles, M, East, R & Lomax, W 2010, 'Market share is correlated with word-of-mouth volume', *Australasian Marketing Journal*, vol. 18, pp. 145–50.

Uncles, M & Ehrenberg, A 1990, 'The buying of packaged goods at US retail chains', *Journal of Retailing*, vol. 66, no. 3, pp. 278–96.

Uncles, M & Hammond, K 1995, 'Grocery store patronage', *International Review of Retail, Distribution & Consumer Research*, vol. 5, no. 3, pp. 287–302.

Uncles, M, Hammond, K, Ehrenberg, A & Davies, R 1994, 'A replication study of two brand-loyalty measures', *European Journal of Operational Research*, vol. 76, no. 2, pp. 375–85.

Uncles, M, Kennedy, R, Nenycz-Thiel, M, Singh, J & Kwok, S 2012, 'User profiles for directly competing brands seldom differ: reexamining the evidence', *Journal of Advertising Research*, vol. 52, no. 2, pp. 252–61.

Uncles, M & Kwok, S 2008, 'Generalizing patterns of store-type patronage: an analysis across major Chinese cities', *International Review of Retail, Distribution and Consumer Research*, vol. 18, no. 5, pp. 473–93.

Uncles, M & Kwok, S 2009, 'Patterns of store patronage in urban China', *Journal of Business Research*, vol. 62, no. 1, pp. 68–81.

USA Today 2020, 'America's favorite coffee brands: Dunkin' Donuts, Starbucks, Folgers and more', 24 March, <www.usatoday.com/picture-gallery/life/2020/03/24/americas-favorite-coffee-brands-dunkin-mccafe-starbucks-and-more/111431110>.

Vaughan, K, Beal, V & Romaniuk, J 2016, 'Can brand users really remember advertising more than nonusers? Testing an empirical generalization across six advertising awareness measures', *Journal of Advertising Research*, vol. 56, no. 3, pp. 311–20.

Vaughan, K, Beal, V, Corsi, A & Sharp, B 2020, 'Measuring advertising's effect on mental availability', *International Journal of Market Research*, pp. 1–17. DOI 1.o0r.g1/107.171/1774/710470875352302909555095

Verdon, J 2020, 'Best Buy worked on its tech before the pandemic and now it's flexing its muscles', *Forbes*, 21 May, <www.forbes.com/sites/joanverdon/2020/05/21/best-buy-worked-on-its-tech-before-the-pandemic-and-now-its-flexing-its-muscles/?sh=35e8733efd90>.

Victory, K, Nenycz-Thiel, M, Dawes, J, Tanusondjaja A & Corsi, AM 2021, 'How common is new product failure and when does it vary?', *Marketing Letters*, vol. 32, pp. 17–32.

Ward, E, Yang, S, Romaniuk, J & Beal, V 2020, 'Building a unique brand identity: measuring the relative ownership potential of brand identity element types', *Journal of Brand Management*, vol. 27, no. 4, pp. 393–407.

Watts, DJ & Dodds, PS 2007, 'Influentials, networks, and public opinion formation', *Journal of Consumer Research*, vol. 34, no. 4, pp. 441–58.

Wentz, L 2013, 'A leader in Latin-influenced food market, Goya enters baby aisle', *Advertising Age*, 12 July, <http://adage.com/article/hispanic-marketing/a-leader-changing-market-goya-enters-baby-food-aisle/243089>.

Wight, S 2010, 'Brand awareness metrics: the underlying awareness of brand users and non-users', Masters thesis, Ehrenberg–Bass Institute, University of South Australia, Adelaide.

Wilbur, K & Farris, P 2013, 'Distribution and market share', *Journal of Retailing*, vol. 90, no. 2, pp. 154–67.

Winchester, M & Romaniuk, J 2008, 'Negative brand beliefs and brand usage', *International Journal of Market Research*, vol. 50, no. 3, pp. 355–75.

Winchester, M, Romaniuk, J & Bogomolova, S 2008, 'Positive and negative brand beliefs and brand defection/uptake', *European Journal of Marketing*, vol. 42, no. 5/6, pp. 553–70.

Wragg, C & Regan, T 2012, 'Marketing food: Quorn's new appeal', *Admap*, November, pp. 32–3, available from *Warc*, <www.warc.com>.

Wright, M & Sharp, A 2001, 'The effect of a new brand entrant on a market', *Journal of Empirical Generalisations in Marketing Science*, vol. 6, pp. 15–29.